THE SOCIALLY RESPONSIVE SELF

THE SOCIALLY
RESPONSIVE SELF

Social Theory and
Professional Ethics

Larry May

THE UNIVERSITY OF CHICAGO PRESS
CHICAGO & LONDON

LARRY MAY is professor of philosophy at Washington University, St.
Louis. He has published numerous articles and is the author of two
previous books, *The Morality of Groups* (1989) and *Sharing
Responsibility* (1992), the latter published by the
University of Chicago Press.

The University of Chicago Press, Chicago 60637
The University of Chicago Press, Ltd., London
© 1996 by The University of Chicago
All rights reserved. Published 1996
Printed in the United States of America
05 04 03 02 01 00 99 98 97 96   1 2 3 4 5

ISBN: 0-226-51171-5 (cloth)
ISBN: 0-226-51172-3 (paper)

Library of Congress Cataloging-in-Publication Data

May, Larry.
    The socially responsive self : social theory and professional ethics /
Larry May.
        p.   cm.
    Includes bibliographical references and index.
    ISBN 0-226-51171-5 (cloth : alk. paper). — ISBN 0-226-51172-3
(paper : alk. paper)
    1. Professional ethics.   2. Responsibility—Social aspects.
    I. Title.
    BJ1725.M35   1996
    174—dc20   96-14866
                                                             CIP

♾ The paper used in this publication meets the minimum requirements of
the American National Standard for Information Sciences—Permanence of
Paper for Printed Library Materials, ANSI Z39.48-1984.

FOR ELIZABETH

CONTENTS

ACKNOWLEDGMENTS

Roger Gibson first suggested to me that I write a book combining my interests in social theory and professional ethics. I am very grateful to him for this suggestion and for giving me leave from my teaching duties early in my tenure at Washington University so as to prepare this manuscript. For similar reasons I am grateful to Rachelle Hollander and the National Science Foundation's project in Ethics and Value Studies for recognizing the legitimacy of this project and providing funding for the time I spent drafting this book. My former dean, Martin Israel, also provided valuable financial support.

Marilyn Friedman and Jim Bohman read early drafts of each of these chapters and patiently listened as I tried to explain what I was up to. At a later stage, Carl Wellman and Hugh LaFollette provided invaluable feedback on a complete draft of the book; and Margaret Walker, William Rehg, George Brenkert, and Joel Anderson provided feedback on the first half. Many people have commented on portions of this book—I here list those whose comments struck me as especially helpful: Ralph Lindgren, Johann Klaassen, Peggy DesAutels, David Chalmers, Andy Clark, Mark Rollins, Jerry Kohn, Diana Meyers, John Deigh, Joan Callahan, Roger Gibson, Paul Gomberg, Dan Wueste, Bill McBride, Bruce Russell, Katherine Goldwasser, and Amy Kennedy. Ron Broach was very helpful as my research assistant during a crucial stage of the project. Kate Parsons constructed the index.

Early versions of these chapters were presented at Saint Louis University, Clemson University, the College of Charleston, Allbright College, and Muhlenberg College, as well as at several meetings of the American Philosophical Association. Chapter 7 was presented as the keynote address at the Central States Philosophical Association meetings. In addition, several chapters were presented while I was the Selfridge Lecturer at Lehigh University. I thank the Lehigh Philosophy Department collectively. I am grateful to the National Science Foundation for recognizing, and supporting, my research.

Three of these chapters (1, 5, and 9) are revised versions of essays that appeared, respectively, as "Integrity, Self, and Value Plurality" in *Journal of Social Philosophy* (winter 1996), as "Social Responsibility" in *Midwest Studies in Philosophy* (1995), and as "Challenging Medical Authority" in *The Hastings Center Report* (January–February 1995). Chapters 4 and 7 appeared in a slightly different form, the former as "Socialization and Institutional Evil" in *Hannah Arendt: Twenty Years Later,* edited by Larry May and Jerome Kohn (Cambridge, MA: MIT Press, 1996), and the latter as "Conflict of Interest" in *Professional Ethics and Social Responsibility,* edited by Daniel E. Wueste (Lanham, MD: Rowan & Littlefield, 1994). All this material is reproduced with permission.

The staff at the University of Chicago Press has been, as usual, good to work with, producing a fine-quality volume. David Brent, my editor, deserves high praise for his patience and professionalism.

Individuals can stabilize their fragile identities
only mutually and simultaneously with the identity of the group.
—*Jürgen Habermas*[1]

Within the flickering inconsequential acts of separate selves dwells
a sense of the whole which claims and dignifies them.
—*John Dewey*[2]

I begin with two facts. First, the sound of a baby crying causes most of us to investigate, to reach out to help, regardless of who the baby is. Second, dolphins will go to the aid of tuna or other dolphins in distress; indeed, dolphins have been known to swim for miles carrying injured human swimmers to shore.[3] Both of these facts lend support for some kind of natural feeling of responsiveness to the needs of others. Social and moral responsibility is much more a matter of responsiveness to others in need than it is a matter of rule following. As David Hume said, morality "is more properly felt than judg'd of."[4] Social and moral theory needs to take seriously how people respond to the world around them.

I was inspired to write this book by my own unease when asked the following question: Since you work in ethics, are you a deontologist or a utilitarian or a virtue theorist? While some of my views overlap with virtue theory, and some with consequentialism, my focus on social responsibility does not easily fit into one of these camps. Over the years, I have discovered that many of my colleagues are in a similar predicament: they are not quite sure how to answer this question, since the way they approach ethics is so different from the approach of those who subscribe to the dominant

---

1. Jürgen Habermas, "Justice and Solidarity: On the Discussion Concerning 'Stage Six,'" *The Philosophical Forum* 21, nos. 1–2 (fall/winter 1989–90): 46.

2. John Dewey, *Human Nature and Conduct* (New York : Henry Holt, 1922), p. 331.

3. For more discussion of such facts see Donald Griffin, *Animal Minds* (Chicago: University of Chicago Press, 1992); and James Q. Wilson, *The Moral Sense* (New York: Free Press, 1993).

4. David Hume, *Treatise of Human Nature,* bk. III, pt. I, sec. II , ed. L. A. Selby-Bigge (1739; Oxford: Clarendon Press, 1968), p. 470.

ethical theories. In this book, I hope to capture another approach to ethics, one not mired in abstract theorizing.[5]

The cornerstone of my view is the socially responsive self. First, I am concerned with the way that selves are socially constituted, that is, the way they are responsive to, in the sense of being a product of, the groups and communities of which they are members. Second, I am concerned with the way that selves conceive of themselves morally, that is, the way they are responsive to, in the sense of how they morally react to, the contexts and situations they find themselves in. This dual sense of the "responsive self," as both passive recipient of social stimuli and active participant in the social milieu, will be of central concern throughout the book.

This is a book about social responsibility, especially in professional life. I explore the nature of social institutions and the role these institutions play in shaping and limiting our responsibilities. The categories of integrity, authority, role responsibility, and advocacy are reexamined in light of very recent work in social and moral philosophy, especially in critical theory. I attempt to defend a progressive communitarian conception of social and moral theory that cuts a path between the extremes of the atomism of liberalism and the collectivism of communitarianism. As in my previous work, the focus of attention is on individuals in relationships.[6]

I. SOCIAL RESPONSIBILITY AND INTEGRITY

The main thesis of the first half of the book is that moral concepts such as integrity and responsibility need to be understood as embedded in social structures and processes such as socialization, solidarity, and collective consciousness. Integrity and responsibility are not the exclusive purview of isolated individual consciences. Rather, these moral concepts are at least partially formed by, and promoted or inhibited in, the interplay of persons that occurs within families, communities, and nation-states. The practical upshot of this thesis is that it is a mistake to judge individuals as if social pressures, both negative and positive, were not morally important. Codes of conduct that stipulate morally required behavior, without any reference to the socialization patterns or degree of solidarity among individuals who fall under the code, are both unrealistic and unfair.

5. Some of the critics of traditional approaches to ethics have chosen the label "antitheory." See the fascinating collection of papers on this topic in *Anti-Theory in Ethics and Moral Conservatism*, ed. Stanley G. Clarke and Even Simpson (Albany: State University of New York Press, 1989).

6. See Larry May, *The Morality of Groups* (Notre Dame, IN: University of Notre Dame Press, 1987), chap. 1; and Larry May, *Sharing Responsibility* (Chicago: University of Chicago Press, 1992), chaps. 1 and 9.

According to the view that is rejected in this book, the socially responsible person is said to be motivated mainly by the dictates of conscience, which provide a bedrock from which the individual can gain a sense of mastery over the world around him or her. While the self does have inner resources from which the strength to resist immoral impulses can be generated, on my communitarian view of the self we must understand that the self itself is largely a product of social factors. Since the self is also a product of the group affiliations of which it is a part, a weak set of affiliations will make it more difficult for the self both to know what is right and to do it. In such a situation it is sometimes unreasonable to expect the self to have resources from which it can resist forces that move it away from what is good or right. This is especially true when the potential harm likely to occur as a result of failing to follow a particular rule is minimal.

For some individuals, their group affiliations also provide a sense of support, a much more common basis than the isolated conscience upon which the individual can find the strength to do what is right. In professional life, the engineer, lawyer, or doctor is a member of many competing groups that pull the professional in different directions. When group affiliations provide a sense of solidarity or of group identity, then it is more likely that a self can resist, for instance, profit-motivated pressures from his or her employing institution. Here the key is the actual or anticipated moral support that an individual feels, a support that gives the strength of numbers to the often difficult struggles of seemingly isolated selves in the contemporary world.

Another theme of the book is that social and moral theory should be understood as closely connected to each other. The concerns of moral philosophers are often expressed solely in terms of abstract duties or ideal norms that are thought to apply universally. On this construal of ethics, no attention need be paid to social theory or practice. But if morality is conceived as closely related to socialization, or if morality is conceived as interconnected with factors such as loyalty, solidarity, or group identity, the plausibility of which will be shown in what follows, then one cannot discuss moral theory without also discussing social theory and practice.

My view is not that morality is only concerned with what societies socialize their members to believe, for morality has a critical function as well.[7] Rather, my view is that morality is at least in part to be understood as framed by the specific socialization of various societies. People first come to have moral intuitions as a result of early childhood socialization.

---

7. H. L. A. Hart distinguished this "critical morality" from what he called "positive morality," the morality of a particular society, in *Law, Liberty, and Morality* (Stanford: Stanford University Press, 1963).

And adults are motivated to act in specific moral ways again because of the socialization patterns to which they have been exposed. Socialization patterns themselves may be subject to moral criticism, to be sure, but we cannot have a morality without some patterns of socialization. It should not be forgotten, though, that despite one's socialization there are almost always choices: one has to accept or reject certain aspects of one's socialization.

Throughout the book an argument is advanced for thinking that morality needs to be discussed in realistic—and that often means restricted—terms. This argument seems to fly in the face of my previous book, *Sharing Responsibility,* where I argued for an expanded realm of responsibility. In that book I argued for extending responsibility as a shared enterprise, in light of what the members of a community could do together to end or prevent various harms. In the present book I also aim to extend the analysis of moral concepts into the social domain in which they are embedded. And while some of the arguments I will advance call for holding people to a less stringent standard of responsibility than is true of other views I discuss, the focus remains on the social groups to which one is connected. But the emphasis now is on how the lack of connections may make it harder and more costly for individuals to know what is right and to do it.[8] The upshot of these two works is that while strong community bonds may increase what can be expected of us, weak community bonds may decrease what can be expected of us. The socially responsive self needs to be understood as *both* passive recipient *and* active participant in its social milieu.

The best previous work on the topics of this book has been done by continental social philosophers over the last century. The work of Emile Durkheim and Max Weber will be frequently cited. In addition, I will be guided by very recent work in contemporary continental social theory that has helped me to see the connections between moral philosophy and social theory. In this context the work of Jürgen Habermas and other contemporary critical theorists, as well as that of Charles Taylor, will be of prime concern. While I will ultimately reject many of the central tenets of Habermas's and Taylor's moral and social theory, many of my views have been worked out while being forced to confront various issues in reading their written views, as well as in actual dialogue with a number of their most able defenders. Finally, I have been guided by past and present work on liberalism, from John Stuart Mill to Joel Feinberg. Feinberg continues to

---

8. In this respect my work falls into the camp of those who have defended a thick, as opposed to a thin, conception of moral agency. See Michael Walzer's *Thick and Thin* (Notre Dame, IN: University of Notre Dame Press, 1994), and Rita C. Manning, "Toward a Thick Theory of Moral Agency," *Social Theory and Practice* 20, no. 2 (summer 1994).

be the social philosopher with whom I engage most productively, as was also true in my previous writings.

Any adequate discussion of social and moral theory should give a detailed indication of how the theory will work itself out in practice. Hence, the book has been divided into two parts: social and moral theory in the first part, and practical application in the second part. In each of these parts, however, both theory and application are discussed. I have divided these chapters based on what the predominant emphasis is in each half, rather than attempting an artificial division in which the two are kept separate.

II. SOCIALLY RESPONSIVE PROFESSIONALS

The second half of the book concerns the central concepts of professional ethics: professional integrity, advocacy, and conflict of interest. The socially responsive professional is often conceived as someone who conscientiously conforms to a set of strict obligations. So, in discussions of professional ethics, quite a bit of time is spent trying to delineate an ideal set of these obligations. Virtually no attention is paid to the conditions that might make it harder or easier for individuals to satisfy these obligations. Indeed, it is often said that the model of the socially responsible professional is someone who disregards all factors except his or her professional obligations. I will challenge this one-sided approach to the central problems in social and professional responsibility.

My contention is that the professional *persona* is such an idealized vision of the professional that it is nearly impossible to be actualized. Professional codes, which embody the self-perceptions of the professional communities, contend that a professional should adhere to a unique and much higher standard of morality than that of nonprofessionals. This often means that the professional should be scupulously loyal to the client and completely avoid conflicts of interest. In addition, the professional is thought to have a kind of privilege, namely, to be excused from certain normal moral requirements so as to be able to devote himself or herself exclusively to the higher duties of the profession, for example, the pursuit of truth, justice, or health. Underlying this conception of the professional is a conception of the professional self, according to which it is possible for a person to be guided exclusively by certain interests to the complete exclusion of self-interested and other motivations. This view of the self as singularly motivated and unconflicted is a paradigmatically modern conception and one in need of serious reexamination.

My view is that it is important that a professional not think that his or her goal is to submerge interests of the self, family, etc., into the professional role. Each person is a member of many communities, and each community has a plurality of often overlapping roles. Important relationships exist for a professional that are not related to the professional community to which he or she belongs. The most significant of these relationships, and the greatest source of difficulties, comes from those corporations and institutions that employ most professionals. These relationships create role responsibilities that often cannot be subjugated to the role responsibilities one has as a professional without serious risk of financial harm to the professional. There are also familial, civic, and national communities in which people who are professionals also assume various roles with corresponding responsibilities.

Engineers, doctors, lawyers, and scientists who work for large organizations will continue to have trouble meeting their professional standards concerning honesty and integrity. Until some form of protection can be established for professionals against possible retaliation by these organizations for doing what the professionals think is right, we should not expect individuals who lack this support to live up to their professional standards in all cases. In attempting to render this thesis plausible I will draw upon the work of existentialist philosophers, especially Hannah Arendt, who have been concerned with ethical dilemmas caused by economic and institutional pressures on individuals.[9]

In the recent book *Responsible Science,* published by the National Academy of Sciences et al., the penultimate recommendation specifically addresses whistle-blowing.

> Individuals who, in good conscience, report suspected misconduct in science deserve support and protection. . . . When necessary, serious and considered whistle-blowing is an act of courage that should be supported by the entire research community.[10]

I will explore some of the theoretical underpinnings that would support such a recommendation. I will be especially interested in defending the claim of the report that the "entire research community" has obligations that arise when one of its members engages in misconduct.

It seems relatively uncontroversial that group membership often does affect an individual's values. Professional associations, as well as the organizations that employ professionals, can have a profound impact on how

9. See Hannah Arendt, *Eichmann in Jerusalem* (New York: Viking Press, 1963), as well as Karl Jaspers, *The Question of German Guilt* (New York: Capricorn Books, 1947).

10. National Academy of Sciences, National Academy of Engineering, and Institute of Medicine, *Responsible Science: Ensuring the Integrity of the Research Process,* vol. 1 (Washington, DC: National Academy Press, 1992).

professionals understand their moral responsibilities.[11] Fledgling professionals need to be provided with a more realistic picture of professional life. In addition, professional norms and rules need to be reconceptualized so that they are consonant with the realities of professional life, especially in light of the fact that many professionals in American society are employed by large organizations.

In the second half of the book I am quite critical of the current methods and goals of professional socialization. Professionals should be brought to understand that professional privilege and loyalty to client are important but must be balanced against other societal norms. Specifically, I argue that lawyers should not place loyalty to client above all other values. Concern for the common good, as well as achieving cooperative settlements, should be as important as adversarial advocacy. And doctors should not put the patient's physical well-being ahead of other values, such as the patient's mental and spiritual well-being. There are serious problems with our current practices of legal and medical socialization. We live in a world where an increasing number of people demand that professionals be more sensitive to the values that are embedded in quite disparate communities. The Christian Science refusal cases are introduced in the penultimate chapter to illustrate this problem. The book ends with a discussion of whistleblowing in science.

Jürgen Habermas has argued that integrity and solidarity must go hand in hand. John Dewey expressed similar sentiments when he said that the self draws both strength and dignity from group affiliations. As the quotations at the beginning of this introduction indicate, these are the ideas that inspire the book that follows. Philosophical ethics in general, and professional ethics in particular, need to face up to the social facts of contemporary life and to change correspondingly their viewpoints and research agendas. I hope that others will explore this approach and provide similar reappraisals of other aspects of social theory and ethics.

---

11. See my essay "Professional Actions and the Liabilities of Professional Associations: ASME vs. Hydrolevel Corp.," *Business and Professional Ethics Journal* 2, no. 1 (fall 1982): 1–14.

I

SOCIAL AND
MORAL THEORY

1

INTEGRITY, SELF, AND
VALUE PLURALITY

This chapter is an attempt to develop a pluralistic, communitarian conception of integrity.[1] The project is a part of the larger project of arguing that moral identity is intimately connected to group identity. Moral identity necessarily involves a consideration of the various values that are espoused by the groups of which one is a member. The main insight here is that the various aspects of the self are constituted from group memberships. Moral integrity is not merely a matter of a conscience that sticks steadfastly to its principles. Integrity is not a withdrawal from the influences of the world into one's own core self. Understanding integrity necessarily involves understanding how groups influence the formation of even the most "essential" aspects of the self.

Moral integrity has three aspects: coherence of value orientation, mature development of a critical point of view, and disposition to act in a principled way. In this chapter I will show that communitarians can embrace each of these aspects of integrity. In the first section, I provide a sketch of a communitarian construal of the self.

In the second section, I explain how the first aspect of integrity, coherence, can be understood according to the communitarian construal of the self. In the third section, I draw on very recent work in developmental psychology as I elaborate on the second aspect of integrity: the development of a critical perspective. And in the fourth section, I discuss the third aspect of integrity: commitment to act on one's principles. In the final section, I draw out some implications of my analysis for understanding how integrity should be understood in professional life.

1. I have previously called this view "liberationist communitarianism" in *Sharing Responsibility*.

Communitarianism is best understood as a social and moral perspective that is based on certain criticisms of liberalism. Allen Buchanan has performed the useful service of clearly summarizing five criticisms that can be found in most communitarian writing. These criticisms are that liberalism

i. devalues, neglects, and/or undermines community;
ii. undervalues political life, viewing political association as a merely instrumental good;
iii. fails to provide, or is incompatible with, an adequate account of certain types of obligations and commitments—those that are not chosen;
iv. presupposes a defective conception of the self, failing to recognize that the self is "embedded";
v. wrongly exalts justice as being "the first virtue of social institutions."[2]

I agree with Buchanan that these are the most important and most common criticisms of liberalism offered by communitarians.

Buchanan's list of communitarian objections to liberalism provides a good springboard for understanding the positive agenda of contemporary communitarians. The five positive theses that I and many communitarians share are these:

i. community is constitutive of any conception of the good life;
ii. participation in politics has intrinsic value;
iii. some of our most important responsibilities are thrust upon us, not voluntarily assumed;
iv. the self is socially constructed;
v. responsibility is at least as important a moral value as is justice.

Accepting one or another of these theses does not necessarily mean that one rejects liberalism. But accepting all of these theses makes it very hard to remain committed to certain forms of traditional liberalism.[3]

A communitarian approach to integrity faces several serious problems. First, one of the most common ways of characterizing integrity is "to be true to oneself." This requires that there be a self; indeed, some would say that there must be a core or essential self. Yet this seems to be ruled out by the communitarian support for the social construction of the self.

2. Allen E. Buchanan, "Assessing the Communitarian Critique of Liberalism," *Ethics* 99 (July 1989): 852–3.
3. The best account of why this is true is provided by Michael Sandel in *Liberalism and the Limits of Justice* (Cambridge: Cambridge University Press, 1982), especially pp. 147–83.

Second, integrity is often characterized as the chief basis of individuality or of the personal standpoint (as opposed to the social). Yet communitarians seemingly must deny that there is a sharp distinction to be drawn between self and society. Third, sticking to one's principles in the face of temptation and social pressure seems to depend on there being principles and commitments of the self that are truly of the self. Yet this is also seemingly denied by communitarians. Fourth, integrity is often seen as a matter of conscientious commitment. Yet it is unclear whether communitarians have a place in their view for anything like what has traditionally been meant by conscience or commitment. I will take up these points as I explore the conception of personal identity and self that is communitarian but does not leave the self without resources to act on its commitments. Charles Taylor has recently explored in some detail a view of identity that I find plausible. He says that

> people may see their identity as defined partly by some moral or spiritual commitment, say as a Catholic, or an anarchist. Or they may define it in part by the nation or tradition they belong to, as an Armenian, say, or a Québécois. What they are saying by this is not just that they are strongly attached to this spiritual view or background; rather it is that this provides the frame within which they can determine where they stand on questions of what is good, or worthwhile, or admirable, or of value. Put counterfactually, they are saying that were they to lose this commitment or identification, they would be at sea, as it were; they wouldn't know anymore, for an important range of questions, what the significance of things was for them.[4]

In this section I wish to explore how a self is constituted out of its group memberships, a topic which most communitarians have skirted. In the next section I wish to explore the similarly neglected topic of the formation of integrity out of the often conflicting principles one is exposed to.

My view is that personal identity is best understood not in terms of an essence or a core, but as a web knit from the various identifications and commitments that one makes with various social groups.[5] These group identifications give us a "frame or horizon," a "background" in terms of which we make sense of our lives. Indeed, Taylor puts his point quite strongly when he asserts that "doing without frameworks is utterly im-

4. Charles Taylor, *Sources of the Self* (Cambridge, MA: Harvard University Press, 1989), p. 27.
5. Taylor tends not to place nearly as much stress on social groups as I will in what follows. But as I suggest, my stress on social groups does not appear to be inconsistent with Taylor's project.

possible for us" insofar as it will create an "identity crisis."[6] The identity crisis will result because of the loss of a sense of the "moral space" in which we reside. The background or orientation provided by our group identifications provides the thread out of which the web of self will be spun. This web creates a kind of personal space within which each of us can stand, but this personal space is best understood as growing out of a common space. As Taylor says, "I am a self only in relation to certain interlocutors."[7] From the perspective of group membership I have been developing, one is a self only in relation to the various social groups with which one identifies.

Here we have the communitarian correlate of the core, or essential, self of the traditional liberal perspectives. But this core is really like the inside of a web or the "core" of an onion, made up of many strands or layers of group identification and commitment, rather than a core or essence that is somehow merely a function of past memories and choices of the individual. Indeed, the commitments people feel are themselves heavily influenced by early childhood training or socialization at a more mature level. Of course, there is more to commitment than this. It is crucial to commitment that a person support or endorse a particular principle, regardless of the source of that principle. But the positive endorsement of a principle which one has received from a particular group is a form of critical judgment that is itself also heavily influenced by social factors.

On the communitarian view I am presenting, one's identity is formed by, among other things, principles and values that one endorses. Both the principles that one is committed to and the judgments of endorsement are strongly influenced, or even constituted, by social factors, namely, the values of the groups one belongs to. These multiple dimensions concern a richer construal of the self than is normally provided in liberal theory with its minimal or thin conception of agency. A number of theorists have tried to make greater sense of the notion of identity that rejects the traditionally narrow liberal self. According to Owen Flanagan, "Identity in this thick, rich sense—let us call it actual full identity—is constituted by the dynamic integrated system of past and present identifications, desires, commitments, aspirations, beliefs, dispositions, temperament, roles, acts, and actional patterns, as well as by whatever self-understandings (even incorrect ones) each person brings to his or her life."[8]

Flanagan allows that these aspects of one's identity will have been ini-

6. Taylor, *Sources of the Self*, p. 27.

7. Ibid., p. 36.

8. Owen Flanagan, *Varieties of Moral Personality* (Cambridge, MA: Harvard University Press, 1991), p. 135.

tially formed as "primarily emergent, relational products rather than pure self-creations."[9] But he claims that identity must be understood both historically (in terms of the social factors that have constructed the material out of which a self is formed) and contemporaneously (in terms of the actual current factors that are ascendant in one's identity). Flanagan finds fault with those communitarians who try to draw normative conclusions from what he acknowledges to be a psychological fact. Flanagan criticizes communitarians for not recognizing that there must be some kind of "core self" at a given moment.[10]

Some communitarians do support the value of homogeneity in community as a vehicle for providing coherence for the otherwise chaotic self. But, as I will argue, communitarians need not make this move to give a coherence to the socially constituted self. Flanagan is right to think that nothing follows from the communitarian claims about the social self in terms of valuing a more homogeneous community over a heterogeneous one. It is important to recognize that a "core self" can be as well formed from disparate as from highly similar social influences. I will say more about this point in the next section.

My communitarian view of the self tries to avoid most of these pitfalls by stressing that an albeit often temporary "core self" is formed in most people that can resist many future social influences and hence maintain a kind of equilibrium over time.[11] That is, I agree with Flanagan that the self is a "dynamic integrated system" rather than a "disunified hodge-podge."[12] The communitarian social conception of the self does not need to rule out unity of the self, at least temporary unity. And the social conception of the self does not need to favor homogeneous over heterogeneous communities or groups of which the self is a member. This will all become clearer in the ensuing discussion of integrity in the next sections of this chapter.

II. ACHIEVING INTEGRITY

One of the key questions faced by the communitarian conception of the self is how the self can integrate itself given that the components of the self have not been chosen by the self. It has become common in philosophical

9. Ibid., p. 142.

10. Ibid., p. 146 and elsewhere.

11. In sec. 4, I will speak of the communitarian "core self" in terms of a "web of commitments."

12. Flanagan, p. 136. But I strongly disagree with Flanagan, as should be already clear, when he says that his arguments have shown that "communitarian claims" about the self are "empirically unsubstantiated, or downright dubious" or "normatively problematic" (p. 158).

discussions of the self to distinguish between two levels of the self: the first-order beliefs, desires, and attitudes that are a product of factors not under the control of the self, such as social influences, and the second-order endorsement or rejection of those first-order beliefs, desires, and attitudes, which is somehow "of the self."[13] The "core self," or the integrating portion of the self, is seen as residing at the second level. I will begin this section by offering some criticisms of this approach to understanding integrity before offering my positive account of how integrity of the self is to be understood.

Gabriele Taylor has provided one of the best accounts of integrity drawn in terms of the two levels of the self.

> To be a candidate for possession of integrity the person's choices and evaluations must be her own: her identifications with her desires must be neither subject to unconsidered change nor be distorted or confused. Her reasons for action must be genuine.[14]

Taylor contends that the best way to understand what it means to have integrity is in terms of being one's own person, where this means having "second order volitions" in which "one is capable of evaluating and thereby controlling her desires."[15] Here it is very clear that there are two levels of the self: one is the core or genuine self, which is in control; the other is controlled and evaluated by the core or genuine self.

There are several important problems with this account, not the least of which is that it fails to explain what is the source of the core self that is claimed to be in control, and thereby fails to explain why the core level is any less influenced by social factors than the other level.[16] This is by now a standard objection to so-called split-level accounts of the self. I have mentioned Gabriele Taylor's account and its most obvious difficulty in order to call attention to a problem that will confront nearly all accounts of the integrated self, including communitarian accounts; namely, that one must give an account of *what* is controlling the integration, as well as of *how* the integration is to take place.

I have argued elsewhere[17] for a self as process rather than essence.[18]

---

13. The most influential work on this topic is that by Harry Frankfurt. See the collection of his essays entitled *The Importance of What We Care About* (Cambridge: Cambridge University Press, 1988).

14. Gabriele Taylor, *Pride, Shame, and Guilt* (Oxford: The Clarendon Press, 1985), p. 126.

15. Ibid., p. 118.

16. See Marilyn Friedman's essay, "Autonomy and the Split-Level Self," *Southern Journal of Philosophy* 24, no. 1 (summer 1986): 19–35.

17. May, *Sharing Responsibility*, especially pp. 3, 18–24, and 173–4.

18. For a similar account, see Mark Johnson, *Moral Imagination* (Chicago: University of

Here the self emerges and changes over time. When the self is seen as an evolving, developing process, it is possible to explain how something that is a product of social influences can itself modify some of those influences such that part of what influences us also allows us to change that which influences us. Our emerging critical skills of assessment, acceptance, or rejection evolve from social influences. Not all of us develop the same critical skills. Also, some people develop critical skills so different from those of the other members of a given community they belong to that they are not able to communicate with the other members of that community.

People develop quite different styles of critical reflection based on the range of different perspectives to which they have been exposed.[19] The more diverse the experiences of the self, the richer a set of resources a person will have to draw upon in critically integrating the various social influences he or she has been exposed to. As one matures, one's ability to reflect upon, and cope with, one's changing experiences increases. Such a view is much more in keeping with the very different ways that the same people, over the course of a life, confront the world around them (through resignation, withdrawal, rejection, cooptation, etc.) than is the view of the self as having an essence that remains fixed and changes little over the course of a life.[20]

The crucial dimension of maturation for integrity occurs when the self is able to make adjustments in its personality: to block certain influences and to add new ones, thereby beginning the task of providing a unifying structure to the self that is in keeping with how one wants to be. The person of integrity does indeed exercise control over his or her life, but the way in which this occurs is quite different from that proposed by those who postulate the split-level conception of the self. On my view, both the self that is integrated and the self that acts to achieve the integration are products of factors (such as the influences of family, teachers, ministers, friends, partners, etc.) that are at least initially outside the control of the self. Maturation is largely a matter of "bootstrapping"—that is, learning to control certain aspects of the self by using other aspects of the self that were initially beyond one's control.

A critic of my view may raise the question of how a self formed by

---

Chicago Press, 1993), pp. 149 and 147. There Johnson provides an account of the "self-in-process" that posits an "evolving identity."

19. On my view it is possible for moral integrity to be found in people who reside in very traditional, nonpluralistic societies. But for moral integrity to develop in a person in such an environment, he or she needs to have some diversity of experience to be able to question his or her primary group's values. A source of that diversity can come from within a segment of one's own group that is at the periphery or margin.

20. As Johnson puts it, "Experience is synthetic all the way down." *Moral Imagination*, p. 164.

social influences beyond its control can itself come to gain control so that something like autonomous choices are possible.[21] This, of course, is an age-old problem that did not originate with communitarian approaches. For just the same question arises if God is the source of all of the features of the self. If God creates the human soul and will, how is it possible for this same soul and will to become an autonomous spring or source of action? When the question had this theological cast, the answer was phrased in "deus ex machina" terms: God simply made it turn out that humans would be *given freedom*. The same is true for any focus on innate features of the self. Those innate features didn't arise ex nihilo, and the question then becomes, How can innate features of the self, which themselves arose outside our control, become the source of an independent control or choice?

So it turns out that my communitarian account of these matters is in no worse shape than the other views that have historically been advanced to account for the self. What makes my approach preferable, I want to argue, is that it is most compatible with the very best psychological accounts of how a personality develops. I am here explicitly urging that at least some ethical disputes be resolved in light of empirical evidence, and in this sense I am squarely in the midst of the new movement that calls itself "naturalized ethics."[22] I come down cautiously in favor of a developmental view of the self. Such a view is not at odds with a view of the self as having certain innate capacities that are actualized or triggered by certain forms of experience. The possible existence of innate capacities does not necessarily pose problems for a communitarian account since, as with Kant's categories of the human mind, there is no substance to the capacities until they are activated. What is denied is that there is some kind of core self that exists somehow independent of experience.

In achieving integrity, what is crucial is that the self have a diversity of experiences as resources to draw upon, both to be integrated and to do the integrating. Since there is no preexisting core self, a well-maturing self needs a wide range of resources for its own self-construction. Psychological accounts of moral development and maturation, as I will next indicate, have stressed this for years. Communitarians have often seemed to embrace just the opposite principle, stressing the importance of homogeneous communities for the development of the self. In the next section I will challenge this notion, but unlike previous critics I will do so from within a perspective that is self-consciously communitarian.

21. This objection was raised by Mark Bickhard.

22. See the introduction to *Mind and Morals*, ed. Larry May, Marilyn Friedman, and Andy Clark (Cambridge, MA: Bradford Books/MIT Press, 1995). Also see the first chapter of Flanagan.

III. THE VALUE OF VALUE PLURALITY

Being exposed to a set of values that are unchallenged by one's community is initially advantageous for the development of self. As the boundaries of the self are first being formed, it is very important that a young child get a clear sense of who he or she is and of what is valuable, at least in a rudimentary way. But in order to mature, a child must move beyond such simple value formation. In a recent textbook on children's cognitive and developmental psychology, Lawrence Kohlberg claims that there is now agreement among psychologists that moral development in children proceeds not by their learning a particular value system and adopting it uncritically, but rather by their embracing a critical standpoint from which they can come to appreciate or reject given values. The development of a critical standpoint is achieved through "democratic and non-indoctrinative" methods in which various ideological positions are presented to children in a way that invites "criticism as well as understanding."[23]

Various other psychologists who have studied moral development support the view that heterogeneity of value perspectives is crucial in the maturation process. The cultural psychologist Carolyn Pope Edwards has argued that

> Children do not simply "receive" knowledge of standards, nor do they autonomously "construct" it without cultural assistance. Rather they "reconstruct" or "recreate" culturally appropriate moral meaning systems. That is, with increasing age and experience, children apply progressively more complex and mobile logical schemas to cultural distinctions and categories; they transform what they are told and what they experience into their own self-organized realities.[24]

I made a similar point about how critical skills develop out of cultural influences when I discussed the bootstrapping effects of moral maturation earlier in this chapter.

Elliot Turiel and Richard Schweder, who have both been critical of Kohlberg on various counts, nonetheless support the view that exposure to cultural diversity is crucial for moral maturation. Schweder bases his claims on cross-cultural research conducted in India and the United

23. Lawrence Kohlberg, *Child Psychology and Childhood Development* (New York: Longman, 1987); see chap. 3, "Development as the Aim of Education," especially pp. 82–3.

24. Carolyn Pope Edwards, "Culture and the Construction of Moral Values: A Comparative Ethnography of Moral Encounters in Two Cultural Settings," in *The Emergence of Morality in Young Children*, ed. Jerome Kagan and Sharon Lamb (Chicago: University of Chicago Press, 1987), p. 149.

States.[25] And in an extensive survey of recent literature, Turiel argues that relativism does not result when children are exposed to quite widely divergent cultural perspectives and values.[26] These psychologists admit that exposure to diverse perspectives and values is not suffcient for moral maturation, but as Kohlberg claims, they all agree that it is necessary for that maturation process to proceed beyond the conventional stage of moral reasoning.

Ego development theorists stress that at a certain stage, development requires, as Erik Erikson puts it, "the capacity to commit [oneself] to concrete affiliations and partnerships and to develop the ethical strength to abide by such commitments, even though they may call for significant sacrifices and compromises."[27] The development of what in other terms can be called integrity is indeed something that is achieved through the life cycle. At earlier stages of development it is important that the self attain an inner coherence, rather than a confusion about how to integrate conflicting ideologies and value orientations. But, perhaps surprisingly, this is best achieved not through cultural homogeneity but through exposure to cultural diversity. While maturation occurs only when a stable self emerges, what is crucial is attaining "the courage to make adult commitments in spite of a relativistic and contradictory world. . . . Critical to identity formation throughout the life cycle is the resolution of the particular polar tension that characterizes each phase."[28]

The self matures by becoming committed to certain values and beliefs as a result of critical reflection, not merely as a result of having been socialized to accept certain values and beliefs. A person attains a mature coherence of values and beliefs through a self-critical process stimulated by confrontation by diverse values and beliefs. Without such a confrontation, the self does not normally have the resources imaginatively to create alternative systems of values and beliefs to counterpose to the individual's own values and beliefs. The mechanism for moral growth is this confrontation process, which causes us to doubt our values and beliefs and then to affirm certain values and beliefs that have stood the test of critical reflection.

25. Richard Schweder, Manawohan Mahapatra, and Joan G. Miller, "Culture and Moral Development," in Kagan and Lamb, *Emergence of Morality*.

26. Elliot Turiel, Melanie Killen, and Charles C. Helwig, "Morality: Its Structure, Functions, and Vagaries," in Kagan and Lamb, *Emergence of Morality*.

27. Erik Erikson, *Childhood and Society*, 2d ed. (New York: Norton, 1963), p. 263. Cited in Kohlberg, p. 375.

28. Kohlberg, p. 375. In these passages Kohlberg is summarizing and expanding on Erikson's views, especially those developed in Erikson's *Insight and Responsibility: Lectures on the Ethical Implications of Psychoanalytic Insight* (New York: Norton, 1964), especially p. 125.

John Stuart Mill recognized the same point more than a century ago, when he argued for exposure to a plurality of values. In *On Liberty,* he argues that a "negative discussion" of whatever a person firmly believed is necessary for the

> purpose of convincing anyone who had merely adopted the common places of received opinion that he did not understand the subject— that he as yet attached no definite meaning to the doctrines he pro- fessed; in order that, becoming aware of his ignorance, he might be put in the way to obtain a stable belief, resting on a clear apprehen- sion both of the meaning of doctrines and of their evidence.[29]

For Mill, as for most contemporary psychologists, the development of a stable, integrated self is intimately linked, among other things, with being exposed to a plurality of value perspectives.

Some communitarians seemingly endorse social homogeneity over heterogeneity. Alasdair MacIntyre talks of the importance of forming communities in which there is a "shared vision of and understanding of goods."[30] Given the consensus among psychologists as to the importance of exposure to value plurality in the development of the integrated self, why have some communitarians seemingly denied it? Homogeneity is valuable in the very early stages of ego development, but a mature sense of self will not easily arise in a homogeneous environment. Communitarians who have embraced a "shared moral vision" for the development of the self do not have to reject the value of value plurality.

Many communitarians are indeed committed to the value of small, close-knit communities. On the usual communitarian view, such commu- nities are especially important for providing a stable and supportive envi- ronment for their members in order that they can more easily come to understand their roles and on this basis do what they ought to do.[31] There is indeed a strong value in having fellow community members who share a perspective on the world. But this is not at all incompatible with also plac- ing a strong value on having many such communities in close proximity to one another, each with its own distinct perspective (as long as these com- munities do not threaten one another's existence). As I indicated above,

---

29. John Stuart Mill, *On Liberty,* ed. Elizabeth Rappaport (1859; Indianapolis, IN: Hackett, 1978), p. 42.

30. Alasdair MacIntyre, *After Virtue* (Notre Dame, IN: University of Notre Dame Press, 1981), p. 240.

31. Michael Oakeshott exemplifies this view when he claims that the plethora of values in modern society creates a moral "Tower of Babel," in *Rationalism in Politics and Other Es- says* (Indianapolis, IN: Liberty Press, 1991).

both homogeneity and value plurality are important for the development of a mature and stable ego. But neither can accomplish this alone.

The development of a critical perspective by means of which integrity can be achieved depends on there being diverse values to which an individual is exposed. This fact has not eluded most communitarians, and it is surely not incompatible with their projects. Indeed, the strong emphasis among many communitarians on participatory democratic forms of government makes the most sense when the communities are heterogeneous rather than homogeneous. And while some communitarians, such as Mac-Intyre, have worried about pluralistic communities, their worries are more about assimilationist societies than about societies where there are diverse communities existing side by side. What communitarians have rejected is the idea that political order should be maintained over such diverse communities without some thread of shared morality being laced through them. I support such a view. But this is not to say that this thread must encompass all values.[32] Without the challenge to many of our values that comes from diversity of perspective, our commitments will not be very strong or, more importantly, understood and reflectively endorsed. Neither communitarians nor their critics envision a world where people are strongly committed to goals and projects merely because everyone else in their communities is so committed.

IV. BEING COMMITTED

As I said at the outset, integrity has three dimensions: coherence of value orientation, mature development of a critical point of view, and disposition to act in a principled way. The third dimension has been characterized as "having a point of no return," a point beyond which one will not go, regardless of the circumstances or the risks to personal well-being. From this third dimension arises the idea that the person of integrity will engage in self-sacrifice in certain cases. Can communitarians embrace this dimension of integrity similarly to the way they can, on my account, embrace the first two dimensions? In this fourth section I will provide an affirmative response to this question.

Let us begin by looking at one influential treatment of the notion of commitment in the context of integrity. Lynn McFall argues that "personal integrity requires unconditional commitments."[33] On this account of in-

32. For a discussion of a case in which there is a conflict between different communities' moral values within a larger pluralistic society, see my discussion in chap. 9, "Challenging Medical Authority," sec. 1, "Two Christian Science Refusal Cases."

33. Lynn McFall, "Integrity," in *Ethics and Personality,* ed. John Deigh (Chicago: University of Chicago Press, 1992), pp. 85 and 90.

tegrity, unconditional commitments are definitive of the self's "core."[34] As she says at the very end of her essay, "Without integrity and the identity conferring commitments it assumes, there would be nothing to fear the loss of, not because we are safe but because we have nothing to lose."[35]

Without some moral commitments we feel compelled to stay with, there is very little to us as moral agents. As we will see, this way of understanding commitment in integrity is in many respects quite compatible with the communitarian picture of integrity I have been sketching, but there are a few aspects of this understanding of commitment that communitarians rightly would reject.

On first sight, it might appear that a communitarian cannot accept a strong notion of stable personal commitment since the self is merely what it has been influenced to become by forces outside its control. Just as these forces have influenced the self's formation in a particular way, in terms of current commitments, so those forces could influence the self to abandon its current commitments, or so it would seem. While there may be a very temporary core of commitments that seem unshakable, the fluidity of the socially constructed self would seemingly rule out such comments as that by e. e. cummings's character Olaf in the poem from which McFall draws, namely, " 'there is some shit I will not eat.' " It could only be true in a relatively trivial sense, namely, "at this moment I will not do X but who can say about tomorrow."

My response to the above challenge to the possibility of a committed communitarian self begins by noting that it is not plausible to think that integrity requires commitments on which a person would *never* renege. Integrity cannot require that people form commitments that are unbreakable, even for very good moral reasons, because this would be both psychologically implausible and morally pernicious. Rather, integrity requires a sense of realistic commitment. According to this construal, commitments are often very strong through a certain period of one's life but become significantly weaker later in life, while other commitments that were once weak become more important and stronger than ones previously thought of as unshakable. It may be important that one have, at any given time, very strongly held commitments. But it is implausible to think that an integrated or committed person must hold certain unshakable commitments over the course of his or her life.

Once we let go of the idea that commitments must be unshakable, it becomes easier to see how a communitarian could endorse the importance of commitment to integrity. Consider someone who has come to believe that "respect for private property" is the most important value in his life.

34. Ibid., p. 87.
35. Ibid., p. 94.

This is held as a strong commitment and forms a major part of the person's self-conception. But now imagine that this person is exposed to the culture of homeless people in America, or is presented with a particularly vivid example such as the Heinz dilemma, employed in moral psychology (a dilemma in which someone finds that his only hope of saving his wife's life is to steal a drug from a pharmacy). No one could plausibly say that the weakening of the commitment to the value of private property must carry with it the charge of lack of integrity. If this man now sees the "harm principle" as more important than the "property principle," and realigns his other beliefs and commitments accordingly, then only on the basis of the most static conception of integrity could it be said that he lacks integrity. Indeed, psychologists would consider the change to be often a sign of moral maturation rather than lack of integrity.

On my view, the self is a *web* of commitments.[36] On this view, the self does not have a core of commitments that are unshakeable. The metaphor of a web conjures up the image of a group of commitments that are all interrelated, but where the form of interrelation and the strength of each part may vary over time. A communitarian conception of self and integrity can encompass a notion of strong commitment, but such commitments are not best understood on the model of an impervious core. A web is pervious to outside factors and is hence a better metaphor for the social self and its commitments than is the metaphor of an impervious core self composed of unshakable commitments.

Consider the example of an engineer who holds the view that service to community safety is of paramount concern, and considers it one of her chief professional values. Now imagine that this engineer is asked to approve a building project that uses materials the engineer deems to be inferior to other materials that would better secure the safety of those who will occupy the building. When the engineer confronts her supervisor, she is told to keep quiet about this or lose her job. The engineer is the sole support of two small children. Loss of her job would be devastating to her family. If after critical reflection she adjusts her values so that service to community safety is somewhat lessened, allowing her to follow the lead of her supervisor, she has not necessarily lost her integrity. Loss of integrity is not a function of change of beliefs or values, but rather of unreflective change.[37] There are no particular strands in the web of commitments that are necessary for the continued identity of a given self. One advantage of holding to my particular communitarian conception of self and integrity is

---

36. Gabriele Taylor has also suggested that we see the self as a web of commitments. See her discussion of this point in Taylor, *Pride, Shame, and Guilt*, pp. 139–40.

37. For a lengthy discussion of such cases see chap. 6, "Professional Integrity."

that it makes it easier to understand how change within the self can be understood as morally beneficial. Victoria Davion, who has argued for a similar position to mine from a radical feminist perspective,[38] contends that

> the idea that moral integrity depends on a core of unchanging commitments is inconsistent with the kind of radical change that many feminists have been trying to encourage. For change to be radical, it must take place at the roots, at the deepest level.[39]

Davion argues that if integrity is associated with having unconditional substantive commitments, then when one has a major change of commitments, coming to reject heterosexism, for instance, then one must literally become a new person. But this seems counterintuitive since, in many cases, there is so much other continuity between the person before and after the radical change of commitment.

On the account I have sketched above, it is the process rather than the substance of one's beliefs that is most important for integrity.[40] What is unique about each of us is often more a matter of how we approach the world, especially of how we adapt to the changing contexts we encounter, than of the specific beliefs we hold. This approach to self and integrity fits well with the metaphor I adopted above of the self as a web of commitments. The holes in the web are as important as the strands, for the holes tell us quite a bit about how pervious and adaptable to changing context a particular self is likely to be.

On my account of integrity it is important that a person find resources within himself or herself to act in a way he or she can live with. The idea that one should be true to oneself is so important in our understandings of conscience and morality generally that if communitarians could not accommodate it, their views should be greatly diminished.[41] But, as I have been arguing, communitarians need not abandon the idea of commitment. What they must do, though—and this is not an easy matter at all—is to comprehend commitment within a sea of often conflicting value orientations that exist within a single self. In the final section of this chapter, I will explore this point in more detail.

38. Victoria Davion, "Integrity and Radical Change," in *Feminist Ethics,* ed. Claudia Card (Lawrence: University of Kansas Press, 1991), pp. 180–92.

39. Ibid., p. 181.

40. Similarly, in searching for a way to characterize what stays the same in even radical changes of commitment, Davion seizes on the idea that "being true to oneself" may depend on a certain kind of commitment "to being careful and paying attention to one's growth process." See Davion, p. 184.

41. See my essay, "On Conscience," *American Philosophical Quarterly* 20, no. 1 (January 1983).

Moral integrity is not best understood as holding steadfastly to a code of conduct or rules that others have provided, even if one endorses the code or rules. Rather, moral integrity is best seen as a form of maturation in which reflection on a plurality of values provides a critical coherence to one's experiences. Achieving integrity means developing a critical perspective that allows at least for a temporarily stable standpoint from which to endorse or reject new social influences. But the person of integrity is just as likely to reject as to accept a given code of conduct or set of rules he or she has been presented with, since the code or rules may indeed be opposed by other values in the society that the person of integrity also regards as important.

The person of integrity, on my communitarian view, is responsive to all of the various social groups that have been instrumental in forming his or her "core" self. Contrary to what is sometimes said, professional integrity does not require that people steadfastly stick to the standards commonly recognized for members of a particular profession.

The paragon of integrity is sometimes someone who heroically upholds these professional standards, but it is more likely to be someone who heroically opposes those standards in the face of more important considerations from some other quarter of society. When a person acts as if only one set of values or principles were important in his or her life, such a person does not display the maturity that is one of the three hallmarks of the integrated self.

Integrity involves a coherent, at least temporarily stable, conception of who one is and what one's commitments are. The self's "core," in terms of which values are accepted or rejected, is itself formed through a process of socialization. The self comes to be a coherent "web of commitments" over time, and the process of development may continue over an entire lifetime. At any given point in the life of a mature person, retaining integrity will often involve some sacrifices so as to live up to one's principles. But during the life of a mature person, being true to oneself may be consistent with radical changes of value orientation. Exposure to differing values is essential to personal growth.

Throughout this chapter I have presented a pluralistic communitarian conception of integrity. According to this account, the self that brings about value coherence and makes commitments is the same self that initially is instilled with values and commitments from the various groups in its social environment. What does the controlling is a developing self, and how control is exerted is through the use of critical skills to accept or reject that which comes to the self from its environment. In this sense, achieving integrity is a form of "bootstrapping," whereby one learns to make use of the very things that one initially has little control over so as to gain control. The principles that one comes to call one's own are endorsed through a process of socialization in which one achieves one's "core" values. And what is most important is that there be a wide plurality of values to which the individual self is exposed in the developmental process of ego formation. Far from requiring homogeneity in societies, pluralistic communitarianism views wide-scale value plurality as crucial in the development of a mature person of integrity. This conception of integrity should hold strong appeal for all of us who find ourselves in a pluralistic world trying both to understand, and to be true to, who we are.

In the following chapters we will explore the importance of moral support and socialization for providing the kind of environment in which it may make sense to expect people to be strongly committed to certain rules or principles. On this count, my version of communitarianism is compatible with certain aspects of critical theory, although this is not necessarily true of other versions of communitarianism.[42] Seyla Benhabib is one critical theorist who has presented a conception of the self very close to my own. She claims that "individuation does not precede association; rather, it is the kinds of associations which we inhabit that define the kinds of individuals we will become."[43] For my view, as for many critical theorists, integrity is achieved through a process of maturation that is greatly influenced by socialization patterns. We will explore this theme in much more detail in the next three chapters.

A view sometimes expressed in codes of professional conduct is that people are supposed to be true to the principles of their profession regardless of the personal consequences. Virtue theorists and communitarians have challenged the legitimacy of such claims, arguing that it is a mistake to expect people to act in a morally heroic or saintly manner. I believe, to the contrary, that it can be legitimate to demand of a person quite high levels of sacrifice for a certain group's principles, but only when one of two conditions is met: either the good to be achieved by the principled conduct is very great indeed, or the person who is expected to sacrifice is given significant moral support from his or her community. I explore the importance of solidarity and moral support in the next chapter.

42. See Seyla Benhabib, "Autonomy, Modernity and Community," in *Situating the Self* (New York: Routledge, 1992), pp. 77–78, where she distinguishes between an "integrationist communitarianism," which stresses the importance of the inculcation of a coherent value scheme, and a "participationist communitarianism," which "does not see social differentiation as an aspect of modernity which needs to be overcome. Rather the participationist advocates the reduction of contradictions and irrationalities among the various spheres, and the encouragement of non-exclusive principles of membership among the spheres."
43. Ibid., p. 71.

2

SOLIDARITY AND MORAL SUPPORT

In the previous chapter I set out a communitarian conception of the self and of moral integrity. In subsequent chapters I wish to investigate how such an account connects with the claims of responsibility and obligation that groups make on their members. The current chapter acts as a bridge between these two tasks. In what follows I will examine the concept of solidarity, the main vehicle by which individuals feel related to the other members of their communities, and one of the main sources of motivation for individuals to come to the aid of these fellow group members. Solidarity provides a basis for the sense of connectedness that builds communities, and it also provides a basis for the kind of security that individuals seek, especially when they are asked to sacrifice their individual interests for the common good.

In this chapter, I argue that solidarity is intimately linked to both moral support and security. Solidarity must exist within a community before its moral demands are likely to be heeded by the members of a community. In this sense, solidarity plays an important, although largely unrecognized, role in ethics. I begin with an analysis of the concept of solidarity and I provide a preliminary argument for seeing bonds of sentiment as crucial to solidarity. I then turn to a discussion of group identity and its importance for those who are oppressed as well as for those in professional life. In the third section, I argue that solidarity plays an important moral role because of its close connection with the concept of moral support. In the fourth section, I discuss the attempt by Richard Rorty and Jürgen Habermas to extend the notion of solidarity to include a community encompassing all humans. While basically in sympathy with this move, I express some doubts about extending the concept of solidarity, even given its moral orientation, to the whole of humanity.

I. SOLIDARITY AND BONDS OF SENTIMENT

Sociologists have used the term *solidarity* descriptively to refer to the extent of cohesiveness within a group. Emile Durkheim, somewhat an exception in this respect, talks of two types of solidarity, mechanical and organic, which have strong moral dimensions. Mechanical solidarity depends on a cohesiveness that is "the result of resemblances."[1] Families and clans are based on "consanguinity," relation by blood or other natural or fictitious similarity. Durkheim claims that there is a great deal of homogeneity in societies where there is mechanical solidarity, and this means that people have little real individuality. As a result, the member "becomes, with those whom he resembles, part of the same collective."[2] The members of such groups come to have very similar consciences. It is this similarity of conscience that seems to account for the fact that members of such groups feel bound to one another. And, reconstructing a bit, Durkheim is thus led to claim that altruism develops on the basis of similarity of conscience, or what he calls "collective conscience."

Durkheim contrasts this mechanical solidarity with organic solidarity. Here groups are "constituted, not by repetition of similar, homogenous segments, but by a system of different organs each of which has a special role, and which are themselves formed by differentiated parts . . . coordinated and subordinated one to another around the same central organ."[3] In such societies the function or role each member is supposed to fill is what binds the individual to the group. The hallmark of such societies is the division of labor and the ensuing interdependence which provides social cohesion. As Durkheim puts it, the member depends upon other members "in the same measure that he is distinguished from them, and consequently upon the society which results from their union." As in mechanical solidarity, altruism also arises out of organic solidarity, but not because of likeness or resemblance but because of "the social division of labor."[4]

Durkheim identifies two ways in which a group can achieve solidarity: through homogeneity and through dependency. In contemporary literature, it is common to talk of these roots of solidarity as both based in an interest that each member of a group has in the group, which is often understood as interests in the interests of one another. I will later say much more about this strategy (in the discussion of Feinberg). But it is interesting

1. Durkheim, Emile, *Emile Durkheim on Morality and Society,* ed. Robert Bellah (Chicago: University of Chicago Press, 1973), p. 63.
2. Ibid., p. 110.
3. Ibid., p. 69.
4. Ibid., p. 110.

to note that Durkheim eschews such analysis, maintaining that "if interest relates men, it is never for more than some few moments. It can create only an external link between them. . . . Consciences are only in superficial contact; they neither penetrate each other, nor do they adhere."[5] For Durkheim, it seems that the bonds formed by mutual self-interest will be very short-lived since no serious attachment to the other is formed on this basis. In order for there to be serious attachment, commonality of conscience must accompany commonality of interest.

For Durkheim the most important concept in understanding group solidarity is "collective conscience." By this he means a system of shared values and beliefs dependent on rituals that facilitate consensus within the group. What binds people together as far as solidarity is concerned is their felt bond with one another and their readiness to act collectively in one another's behalf,[6] that is, their adherence to one another rather than to a set of rules.[7] Indeed, Marx was quite correct, in my view, when he said that a revolutionary class must develop "radical chains" if it is to be successful.[8] These chains or bonds are characterized by a mutuality of interest that is conjoined with a mutual willingness to offer support to one another. The bonds that so develop often persist even as self-interests change.

Solidarity is unlike compliance to rule or law in that mutuality of interest is tightly intertwined with mutuality of support. Groups can surely cohere without achieving solidarity, and this is especially evident when very large groups achieve a temporary coherence. Often it is impossible for each member of the group to feel attachment to, or even to know, the other members of the group. Here compliance to a central authority can produce coherence for the group. Rational choice theorists and others who follow Thomas Hobbes are correct in thinking that, because of the free rider problem, such groups may need strong controls, such as rule socialization or coercion, in order to maintain this coherence over time.[9] But when coherence is so achieved it is not best understood as depending on solidarity.

5. Ibid., p. 89.

6. See Rick Fantasia's discussion of what he calls "transformative associational bonding." *Cultures of Solidarity: Consciousness, Action and Contemporary American Workers* (Berkeley: University of California Press, 1988), pp. 8–11.

7. I explore the idea that morality is not best understood as a matter of following rules in chap. 5, "Social Responsibility."

8. Karl Marx, introduction to *Contribution to the Critique of Hegel's Philosophy of Right*, reprinted in *The Marx-Engels Reader*, 2d ed., trans. and ed. Robert C. Tucker (New York: W. W. Norton and Co., 1978), p. 64.

9. For a very good discussion of this point see Tony Honore, *Making Law Bind* (Oxford: Clarendon Press, 1987).

Controls do not produce the feelings of connectedness, adherence to one another, or personal bindingness that since the time of Marx and Durkheim have been recognized to epitomize solidarity. This is most obviously true because controls do not create an autonomous sense of responsibility since it is the external control rather than an internal choice or decision that binds.

It is now time to become much more specific in ascertaining the main elements in solidarity. Joel Feinberg provides us with a good start when he isolates three "intertwined conditions" that must "be satisfied to some degree."[10] He contends that first of all "there must be a large community of interest among all the members. . . . A community of interest exists between two parties to the extent that each party's integrated set of interests contains as one of its components the integrated interest-set of the other."[11] While a useful place to start, this condition is stated too strongly. Surely, each individual member of a group that coheres by solidarity does not have to have the entire interest-set of his or her fellow group members as one of his or her own interests. While I may feel strongly that my fellow faculty members should do well, this does not mean that I specifically want them to get the university's internal summer grant that I am also interested in. Indeed, many of my fellow faculty members may have an interest in the election of a Republican president, which is not at all my interest. Nonetheless, on matters of academic freedom we may all stand united in solidarity with a colleague whom the university administration is trying to silence.

Rather than contending that each member must have the integrated set of interests of all other members as one of his or her interests, I would contend that for solidarity the relevant condition (among several others) is that each member have an interest in the general well-being of the group, but not an interest in each of the things that the other member has an interest in. In addition, as I said above, I agree with Durkheim that we should not stress mutuality of interest over mutuality of attachment or mutual willingness to offer support. Indeed, mutuality of interest is far too weak, in any event, to account for the bonds of sentiment or attachment that develop where solidarity is present. But Feinberg recognizes this in that he discusses two other conditions that are intertwined with mutuality of interest. In my opinion, it is the second of his three conditions that is the most important.

As his second condition of solidarity, Feinberg identifies "bonds of

10. Joel Feinberg, "Collective Responsibility," in *Doing and Deserving* (Princeton: Princeton University Press, 1970), p. 234.
11. Ibid.

sentiment directed toward common objects, or of reciprocal affection between parties."[12] This is the element of solidarity missing in the accounts
of solidarity that focus exclusively on the interests of the individual members. It is important to note that Feinberg separates these bonds into two
groups: reciprocal affection, and sentiment directed at a common object.
In the latter group we will find fear of a common enemy. I would add that
there is at least one more possibility: attachment based not necessarily on
mutual affection or liking but rather on interdependency. This is the category that encompasses Durkheim's organic solidarity, that is, solidarity
based on the interdependence that arises out of the division of labor.

Feinberg also mentions, as his third condition, that group solidarity is
"ordinarily a function of the degree to which the parties share a common
lot, the extent to which their goods and harms are necessarily collective
and indivisible."[13] Such a condition is sometimes present, but we should
not regard this as necessary or even common in cases of solidarity. Poverty
is indeed the kind of "common lot" that will intensify solidarity, as is also
true of membership in a particular profession. But having a common lot
does not necessarily mean that goods or harms are collective and indivisible. Indeed, this is often just the problem: it turns out that there can be
significant subgroup differences that cause goods or harms to be distrib-
uted so disparately that some members are not benefited or harmed at all,
while others are. Yet, regardless of benefit or harm, the members may feel
morally driven to support one another. Because of my status within the
university, I may be insulated from recent budget cutbacks. Nonetheless, I
may feel solidarity with the untenured members of the faculty and hence
feel morally driven to speak out against these cutbacks.

A consideration of various cases will show that Feinberg has somewhat mischaracterized solidarity and this has allowed him to claim that
group solidarity is no longer very common.[14] Feinberg thinks that solidarity exists primarily where individual group members display "vicarious
pride and shame."[15] While it is often true that solidarity goes hand in hand
with vicarious pride and shame, solidarity may also exist when these vicarious feelings are absent. The bindingness felt is based on a willingness of
the members to offer moral support to one another, even when they do not
feel so deeply committed to one another's lives as to feel pride or shame
through them. One may feel motivated to take responsibility for the other
even though one disapproves of what the other is doing, thereby blocking

12. Ibid.
13. Ibid.
14. Ibid., p. 235.
15. Ibid., p. 236.

any feelings of vicarious pride or shame. This is because in solidarity one can make at least two forms of identification: an identification with the other's behavior, and an identification with the other's characteristics. My brother who commits a crime and is sent to prison is still my brother even as I strongly disagree with his past behavior. I can decide to display solidarity with him as a fellow family member and yet feel not the slightest vicarious shame in what he has done. Of course, if I could easily imagine myself as the one who had committed the crime, I may feel vicarious shame since I identify now with his behavior as well as with who he is.

In the next section, I will examine in more detail the notion of group identity and in the third section, the notion of collective conscience that Durkheim believed to be the key to solidarity. I will attempt to explain how collective conscience is linked with a certain form of conscious group identification. I will also explain the link between collective conscience and a willingness to show moral support for the fellow members of one's group. In the fourth section, I address the question of whether collective conscience and solidarity generally can extend to the group of all humans, as has been recently claimed in various quarters, especially by the social philosopher Jürgen Habermas.

II. SELF-PERCEPTION AND GROUP IDENTITY

One of the standard ways to characterize group identity is in terms of whether individuals perceive themselves as related to each other as group members. On this view, group identity is thought to turn on the question of whether certain individuals regard themselves as related to each other as members of the same group. It will not matter that society perceives a particular person as a member of a certain group. All that matters is whether the person consciously so categorizes himself or herself. Whether based on mere subjective feeling or not, group identity is often said to be determined by the individual member, either in terms of self-perceptions or in terms of the member's recognition of commonalities with others.

This approach privileges the claims of the individual group member, rather than leaving the determination of collective identity and group membership in the hands of societies or governments. There are many good reasons initially to support such a position. But this approach can often obscure various kinds of harm that are based on the categorizations made by other persons. Self-perception can be a problematic basis for the assignment of group identity, especially when such a determination affects the assignment of group rights. Many people who may need the protection of a group right will not be afforded this protection in those cases where they do not identify with the group because of their own self-deception or societally produced deception about their shared group identity or common interests with the group.[16] So, while it is a good thing generally to empower people to decide for themselves who they are and which claims to press, in the case of group identity this is not always the best policy. Other criteria for the determination of group identity and for corresponding claims of group rights should be employed, especially in cases where self-perceptions are fragmented but societal perceptions are not.

Understanding group identity by reference to self-perceived identifications has some appeal, but it is not the only possible basis for the establishment of group identity. Indeed, the exclusive reliance on what the group members themselves think or desire ignores the fact that how a group is treated is often as much a function of societal perception as of individual perception. Group identity cannot be based solely on self-perceptions since this would lead to the absurd result that a person's merely thinking of himself as Black or Jewish would make it plausible to say that he is Black or Jewish, regardless of what his actual characteristics were and regardless of how the rest of the group, or the society at large, perceived him.

There are at least two distinct approaches to the determination of group identity: an observer perspective and a participant perspective.[17] The observer approach would identify groups and members of groups by reference to how the putative individual members act and to how they are perceived by others. The observer perspective focuses on how groups interact both with their members and with other groups and stresses the "resources" that groups have to impose their views on others. On this view, solidarity is merely a resource employed by some groups to maintain group cohesion and thereby to gain more power. The societal or outsider voice, rather than the group member's own voice, is privileged.

Generally, we are no better off, indeed we may be quite a bit worse off, when the shift is made from a participant perspective to an observer per-

---

16. Jürgen Habermas has recently written about this problem and has taken a position opposed to affording group rights to minorities. See his essay "Struggles for Recognition in Constitutional States," *European Journal of Philosophy* 1/2 (1993).

17. Habermas has argued that a good social theory, especially one that hopes to have an emancipatory effect, must integrate two different perspectives. On the one hand, "society is conceived from the participant's perspective of the acting subject *as the lifeworld of a social group.* On the other hand, from the observer's perspective of the non-participant, society can be conceived as a *system of actions* in which a functional significance accrues to a given action according to its contribution to system maintenance." Jürgen Habermas, *The Theory of Communicative Action,* vol. 2, trans. Thomas McCarthy (Boston: Beacon Press, 1987), p. 117. McCarthy has corrected his own translation and offered a commentary on this passage. See his essay "Complexity and Democracy: or the Seducements of Systems Theory," in *Communicative Action,* ed. Axel Honneth and Hans Joas (Cambridge: MIT Press, 1991), p. 120.

spective of group identity. The voice of those who are builders of social systems should not drown out the voices of the individual members of social groups whose lives we are attempting to explain and understand. But there is one aspect of the observer orientation that is worthy of attention, namely, that this approach allows us to understand the basis of mistreatment of and discrimination against the members of groups in ways hard to fathom from a participant perspective only. Group oppression is often hard to understand or even recognize without taking account of how the society at large categorizes the oppressed group, rather than how the oppressed group members view themselves.

Consider, for example, a recent controversy about the practice at the Smithsonian Institution of returning American Indian bones from the Smithsonian's archives only if the bones were requested by the members of the same tribe or of a tribe with close connection to the tribe of the Indian whose bones were in question. This policy was defended by the claim that American Indians do not identify themselves as Indians but rather as members of particular tribes. From a participant perspective, tribal affiliation was the key to identifying who should have claims on whether or not to rebury these bones. But from an observer perspective, in which the dominant society regards Indians as virtually an undifferentiated mass, the policy could not be defended.

A group can suffer regardless of whether the group has enough coherence to be able to act, and regardless of whether the members identify themselves as group members. Indeed a group, such as American Indians, can suffer even though the members of this group do not conceive of themselves at all as connected to one another. This is because it is sufficient for suffering as a group if others characterize and categorize people as an undifferentiated mass, and thereby react in the same harmful way to all of the people they perceive as members.[18] It is in this sense that the observer perspective contains an important grain of truth. We should not focus exclusively on the participant perspective, for this makes it very hard to account for, and to redress, the way that some groups are oppressed and harmed on the basis of characteristics recognized by the oppressor group although not necessarily by the group members who are being oppressed. It is in this way that solidarity is seen to be a *political* as well as a moral concept. The struggles for power within a society often determine who achieves solidarity and who does not, and solidarity is also often something that must be achieved through difficult political coalition building.[19]

But we should also not focus exclusively on the observer perspective.

18. See my extended discussion of this notion in *The Morality of Groups,* chaps. 5 and 6.
19. I am grateful to Diana Meyers for this point.

To do so would allow the society or the social scientist to have the privilege of deciding who is a member of a given group by completely ignoring the way in which individuals conceive of themselves. This would have the effect of denying the individual the ability to participate in an enterprise that is important for the formation of individual identity, not just of group identity. As we saw in the first chapter, one's identity is tied up with the associations one makes with the groups one identifies with.[20] It is important not to deprive an individual of at least some control over the determination of his or her identity in terms of the associations he or she makes with various groups.[21]

Charles Taylor has proposed a counterfactual assessment that supplements the participant perspective by asking how the participants would identify themselves "if they were to understand themselves well and all false consciousness were to be eliminated."[22] Taylor's proposal has the advantage of supplementing the participant perspective with some reference to the social reality. Because of self-deception and other problems, participants are often not able to understand fully their own identities vis-à-vis various groups. By taking this into account, Taylor attempts to blend participant and observer perspectives. But such a supplement, in my opinion, does not quite accomplish an integration of these perspectives. Eliminating false consciousness will allow us to capture the cases in which individuals refuse to see themselves as group members even though they are aware, on some level of consciousness, that they are being identified as group members. But the extreme case, in which the members of a group are not aware that they are seen as constituting a group by those external to the group, will not be captured by Taylor's counterfactual analysis.[23] Taylor still relies too heavily on the participant perspective, even in this augmented version of that perspective.

Instead, we need an additional supplement that adds a further counterfactual, asking how the participants would identify themselves "if these individuals were aware of how others in society categorized them." Such a supplement truly coordinates the two perspectives since it requires us to

---

20. See my discussion of this point in *Sharing Responsibility,* especially chaps. 4 and 9.

21. It may be instructive to consult the classic study on the relationship between group affiliation and the development of individual identity. See Sigmund Freud, *Group Psychology and the Analysis of the Ego,* trans. and ed. James Strachey (1922; New York: W. W. Norton and Co., 1959), especially chaps. 7 and 10.

22. Charles Taylor, "Language and Society," in Honneth and Joas, eds., *Communicative Action,* p. 26.

23. Nonetheless, Taylor's insight is helpful in the understanding of solidarity, as we will see later, by pointing up the major challenge: to get people to bring their own self-perceptions into line with the way that society perceives their behavior.

consider how the individual's perception of his or her group affiliations would change if he or she were aware of how others in the society viewed his or her behavior.[24] This supplement suggests that the individual is still, as it were, the focus of our analysis of group identity, but it seeks to offset the possibility that the individual is simply unaware of important facts about how he or she is behaving or how this behavior is being perceived by others.

The observer perspective brings out the fact that the behavior of certain group members is not regarded by society in the same way as it is by the group members themselves, as well as the fact that economic and social factors interfere with the independence of the group members. Until individuals take a group-oriented approach, it will appear as if the participant and observer perspectives were mutually exclusive, when in reality they can be coordinated.[25] This is why, for Marxists and other social theorists, solidarity necessarily involves the oppressed's overcoming false consciousness and recognizing how the oppressor class treats the oppressed class. Without this understanding, an important motivational dimension will be lacking.

As we have seen, solidarity is more than group identity felt by individuals from the participant perspective. Individual group members need to understand how others perceive and treat them in order to understand their true interests and to be most likely to identify with one another sufficiently to feel motivated to come to one another's aid. Solidarity involves a moral dimension, namely, willingness of the members of a group to engage in individual or collective action so as to aid fellow group members. Not all groups display these moral dimensions, even when their members identify themselves as group members. I next present an argument for seeing solidarity as a moral notion.

III. COLLECTIVE CONSCIENCE AND MORAL SUPPORT

In the previous sections, it was contended that solidarity involves rather strong bonds of sentiment among group members. The examples considered so far support the commonly held intuition that solidarity is more than mere group identification. In addition, solidarity enables individual and collective moral action because of the strong ties that exist within the group. Specifically, in solidarity the members of a group feel motivated to

24. To say that these perspectives are coordinated is not to say that they are melded. It may still turn out that in any particular case one or the other perspective dominates. What is coordinated is the consideration of both perspectives.

25. I am grateful to Jim Bohman for pointing this out to me.

engage in individual or collective action in support of one another because of the felt commonality within the group. In this sense, there is a strong altruistic or moral dimension in solidarity, and it is thus a mistake for social theorists to think of solidarity as merely a matter of collective (especially class) consciousness.[26]

On my account, as on Durkheim's, the bonds of sentiment characteristic of solidarity are, at least in part, moral. By this I mean that when solidarity exists people feel motivated (by feelings of obligation or responsibility) to aid one another, at least within a circumscribed realm of behavior. When people feel solidarity with one another they do identify on some level with one another, but in addition they stand ready to go to one another's aid. Most characteristically, this readiness displays itself in offers of moral support. Forms of aid or moral support range from various forms of helping behavior (such as assisting, facilitating, or cooperating) to direct action to confront harm to the other (such as retaliating, boycotting, or engaging in a strike). What is crucial is not the kind of behavior but, rather, the degree of seriousness with which the group members resolve to help one another, or react to harm. In this section I will explore more fully two dimensions of the kind of moral support that is associated with solidarity.

The recognition of how one's identity is intertwined with that of a group will sometimes make explicit what was perhaps only implicit or subliminal, namely, the degree of convergence between values of the self and values of the other members of one's group. This recognition does not necessarily lead to greater altruism toward the others, but it often can do so. In this sense, conscious group identity and solidarity can be at least contingently linked. As the linchpin of solidarity, collective conscience remains a thoroughly other-directed notion. But in what sense is it moral? The key is to understand how collective conscience is intertwined with feeling motivated to provide a member of one's group with moral support.

In the remainder of this section I wish to build on some of Durkheim's insights in attempting to explain the importance of the altruistic or moral dimension of solidarity. In doing so, I will also be guided by the following remark made by Freud in *Group Psychology and the Analysis of the Ego*:

> The psychology of such a [human] group, as we know it from descriptions to which we have so often referred—the dwindling of the conscious individual personality, the focusing of thoughts and feelings into a common direction, the predominance of the affective side of the mind and of unconscious psychical life, the tendency of the

26. Some sociologists have recently criticized the heavy reliance in their discipline on class consciousness instead of readiness to engage in collective action as the identifying characteristic of solidarity. See Fantasia, *Cultures of Solidarity,* especially chap. 1.

immediate carrying out of intentions as they emerge—all this corresponds to a state of regression to a primitive mental activity. . . . Thus the group appears to us to be a revival of the primal horde.[27]

While I find most of this to be overstated, it turns on the psychological insight that people in some groups tend to focus more on what is good for the group (that is, the common good) than is true when solidarity is lacking.[28]

The social category that contrasts with solidarity and collective conscience is alienation, in which a person finds little or no commonality of beliefs or values with the members of a group.[29] The alienated person tends not to think about the common good, rather focusing on his or her own individual good.[30] If a person feels unconnected to a group, he or she will in all likelihood have no feelings of attachment to the group or even to the members of the group. On the other hand, when one feels connected to others by common beliefs and values, as is true in collective conscience, there is a tendency to think about the common good as a result of feelings of attachment with the group and with its members. This focus on the common good is related to two different dimensions of moral support in solidarity. First, solidarity provides an impetus to various members of a group to feel motivated to go to the aid of fellow members who are in need. Second, and perhaps because of the first, solidarity also provides an impetus for a particular group member to feel motivated to overcome egoistic concerns in favor of concerns about the common good.[31]

Solidarity is one of the major forces counteracting the feelings of egoistic alienation that many people feel when faced with a certain kind of moral dilemma. When a person feels alienated from any possible community of which he or she could be a member, that person often lacks the resources to stand on her or his principles and act for the common good. Consider the case of a professional engineer who is faced with a dilemma: either to conform to a demand by her corporate employer to sign a statement saying that a product is safe, or to decline to sign, as is required by her code of professional conduct, because she believes that the product is actually unsafe for the people who will most likely buy it. Without the support

27. Freud, pp. 54–55.

28. In chap. 10 I take up the question of whether solidarity can itself lead to morally problematic results. Not all forms of solidarity result in "moral" support.

29. Alienation can coexist with solidarity, although such occasions are rare. This is because solidarity often provides a person with a sense of belonging.

30. See Richard Schacht's discussion of this point in *Alienation* (Garden City, NY: Anchor Books, 1971), especially pp. 165–6.

31. I am not suggesting that solidarity is the only basis for such feelings of altruism.

of her professional group, such a person may feel that she has too high a price to pay for doing what her profession declares to be morally right.[32]

Solidarity increases the resources that the self has to draw upon to counteract the self-interested motivations to violate one's principles that are based on a worry about retaliation when one acts as one thinks one should. Such self-interested motivations are supplied by oppressor groups and employing organizations that put strong pressure on the individual to conform to the normative standards of these oppressor groups or employing organizations. Such groups and organizations are often successful because they rely on the feelings of alienation and lack of connectedness of those they seek to pressure. Indeed, it seems to be too much to expect of an isolated individual that he or she act on his or her principles in the face of strong pressure. What is needed is moral support that can supply countervailing pressure on behalf of the principled response, which is often drawn in terms of the common good.[33]

As a result of knowing that there is a support group, the individual group member is made more likely to look to the group's common good. Solidarity unifies a group in a particular way, through what we have been calling bonds of sentiment and moral support. Conscious group identity and bonds of sentiment are needed for solidarity, and the lack of such factors is one of the major causes of alienation and lack of morally principled behavior. But is such solidarity likely in a very large group, indeed in the largest group—the group of all humans? In the next section, I will cast some doubt on the feasibility of such solidarity in spite of what philosophers such as Jürgen Habermas and Richard Rorty have recently claimed.

IV. SOLIDARITY AND HUMANITY

Joel Feinberg has made a very interesting remark concerning solidarity in very large groups:

> I, for one, am quite incapable of feeling the same kind of solidarity with all white men, a motley group of one billion persons who are, in my mind, no more an "organization" than is the entire human race as such. I certainly feel no bonds to seventeenth-century slave traders analogous to those ties of identification an American Negro must

---

32. See chap. 6, "Professional Integrity," for an extended discussion of examples such as this.
33. See my discussion of this point in the monograph *Professional Responsibility for Harmful Actions,* which I coauthored with Martin Curd (Dubuque, IA: Kendall/Hunt Publishing, 1984).

naturally feel with the captured slaves. Precisely because of this failure of imagination, I can feel no shame on their behalf.[34]

I have already taken issue with using vicarious pride or shame as a test of solidarity; but it seems to me nonetheless that Feinberg has put his finger on something important here that I shall try to explicate in what follows.

Consider the case of someone who feels solidarity with the peasants in El Salvador who are struggling to end their oppression. There are at least two possible roots of solidarity here: one based on an identification with the peasants' revolutionary activities, and one based on who the peasants are, perhaps focusing on their suffering or on their minority status within their home country or on their ethnicity. The bonds that are felt with these peasants may be based on an identification one makes with their revolutionary activity, which gives rise to feelings of vicarious pride with each victory the peasants achieve over the oppressive government forces. Or the bond may arise from identifying with their plight. This latter, possible basis for solidarity may not give rise to vicarious pride or shame but may move one to act collectively in another's aid. Such bonds may be based on common beliefs and feelings that we should take responsibility for helping those whose need is based, at least in part, on our own government's complicitous acts. We may feel drawn to join in demonstrations against United States policy, which is supportive of the ruling government, or to write a letter to our congressional representative urging that the United States cut off funds to the ruling government in El Salvador.

Some people seem to have felt solidarity with the peasants of El Salvador, but many more could not identify with either the peasants' revolutionary activity or their terrible plight. At least in part, this is probably due to a failure of imagination on the part of the majority. And in part, this is also due to the quite different patterns of socialization that people are exposed to. As I have argued elsewhere, exposure to a plurality of values and a plurality of life contexts will make it easier to be able to place oneself into the shoes of another person who is very different from oneself.[35] Could we have been socialized differently? Could our socializations have been so different from what they are that all of us would identify with these peasants, or with our fellow humans? The answer is probably yes, but we are far from that time, so far indeed that it is difficult even to speculate about what we would need to change to bring it about.

Just as Feinberg has trouble feeling solidarity with all white men, and just as many people have trouble feeling solidarity with the peasants of El

---

34. Feinberg, *Doing and Deserving*, p. 238.

35. See my discussion of this issue in chap. 1, "Integrity, Self, and Value Plurality."

Salvador, most people seem to have difficulty feeling solidarity with all humans. But several philosophers have recently argued that solidarity can and should be extended to all of humanity. For Richard Rorty "human solidarity" is not based on a recognition of a human essence, but rather "it is thought of as the ability to see more and more traditional differences (of tribe, religion, race, customs, and the like) as unimportant when compared with similarities with respect to pain and suffering—the ability to think of people wildly different from ourselves as included in the range of 'us.' "[36] Rorty allows that solidarity of smaller groups will be much more potent a motivator than is true for the group of all humans; and he also acknowledges that human solidarity is an ideal rather than a reality. The question to be raised, though, is whether it is plausible to think of solidarity's being extended to the whole of humanity.

Jürgen Habermas has also talked about humanness as the basis for a particular type of solidarity ("of a concrete lifeworld of family, tribe, city, or nation"[37]) that "has been transformed in the light of the idea of the general discursive will formation."[38] For Habermas "membership in an ideal communication community" can generate "a consciousness of irrevocable" human solidarity.[39] But it seems to me that this is precisely the problem. Can a true sense of solidarity be generated from a dialogue in an ideal community? Habermas thinks that one can go through a process whereby one increasingly abstracts oneself from the particularities of life so that all that is left is one's common humanity. But is it plausible to think that such an abstract connection among people could generate the bonds of sentiment and attachment that both Habermas and Rorty recognize as the hallmark of solidarity?

Of course, it is quite common for people to claim that they have acted out of a sense of fellowship with humanity. Solidarity with humanity may occur when "one displays civility and a willingness to cooperate with strangers, or as often as one willingly contributes to those in need."[40] But most of the time such actions are motivated by the particular relationships or situations in which one encounters the other, not out of an abstract feel-

---

36. Richard Rorty, *Contingency, Irony, and Solidarity* (Cambridge: Cambridge University Press, 1989), p. 192.

37. Habermas, "Justice and Solidarity," p. 48.

38. Ibid., p. 47. For an interesting critique of Habermas's conception of solidarity, drawn in terms very different from my own, see Nanette Funk's essay "Habermas and Solidarity," in the Greek journal, *Philosophical Inquiry* 12, nos. 3–4 (1990).

39. Habermas, "Justice and Solidarity," p. 48.

40. William Rehg, *Insight and Solidarity* (Berkeley: University of California Press, 1994), p. 111.

ing of love for all of humanity or out of an ideal communicative process.[41] Indeed, in the case of the Salvadoran peasants, people may find themselves able to identify with the plight of these particular poor people but not moved by the plight of poor people in the Sudan or in Palestine. Such common facts cast doubt on the likelihood that many people at all feel a solidarity for all of humanity.

While I applaud the attempt by Rorty, Habermas, and their followers to urge that people try to adopt an ideal of human solidarity, it seems to me that at best what this is likely to generate is what Konstantin Kolenda has called "incremental solidarity," in which "we manage to extend somewhat the reach of our interest and concern, to include among *us* at least some of *them*."[42] What is important is that people be motivated to take responsibility for ending one another's suffering.[43] But I am much less optimistic about such a sense of global responsibility arising out of a sense of solidarity since solidarity is so deeply rooted in the particularities of a specific life context.

We are much more likely to make progress at the "local" than at the "global" level; that is, we are most likely to make progress at the level of increasing the sense of solidarity (and of responsibility) that members of particular local groups feel for one another. This is because solidarity involves more than conscious group identification, for example, more than the realization that one is a fellow member of the human race. Solidarity involves bonds of sentiment that are very hard to establish and even harder to maintain in large groups, let alone in the largest of all human groups, the human race.[44] This is why Feinberg did not feel solidarity with fellow white men. Perhaps empathy can get us to have respect for each fellow human being we meet, but solidarity would involve not merely *seeing* ourselves as similar to one another but also *feeling* drawn to offer moral support.

Let us return to the passage from Freud I cited earlier. In attempting to

41. It appears that those who engaged in rescue activities of Jews under the Nazis either rescued Jews they knew personally, or were personally acquainted with the plight of other Jews. See Lawrence Baron, "The Dutchness of Dutch Rescuers: The National Dimension of Altruism," in *Embracing the Other*, ed. Pearl Oliner et al. (New York: New York University Press, 1992), pp. 315ff.

42. Konstantin Kolenda, "Incremental Solidarity," *The Humanist* 49 (September/October 1989), 43.

43. I have devoted an entire book to just such a project. See *Sharing Responsibility*, especially chap. 6.

44. Diana Meyers has argued that the lack of global solidarity is due to the fact that certain political ties, necessary for solidarity, cannot be formed by all of humanity. See her discussion of related issues in *Subjection and Subjectivity* (New York: Routledge, 1994), pp. 100–6.

identify the elements in the psychology of a human group, Freud mentions (but does not discuss) "the tendency of the immediate carrying out of intentions as they emerge."[45] Here Freud is groping for the motivational dimension that seems to separate groups into those that remain relatively loosely connected and those that have solidarity. It is not enough that a person identify himself or herself with a particular group, or even that he or she have bonds of sentiment with that group and its members. For it may be that the person will still not feel motivated to go to the aid of a fellow member. The person may even form intentions to go to the aid of fellow members but never act on those intentions. What is essential, as Freud seemingly recognized, is that one have the disposition to act on such intentions. Feinberg was also moving toward the notion of moral support in discussing vicarious feelings of pride or shame. Such feelings are rather direct and immediate as well, although, as I indicated, they are not necessarily the feelings of immediate response to a fellow group member that are characteristic of solidarity.

Members of the human race lack this immediacy of response to a fellow group member. Habermas and Rorty are on the right track in arguing that people need to feel a part of a community with strong ties among its members in order for solidarity to extend to large groups such as the human race. But it is hard to imagine that such a community could be formed given the tendency of most people to identify so strongly with race, religion, and nation, identifications that accentuate the differences rather than the similarities of humans. Such identifications limit the extent of our ability to abstract imaginatively from our particular group characteristics and to think of ourselves only in terms of our common humanity. Until such tendencies are diminished, it is unlikely that anything other than "incremental solidarity" can be realistically hoped for. Let us next pull all of the threads together into a coherent picture of solidarity.

V. SOLIDARITY AS A MOTIVATIONAL FORCE

The discussion has identified the following overlapping threads that normally come together in solidarity:

1. conscious group identification,
2. bonds of sentiment,
3. interest in the group's well-being,
4. shared values and beliefs, and
5. readiness to show moral support.

I will conclude by discussing how a consideration of these elements can

45. Freud, p. 54.

lead to a better understanding of solidarity as a motivational force moving individuals to follow a community's moral demands or norms. This discussion will also pull together some of the chapter's main themes.

Our deepest sense of moral commitment often comes from our sense of self.[46] When an individual identifies himself or herself in terms of a specific group membership, he or she becomes personally invested in that group. The investment takes on a moral character the more the individual identifies with the group's moral values. But such identifications are hampered when there are conflicts of value among the groups to which a person belongs. If one of the groups not only offers an appealing set of values but also offers a readiness to come to the person's aid, especially in difficult times, then the conflict of values will often be resolved in favor of the supportive group's values. Solidarity is achieved through these supportive associations, not merely through personal group identification. Each of us belongs to too many groups, to which we feel somewhat attached, for solidarity to result merely from conscious group identification.

This raises an issue which Habermas has stressed: we must be somewhat wary of solidarity because fellowship and loyalty too often turn into "followership."[47] The bonds of sentiment characteristic of solidarity may become so strong that the members of a group give up their autonomy. For this reason it may be a good thing that some aspects of morality are not intertwined with solidarity. Nonetheless, solidarity can stand as a very important counterweight to the tendency to view morality as merely a matter between the individual and his or her conscience.[48] Solidarity and conscience are each undeniably significant sources of morality, yet solidarity has been greatly underappreciated.

My discussion of solidarity was not meant to collapse all moral virtues or sentiments into solidarity. Indeed, in the last section I specifically sought to distinguish a general "humaneness" from solidarity. Virtues such as compassion and empathy can motivate individuals to come to one another's aid. But such virtues are rarely able to build a sense of community from which one can draw moral support and find motivation to pursue the common good. If one cares about another's pain but doesn't identify with the plight of the person who is in pain, then one may be motivated to help remove the pain, or one may be motivated merely to pity the one who is in pain. On my analysis, it is the identification with the other that strongly motivates us to do something for the other.

In *Sharing Responsibility* I argued that people *should feel motivated* to

46. I argued for this thesis in chap. 1, "Integrity, Self, and Value Plurality."
47. Habermas, "Justice and Solidarity," p. 47.
48. See my essay "On Conscience."

help one another out of a shared commitment to the general common good.[49] Now I am taking a step back from that position to wonder why people *do not often feel motivated* merely by the common humanity that is expressed by the starving, poverty-stricken face on television who is in a community on the other side of the world. In this current work I argue that shared commitment to the common good is linked to community involvement and identification. In this sense, the context really does matter much more for morality than has generally been recognized.

It is the bonds of sentiment and the readiness to show moral support that are most lacking in anything approaching "human solidarity." Rorty and Habermas have attempted to lead us to a better appreciation of how similar our interests are as humans. But, as this chapter has shown, there is more to solidarity than common interest. In addition, solidarity is more than identification with a group. Solidarity involves felt bonds of sentiment and shared values. It is still to be hoped that people will come to see their fellow humans and themselves as sharing enough in common to develop a sense of solidarity with these others and concern for their plight. The achievement of local solidarity by more and more groups may indeed increase the likelihood of humanity's achieving global solidarity one day. Until that time, local solidarity will nonetheless play a profound role in moral life. In the next chapter, I will explore how collective identification and consciousness affect an individual's conscience and sense of responsibility.

49. See especially chap. 9 of *Sharing Responsibility*.

3

COLLECTIVE CONSCIOUSNESS
AND MORAL AUTHORITY

Are integrity, solidarity, and responsibility to be understood merely in terms of the belief states of individuals? Or is there some kind of social transformation of belief that occurs at the group level? In the previous chapters I sketched an account of integrity and solidarity that is group-oriented, stressing the importance of the role of community in forming the moral beliefs of individuals. In the succeeding chapter I will examine the concept of socialization, the key concept for the transference of norms from a community to its members. In the current chapter I examine the conception sometimes thought to be prior to socialization, collective consciousness. Collective consciousness is the basis for social relationships and also, possibly, a source of moral knowledge that accounts for similarity of belief in given communities. I will be especially interested in how moral authority is linked to collective consciousness.[1]

Consciousness is one of many states attributed to a human organism, to a person. Does it make any sense to attribute consciousness to a group of persons? When members of a mob rally together and act in a concerted fashion without any communication, is this because the mob has a kind of collective consciousness of what needs to be done and how to do it? Was there a Polish spirit of solidarity that moved the Gdansk ship workers to oppose Polish communism? Why do many doctors in the United States seemingly have such a single-minded approach to their status as experts in physical well-being that they have a visceral reaction to Christian Scientists who refuse to acknowledge their authority? Are these conceptions of

---

1. In this chapter I am not really interested in "group mind" so much as those social practices that bring individual minds together.

"mob mentality," "Polish spirit," and "single-mindedness" merely meta-phors, or do they belie a deeper reality?

This chapter is an attempt to investigate various answers to the above questions by relating two largely disparate literatures: continental social and moral theory, on the one hand, and recent analytic philosophical work in cognitive science, on the other. The goal is to piece together some in-sights about the possibility of a conception of collective consciousness that will allow us to begin to make sense of such phenomena as solidarity, so-cialization, and moral authority so as to answer rather perplexing specific questions in applied ethics and sociological theory. To this end, in the first section, I will survey some of the most important views of collective con-sciousness that continental philosophers have espoused since the turn of the century. In the second section, several prominent contemporary philos-ophers who have worked on the concept of consciousness will be brought into dialogue with the earlier continental thinkers. Then, in the third sec-tion, some moral and political implications of these views of collective consciousness will be sketched. In the final section, special attention will be paid to examples of taboos and medical socialization.

I. WHAT SOME MAINLY DEAD, AND LARGELY FORGOTTEN, FOLKS HAD TO SAY

In this section I want briefly to survey some of the most important uses of the term *collective consciousness,* especially in the writings of Carl Jung, Alfred Schutz, and Emile Durkheim. These thinkers are now largely ig-nored by analytic philosophers, and if their views are mentioned at all it is normally in terms of ridicu.e. For all three thinkers, collective conscious-ness was the medium through which mind and society were connected. In each case, collective consciousness had a strong moral or normative di-mension; it was not merely a cognitive category.

Carl Jung spoke of the collective unconscious as involving "a 'perceiv-ing' which consists—or to be more cautious, seems to consist—of images, of subjectless 'simulacra.' " This form of consciousness, insists Jung, is nei-ther a form of cognition nor a form of "conscious knowledge as we know it."[2] Jung believed that certain images of our early ancestors were some-how accessible through the collective unconscious. To believe as he did, there would have to be some connection among the states of consciousness of various people over time. States of consciousness are influenced by what Jung called "archetypes." The archetypes "are formal factors responsible

2. Carl Jung, *Synchronicity,* trans. R. F. C. Hull (Princeton, NJ: Princeton University Press, 1973), pp. 77–8.

for the organization of unconscious psychic processes: they are patterns of behavior."[3] These patterns of behavior manifest themselves as having an "inferior or primitive nature," which seems to explain certain widespread similarities or coincidences throughout all of recorded history.[4]

Before one would wish to assess such a strong claim as that made by Jung, it seems reasonable to ask whether there is any sense to be made of saying that there are connections among these states of consciousness that could constitute anything like a collective unconscious that generates similarity of consciousness among members of a group. One explanation sometimes offered by Jungians is that the collective unconscious "archetypes" are housed in the genetic makeup of various groups of people, or perhaps in the human race in general. Regardless of how these archetypes are supposed to produce similarity of consciousness, Jung claims to have quite a lot of empirical support for his thesis, writing that "the psychologist is continually coming up against cases where the emergence of symbolic parallels cannot be explained without the hypothesis of the collective unconscious."[5]

Jung contends that all peoples have a "God-image" and that this image is a "complex of ideas of an archetypical nature." Its origin is a primitive image which all peoples have stored deep in their psyches. The image of God is an archetype, that is, "an unconscious psychic image" that has reality "independent of the attitude of the conscious mind."[6] Archetypes are psychological rather than metaphysical facts for Jung. And each archetypical image is itself also symbolic of a realm of experience that is shared by all peoples. The archetypes convey a kind of knowledge, but it is not knowledge gained in any deductive or inductive manner; rather, it is more like a form of direct perceptual knowledge.

Leaving aside the mystical elements of all of this, Jung, in my opinion, captured something important in his claim that collective unconscious insights are not forms of knowledge but are rather more like forms of perception. If consciousness were largely explicable in terms of perception, then collective consciousness and collective unconsciousness might begin to make sense, for we would not need to posit a collective mind that does the knowing for the group, but only a standpoint of perceiving that is unique to a group rather than to an individual. Such a view, although with very different consequences, can also be found in the writings of Alfred Schutz.

3. Ibid., p. 20.

4. Ibid., p. 21 and 23.

5. Ibid., pp. 23–4.

6. Jung, *Symbols of Transformation*, 2d ed., trans. R. F. C. Hull (Princeton, NJ: Princeton University Press, 1956), p. 56.

For Schutz, collective consciousness is not related to deep-seated un-conscious archetypes, but it is connected to common experiences. This can best be seen in the intense face-to-face encounter that one person has with another during which a "we-relationship" is established through a "com-mon stream of consciousness,"[7] as in the following illustration from his seminal work *The Phenomenology of the Social World*:

> Suppose that you and I are watching a bird in flight. The thought "bird-in-flight" is in each of our minds and is the means by which each of us interprets his own observations. Neither of us, however, could say whether our lived experiences on that occasion were iden-tical. In fact, neither of us would even try to answer that question, since our own subjective meaning can never be laid side by side with another's and compared.
>
> Nevertheless, during the flight of the bird you and I have "grown old together"; our experiences have been simultaneous. Perhaps while I was following the bird's flight I noticed out of the corner of my eye that your head was moving in the same direction as mine. I could then say that the two of us, that *we*, had watched the bird's flight. What I have done in this case is to coordinate temporally a series of my own experiences with a series of yours. . . . And if you have in a similar way coordinated my experiences with yours, then we can both say that *we* have seen a bird in flight.[8]

What Schutz is here describing is the complex way that one comes to make simple inferences about the behavior of others. I assume that the other per-son, as a fellow human being, will respond to the environment in ways sim-ilar to the way I do. So that when I see another person incline his head toward the sky, seemingly following the path of a bird, and I realize what I would be doing in that situation, I am led to believe that he and I are both engaged in the same experience. And from this, I form a belief or an image about the similarity of consciousness that both of us are in.

Schutz contends that the pure form of the we-relationship is the recip-rocal "pure awareness of the *presence* of another person," and also the "knowledge of each that the other is aware of him." For this initial rela-tionship between two people to become a basis for a truly social relation-ship, one must step out of the face-to-face relationship, while in some sense remaining a participant in it. The social relationship requires that I become aware not only of another's presence but also of the specific manner in which the other is regarding me. From the general knowledge of someone's

7. Alfred Schutz, *The Phenomenology of the Social World*, trans. George Walsh and Freder-ick Lehnert (1932; Evanston, IL: Northwestern University Press, 1967), p. 167.
8. Ibid., p. 165.

presence, one must move to specific knowledge of who this other is. Only then can it be said that these two know each other directly and come to an intersubjective understanding of each another. The love relationship is the hallmark of such an intense mutual knowing of the other directly.

In the social relationship, two individuals come to an understanding of each other's presence initially in terms of the similarity and difference in perceptual standpoint. Indeed, I come initially to know the other not only as an object of my perception but as a subject of a relationship that I enter into. And as I grow in understanding of the other person, I take account of an increasing body of new experiences, both experiences of the other and experiences of my experiencing the other. In this process, the knowledge of the other person, as well as knowledge of the self, will "undergo continuous revision as the concrete experience unfolds."[9] A person is able to check his or her "interpretations of what is going on in other people's minds, due to the fact that, in the We-relationship" he or she shares "a common environment with them."[10]

Schutz contends that the common environment creates the possibility that people can have knowledge of the social world as a greatly enlarged common stream of consciousness. This account, though, does not explain the common feelings of connectedness that people also feel when they encounter groups of other persons, or why they feel so strongly connected to each other in social relationships. The collective consciousness is really only each person's belief that both share the same ideas. Hence, Schutz's conception of collective consciousness is ultimately reducible to individual psychological states and does not do justice to phenomena such as love, friendship, and familial relationships, as well as other forms of the we-relationship that he was trying to account for.

Emile Durkheim provides a better basis for accounting for these phenomena when he discusses mechanical solidarity, which depends on a cohesiveness that is "the result of resemblances."[11] As we saw in the previous chapter, families and clans are based on "consanguinity," relation by blood or other natural or fictitious similarity. For Durkheim, collective consciousness is intimately connected to a collective conscience. This involves a system of shared values and beliefs that depend on rituals and that facilitate consensus within the group. In organic solidarity, the individual parts fit together to such an extent that they come to act together as a seamless unit, in which the uniqueness of the parts dissolves. In both cases, the whole is bound together by collective consciousness and conscience.

For Durkheim, collective consciousness and conscience involves "a

9. Ibid., p. 169.
10. Ibid., p. 171.
11. Durkheim, *Emile Durkheim on Morality and Society,* p. 63.

system of shared values and beliefs."[12] In determining whether and to what extent collective consciousness and conscience exists in a particular group, Durkheim was principally concerned to understand the extent, duration, and intensity of consensus on certain key moral beliefs within that group. But consensus is somewhat misleading in this respect since there are no votes taken, nor is there any agreement in the normal voluntarist sense of that term. Furthermore, Durkheim rightly distinguishes between what he calls "corporate egoism," the mere convergence of self-interests of the members of a group, and "collective consciousness or conscience," which is largely altruistic in orientation.

Collective consciousness and conscience is a coincidence of values and beliefs of the members of a group directed at the well-being of fellow group members. If this concept merely referred to a coincidence of belief sharing, this consensus would initially lack stability. Rituals and institutions provide a way to add a bit of stability, but Durkheim was well aware that the self-interests of individual members of a group would constantly tug against the collective conscience. These rituals help intensify the feelings of group identification that can increase feelings of consensus concerning not only shared beliefs but also shared values.[13]

Here we have a spectrum of views about collective consciousness: from Alfred Schutz's virtual equation of collective consciousness with individualized shared belief, to Carl Jung's view that there is something, probably in our genes, that conveys content to our consciousness from the stories our ancestors learned around the prehistoric campfire. The most plausible views are those of Durkheim, who clearly tried to sketch a coherent middle ground. But his views suffer from an impoverished understanding of how consciousness is achieved. Recent work in cognitive science and philosophy has begun to focus on this question, with interesting results in understanding similarity of individual consciousness. In the next section we will see whether some of these results will provide insights also useful for an understanding of collective consciousness.

II. WHAT SOME EMINENTLY ALIVE COGNITIVE PHILOSOPHERS ARE SAYING

I will briefly look at some work by Ruth Millikan, Daniel Dennett, and John Haugeland, philosophers who have all questioned the individualistic

---

12. See David Lockwood, *Solidarity and Schism* (Oxford: The Clarendon Press, 1992), p. 21ff., from which I draw in some of my remarks about Durkheim's conceptions of collective conscience.

13. For more discussion of Durkheim's views, see chap. 2, "Solidarity and Moral Support."

bias in the cognitive science of consciousness. Several have worried openly that the reigning models of cognitive science do not allow us to understand the way people actually learn from and relate to one another socially. But as far as I can tell, none of these theorists has suggested that we need to think about the possible moral and political implications of the theories of consciousness that we embrace.

Ruth Millikan argues that mental states are not, strictly speaking, in the head. She takes seriously the view that mental states reside in the "relations between one's head and the rest of the world."[14] Millikan argues that an attention to history, especially evolutionary history, is needed to help us understand what are the proper functions of such things as the brain and other human organs. The evolutionary history of the brain is, on Millikan's view, more important than the current state of this organ, especially its current properties or dispositions.[15] As she develops her argument, it appears that certain mental states are to be understood in terms of various built-in mechanisms that give a reproductive advantage to certain individuals over others.

Millikan thinks that mental states such as consciousness have something to do with the structures of the mind that are the product of evolutionary history. Indeed, she argues that we should think about organismic processes rather than discrete organisms. Here it is important that Millikan claims that this "organismic process has no skin. It is constantly sucking in matter from its surroundings and spewing it out again." Millikan draws on the empirical work of the evolutionary biologist Richard Dawkins in looking to spider webs as an extension of the skin of the spider. And she contends that

> spider webs and moth cocoons, bird nests and beaver dams, are reproduced by the genes out of environmental material exactly as are bones, wings and eyes. Richard Dawkins discusses the phenomenon of "the extended phenotype," through which boundaries between biological individuals or species become blurred, the biological projects of (the genes of) one individual or species being carried out through opportunistic manipulation of the bodies or behaviors of others.[16]

Millikan comes to the conclusion that the "extended phenotype may thus reach yards or even miles beyond the animal's body. The unity of the or-

---

14. Ruth Garrett Millikan, *White Queen Psychology and Other Essays for Alice* (Cambridge, MA: MIT Press, 1993), p. 29.

15. Ibid., p. 13.

16. Ibid., p. 179.

ganismic process might better be compared, then, to a wave or, say, a whirlpool than to that of an ordinary physical object."[17]

Millikan's concept of the extended phenotype bears some resemblance to Jung's concept of the archetype. For example, the extended phenotype of beavers allows the species to pass characteristics and even information—about the building of dams, for instance—from one generation of beavers to another. For Jung, the collective unconscious archetype, such as the image or idea of God, is deeply instilled in the psyche of each person, allowing symbolic information to be passed from one generation of humans to another. Specifically, various kinds of mental processes or content are evolutionarily passed from generation to generation. Just as the ability to build a nest, a web, or a dam is a bit of collective instinctual information, so too might be various ways that people process stimuli or come to understand themselves in relationship to a more powerful being. While I do not necessarily endorse this view of a possible basis for collective consciousness (nor do I think that Millikan would necessarily endorse it), it is interesting to me that such matters are not far off the agenda of some contemporary cognitive philosophers. We turn next to an account of consciousness that explicitly takes up the possibility of collective consciousness.

Daniel Dennett has advanced the debate about consciousness in interesting directions by countering the idea that there must be a center of consciousness for each human person that is somehow localized in the brain. He urges that we replace this model of consciousness with what he refers to as the Multiple Drafts model.

> According to the Multiple Drafts model, all varieties of perception—indeed all varieties of thought or mental activity—are accomplished in the brain by parallel, multitrack processes of interpretation and elaboration of sensory inputs. Information entering the nervous system is under continuous "editorial revision."[18]

The multiple drafts result in different narratives, and all that binds these narratives together is that they refer to the same self or agent. This is very similar to the account of the self as process that I described in chapter 1.

Dennett is surely one of the most innovative of the people working in contemporary cognitive science. Perhaps because of this, he has occasionally wondered whether consciousness maps onto single or multiple physical bodies. In his book *Consciousness Explained,* Dennett talks critically about the common assumption that there is only one self per human body,

17. Ibid., p. 180.
18. Daniel Dennett, *Consciousness Explained* (Boston: Little Brown, 1991), p. 111.

and even considers the possibility that there could be one self stretched over more than one human body. Dennett says that the self is "an abstraction defined by the myriads of attributions and interpretations (including self-attributions and self-interpretations) that have composed the biography of the living body whose Center of Narrative Gravity it is."[19] On this view, different narratives could apply to the same self, as is true in cases of multiple personality disorder, in which two selves with very distinct identities seem to coexist in the same human body.

Interestingly for our purposes, Dennett also discusses the possibility of "two or more bodies sharing a single self!"

> There may actually have been such a case, in York, England: the Chaplin twins, Greta and Freda (*Time*, April 6, 1981). These identical twins, now in their forties and living in a hostel, seem to act as one; they collaborate on the speaking of a single sentence, finishing each other's sentences with ease or speaking in unison, with one just a split second behind. . . . Some who have dealt with them suggest that the natural and effective tactic that suggested itself was to consider *them* more of a *her.*[20]

Dennett suggests that since these twins are already genetically predisposed to interpret the world's stimuli in similar ways, "there are plenty of subtle, everyday ways of communicating and coordinating" that may "keep them homing in on some sort of loose harmony."[21] This is all in keeping with Dennett's view that consciousness and the self are both "gappy," only loosely connected with their previous manifestations or narrative structures.[22]

Understanding consciousness as a loose harmony of narratives is quite consistent with a certain understanding of collective consciousness. As Schutz suggests, when two people have roughly similar experiences, especially intense experiences with an "other" as occurs in a love relationship, it is surely plausible to speak of a loose harmony of narratives of several selves and of some kind of collective consciousness among them. That there might be something more going on than merely a loose harmony is suggested by Dennett's example of the York twins. As we have seen, Ruth Millikan has taken things further yet by her suggestion that states of mind need not be confined by the skin as the form of the individual's sensory process. To complete our brief journey into some recent literature in the

19. Ibid., pp. 426–7.
20. Ibid., p. 422.
21. Ibid.
22. Ibid., p. 423.

philosophy of cognitive science, I turn finally to a position that seems to fall between the two rehearsed above.

In a recent paper, John Haugeland argues for a view of mind, and by implication of consciousness, that is intimately, inseparably connected to a social world.[23] Haugeland has been deeply influenced by some of the work in continental thought that I discussed earlier in this chapter. Here he draws on work in organizational behavior and systems theory, especially the work of Herbert Simon, in which "the primary division is not into mind, body, and world, but rather into 'layers' that cut across these in various ways."[24] Haugeland uses the analogy of the business corporation, in which the "mind" of the corporation is not to be found in any particular spot or aspect of the organization but is in many parts of the organization and also in things that are outside the corporation (perhaps part of its self found in the laws of the society in which it operates).

Haugeland is also interested in how the social world aids in learning. He asks the rhetorical question "How much of what a culture has learned about life and its environment is 'encoded' in its paraphernalia and practices?" He suggests that social practices are the repositories of cultural learning. "Crucial elements of that heritage, I want to claim, are embodied in the shapes and strengths of the plow, the yoke, and the harness, as well as the practices for building and using them."[25] Social institutions play an integral part in various forms of learning, such as learning how "to build cars or manage a city."

Haugeland comes ultimately to a conclusion that could have been written by a modern-day Durkheim.

> The point is not merely that organizations evolve in functionally effective ways, as do insects and trees, but rather that the structure of an institution is implemented in the high-bandwidth intelligent interactions among individuals, as well as between individuals and their paraphernalia. Furthermore, the expertise of those individuals could not be what it is apart from their participation in this structure.[26]

As a result, Haugeland comes to say in the end that mind is "intimately embodied and intimately embedded in its world."[27] Haugeland does not

23. John Haugeland, "Mind Embodied and Embedded," final draft, 1993, unpublished.

24. Ibid., pp. 13–14.

25. Ibid., pp. 31–2.

26. Ibid., p. 32.

27. Ibid., p. 34.

spell out the implications of this view for social and moral theory,[28] but it seems to me that some of the implications may be consistent with what Durkheim and the social theorists who follow him have held. I will explore this point, among others, in the next section.

III. SOME GENERAL IMPLICATIONS FOR SOCIAL AND MORAL THEORY

As I said at the beginning of this chapter, my interest in this topic is fueled by a desire to work out the relationships among integrity, solidarity, and responsibility, especially as they relate to some current issues in professional ethics. One of the questions that has come up is how one accounts for the authority of codes of conduct, as well as for the sense of solidarity that exists within a professional community, or any community for that matter. It was in trying to answer this question that Durkheim posited a collective consciousness and conscience.

As I have framed the discussion so far, at least three different meanings of collective consciousness can be ferreted out from the older continental literature and the newer cognitive science literature.

First, collective consciousness can refer to the forms, and possibly the content, of reasoning that are genetically transferred to each member of a group of humans. Many philosophers, including Kant, believed in inherited structures of the mind. Jung, and possibly Millikan, think that there is some content that is also inherited.

Second, collective consciousness can refer to various forms of shared or common belief. The shared beliefs may constitute a common stream of consciousness where the identities of the respective individuals are formed by mutual awareness. If the common experiences are extensive enough, there may be formed what Dennett calls a "loose harmony" or what Schutz called a "social relationship."[29]

Third, collective consciousness can refer to cognitive and emotive content collectively shared by members of a group, as seems to be contained in certain institutions, especially rituals and social traditions, as Durkheim and Haugeland believe.

These are overlapping views, to be sure, and do not mutually exclude

---

28. Haugeland cites Hubert Dreyfus quite extensively in this and other of his essays, and Dreyfus has recently written about some of the implications of this general view for ethics and social theory. See Hubert Dreyfus and Stuart Dreyfus, "What Is Morality? A Phenomenological Account of the Development of Ethical Expertise," in *Universalism vs. Communitarianism,* ed. David Rasmussen (Cambridge, MA: MIT Press, 1990), pp. 237–64.

29. For more discussion of the shared nature of social understanding see George Lakoff, *Women, Fire, and Dangerous Things* (Chicago: University of Chicago Press, 1987); and Mark Johnson, *Body in the Mind* (Chicago: University of Chicago Press, 1987).

one another. Let's work briefly through the first two, ending with the third, and most interesting, of these interpretations of collective consciousness.

Those who occupy various social roles, such as the role of mother or father, have a very strong sense of paramount obligation to protect and nurture their young children. Granting that some of the obligatoriness of social roles is socially learned, might not some of it also be based on arche-typical or extended phenotypical inheritance that is passed on to genera-tion after generation of humans? In the introduction, I referred to evidence of dolphins who display helping behavior not just toward their young but also toward human swimmers.[30] It does not seem odd at all to think of these dolphins as exhibiting instinctual behavior in this regard. Might it be that human mothers and fathers, as well as strangers who exhibit altruism to those who are in very dire straits, also display a kind of inherited respon-siveness to certain situations or roles? If so, then the felt obligatoriness of helping those we are in a position to help may be based, at least in part, on a collective consciousness about these helping roles.

Of course, it will be objected, an individual's ideas come from many different sources, but all of our ideas are in our own minds and not housed in some kind of collective mind. There is no need to look beyond the indi-vidual human mind to explain helping behavior, especially since phenome-nologically our drive to help someone who is our child is experienced as a deeply personal feeling. But how things appear phenomenologically may not be a good indication of how they in fact are. Jung would point out that there is a great deal of coincidence of similar behavior in human parents, a coincidence that is hard to explain if there is no connection between these feelings of obligatoriness.

In addition, it might be objected that genetic theories linking respon-siveness with role or situation do not mesh well with the facts. As Max Scheler observed, "Our flow of sympathy . . . fluctuates widely . . . it of-ten fails us when confronted with the fact and the evidence of intense suf-fering, and then often without any such powerful inducement, some trifle may open all our soul."[31] If helping feelings are genetically determined, it is hard to know why some people seem not to have them, and why these feelings fluctuate so widely even in the life of a single person.

Nonetheless, we need to try to account for the feelings of solidarity and moral authority that many people experience in quite similar ways. Perhaps the route sketched by Schutz and Dennett will fit the bill. Perhaps there is a loose harmony among those who have had very similar experi-ences, especially early childhood experiences, that would account for the

30. Griffin, *Animal Minds,* p. 214.

31. Max Scheler, *The Nature of Sympathy,* trans. Peter Heath (1913; Hamden, CT: Archon Books, 1970), p. 50.

coincidence of views about the moral authority of social roles and might also account for the solidarity within certain groups. An account of these examples of collective consciousness based on shared belief has the advantage that it does not even suggest any mysterious group minds or genetic forces operating behind the backs of all humans; hence, such a view does not have to worry about why there is such a wide variation in the way that people react to their social roles.

But the difficulty is that a mere loose harmony has a lot of difficulty providing the basis for the strength of feelings and the role of institutions and rituals in maintaining these feelings among group members. Indeed, I have argued elsewhere in a similar vein that individualistic theories of intention and action fail to capture the way that social relationships change and coordinate individual intentions and actions in group behavior.[32] (In the next section, I rehearse some of those arguments when considering two particular cases.) When collective consciousness is understood merely as shared belief and loose harmony among isolated individual minds, a similar loss of explanatory power results. This is why I feel that some kind of a middle position between these two extremes is called for, namely, a view of collective consciousness that stresses the transmission and transformation of belief that occur through institutional socialization. In the next chapter I will set out an account of how socialization is able to transform belief states.[33]

Solidarity, socialization, and role-based moral authority operate upon an individual's consciousness, but they originate and ultimately reside, as it were, in the relationships, not in those individual consciousnesses. Institutions, by which I mean only the conventions and customs that organize individuals through the assignment of roles, are themselves a function of relationships. We might adopt a strategy of Sartre here in speaking of institutions as "fused" relationships,[34] in which is contained a relatively fixed source of common knowledge formed out of what was once a "fluid" set of interrelations. As such, knowledge and understanding can come from and be transformed by institutions. Solidarity, socialization, and role-based moral authority depend on this interplay between institutions and individuals.

Institutions play a role for humans similar to the role books play. They

---

32. May, *The Morality of Groups,* especially chap. 1.

33. See chap. 4, "Socialization and Institutional Evil." In this context, consider once again the dual aspect of the socially responsive self, the title of this book.

34. Sartre talks of a "fused group" as a group composed of individuals that, at least for a short period of time, can act as a unit. See the discussion of this point in his great work *The Critique of Dialectical Reason,* trans. Alan Sheridan-Smith (1960; London: NLB, 1976), pp. 345–404.

are cultural artifacts, created by individual consciousnesses, which are able to exert terrific influence on other individual consciousnesses but are themselves separate from any particular individual consciousness. In this respect if no other, it makes sense to talk of an institution as an embodiment of collective consciousness. Institutions are embodiments of collective consciousness in that they are both a repository and source of authority for many individual consciousnesses, but where what was true of these individuals taken singly has now disappeared from view. Traditions also may operate this way. Traditions are formed over many generations, and thus necessarily are formed by more than one individual's consciousness.

Moral authority, especially the sort that is embedded in a social role or a code of rules, can also be understood as an embodiment of collective consciousness. There are two kinds of evidence for this view. First, the sources of morality that people refer to (customs and traditions, rules and roles, theories of ethics and conceptions of religion) are formed over time by a process that, as I've argued, is best understood as collective. Second, the feelings of obligation that are generated by these sources of moral authority are also social and, to a certain extent, collective as well. I turn to this second point in the remainder of this chapter. In doing so, though, it is not my intent to blur the distinction between moral authority and a person's feeling of moral authority. Nonetheless, I will be assuming that the way people regard their sources of moral authority will normally tell us some important information about the status of that authority itself.

When a person feels that he or she should conform to a social role, that person takes on a set of beliefs that are clearly felt in the individual self. But the moral authority conveyed by the social role is based on what, following Wilifred Sellers and Raimo Tuomela, we might call a "we-belief."[35] Here the social force of an individual's feeling of obligation comes from a complex set of beliefs, for instance, believing that he or she is a member of a particular group, believing that the members of a group have agreed that a certain type of conduct is required for continued group membership, and believing that one wants to remain a member of that group.[36]

It is a mistake, though, to focus exclusively on the individual belief-states and not to recognize that the relationships created and sustained by the institutions and traditions are also important, and ultimately not reducible to individual belief-states. The obligatoriness we feel when we as-

35. See Raimo Tuomela and Kaarlo Miller, "We-Intentions," *Philosophical Studies* 53 (1988): 367–89. Also see Michael Bratman, "Shared Intention," *Ethics* 104, no. 1 (October 1993): 97–113.

36. On this point it is worth reconsidering David Lewis's seminal work on social rules and norms, *Convention* (Cambridge, MA: Harvard University Press, 1969), pp. 97–108.

sume or are thrust into a social role is not fully explainable by reference to singular beliefs of isolated individuals. As I said in chapter 1, many communitarian theorists have recently argued that this is true, most notably Charles Taylor and Alasdair MacIntyre. What is missing in traditional accounts of obligatoriness is the social basis of feelings of motivation and the common source of this motivation: the institutions and traditions of a particular community.[37]

IV. TWO EXAMPLES

Let me end this chapter with two examples that might help to clarify my points and to focus our attention. My first example is of a social taboo, such as the taboo in Jewish or Muslim societies against eating pork. In examining such practices, the anthropologist Claude Lévi-Strauss came to the conclusion that

> phenomena involving the most fundamental structures of the human mind could not have appeared once and for all. They are repeated in their entirety within each consciousness, and the relevant order falls within an order which transcends both historical successions and contemporary correlations.[38]

Lévi-Strauss believed that structures of taboo formation paralleled structures of grammar formation within each person. Both structures explained how people were able to act and communicate with one another so easily. For Lévi-Strauss, "speech and alliance" were facilitated by the common structures of the mind.[39]

For many anthropologists who have written on this subject, taboos constitute a form of collective practical knowledge that shapes individual behavior. Pierre Bourdieu, for instance, has developed the category of "habitus" to help explain such phenomena. The habitus is a sign or series of signs that connect to "a system of practice-generating schemes which express systematically the necessity and freedom inherent in" a certain social condition.[40] The taboo is a social marker of collective knowledge about what one is excluded from doing in a given society. Bourdieu has been enormously influential, and many anthropologists have claimed to uncover the far-reaching influence of taboo and other forms of habitus in the seemingly rational judgments that people make in many aspects of social life.

---

37. See my detailed discussion of this point in chap. 5, "Social Responsibility."

38. Claude Lévi-Strauss, *The Elementary Structures of Kinship*, trans. James Bell, John von Sturmer, and Rodney Needham (1949; Boston: Beacon Press, 1969), p. 491.

39. Ibid., p. 496.

40. Pierre Bourdieu, *Distinction: A Social Critique of the Judgment of Taste*, trans. Richard Nice (Cambridge, MA: Harvard University Press, 1984), p. 172.

Taboos are difficult to account for by explanations that involve only an individual conception of consciousness. Indeed, there are a whole range of attitudes that people seem incapable of acquiring on their own by individual conscious efforts. The similar visceral and aesthetic reactions that people have when confronted with the possibility of breaking a taboo (as is seen in the actual nausea that some Jews and Muslims feel when they have pork placed before them) is very difficult to explain merely in terms of individual attitudes or beliefs. At least part of what is missing is the history of various religious practices as well as the effect of these practices on anyone who is a member of groups with a certain relevant history.

John Searle has recently joined this debate. One point he has made seems to get at what I was just suggesting. He claims that any attempt to reduce collective intentionality to individual intentions will fail unless the analysis refers to a background in which individuals have a "sense of others as more than mere conscious agents, indeed as actual or potential members of a cooperative activity."[41] He elaborates on this point by saying that "collective intentionality seems to presuppose some level of sense of community before it can ever function."[42] This reason leads Searle to conclude that "collective intentional behavior is a primitive phenomenon that cannot be analyzed as just the summation of individual intentional behavior."[43]

Jerry Hobbs has offered a strong criticism of Searle's views, purportedly in the name of cognitive science. To explain something like Searle's sense of community, Hobbs offers the following reduction:

> From a hardcore AI [artificial intelligence] point of view . . . I have a sense of community with a set of other agents if I believe it is mutually believed by me and the members of that set that we are all "actual or potential members of a cooperative activity," and moreover I have a long-term goal of maintenance that this remain true. This may not explain the warm feeling often associated with some of my senses of community; AI and cognitive science generally have little to say about warm feelings.[44]

In my view, it is the inability to deal with so-called "warm feelings" that betokens a deeper problem with such accounts.

---

41. John Searle, "Collective Intentions and Actions," in *Intentions in Communication,* ed. Philip Cohen, Jerry Morgan, and Martha Pollack (Cambridge, MA: MIT Press, 1990), p. 414.

42. Ibid., p. 413.

43. Ibid., p. 401.

44. Jerry R. Hobbs, "Artificial Intelligence and Collective Intentionality: Comments on Searle and on Grosz and Sidner," in Cohen, Morgan, and Pollack, eds., *Intentions in Communication,* p. 451.

Taboos function only when individuals are in certain relationships with one another. Indeed, I would want to go further than Searle and suggest that the "warm feelings" of, for instance, a sense of solidarity in a community convey a sense of what is appropriate and what is forbidden for these members. Taboos often feel phenomenologically like visceral or aesthetic compulsions because of what is conveyed in the relationships of certain communities. So it is not only the sense of community that is important but also what the relationships in the community convey that is not captured in the reduction of collective consciousness to individual consciousness. And it is these two dimensions of relationships that account for the similarity of values and moral beliefs held by members of various tight-knit communities.

My second example is drawn from contemporary medical practice. In U.S. society, doctors are single-minded in their pursuit of the physical health of their patients. Single-mindedness here refers to two things. First, doctors are socialized to focus very particularly on the disease or other problem that adversely affects the physical body of a patient, and to pursue a cure for the disease or problem with steadfastness. Second, doctors as a group have an ethos that puts such a high premium on physical wellness, and on their expert abilities to cure, that as a group these doctors act as if they had a single mind. This is best seen in those cases in which their expertise or physically curative authority is thrown into question, as is true when groups such as Christian Scientists seek to downplay the curative power of doctors and to put in its place the curative power of prayer. In my experience working with doctors at St. Louis Children's Hospital, I have found the single-mindedness of this second variety to be so strong that discussions of Christian Science elicit only visceral reactions from virtually all doctors.[45] How are we best to account for this phenomenon?

Socialization is surely one of the key dimensions in any account of the single-mindedness I have illustrated above. But how are we to explain socialization? On one level it is merely the conveyance of a certain form of information from one person to another, from a medical school teacher to a first-year medical student, for example. But on another level, socialization involves at least a loose harmony among members of a group, for without this the beliefs that are taught or instilled will lack the motivational force characteristic of most forms of socialization. Here is where an element of affective learning is intertwined with belief formation. Simple forms of learning, unlike socialization, can be counteracted or unlearned relatively easily. But socialization is a process of learning that involves strong mutual support for the authority of the educator, and this support

---

45. See chap. 9, "Challenging Medical Authority," for a detailed discussion of this case.

accounts for the strength of motivation that is felt to continue to attach to what one has learned, even in the face of strong motivations against it.

To account for the strength of motivational support as an affective rather than a cognitive factor, loose harmony among doctors and potential doctors may not be enough. For in some cases, socialization may have to be explained by reference to the history of various practices and the kind of commonality of feeling generated by these practices that one finds only in various forms of solidarity. Indeed, it is situations such as this that make it tempting to talk of collective consciousness in attempting to explain how these forms of learning are different from simple forms of learning. Collective consciousness gives an affective strength to the authority of the person or group that is the socializer. Yet collective consciousness is not itself a mere feeling within a person or even a single belief-state within several persons. Indeed, collective consciousness is not itself a single belief-state or a feeling at all but rather is a combination of affective and cognitive factors that are embedded in institutions.

Doctors in the United States feel a strong sense of commitment to one another and to their profession, and this fact helps us account for how they are socialized to have a single-minded reaction to perceived external challenges such as that posed by the Christian Scientists. The social roles into which doctors are socialized, and the solidarity that comes to characterize the interrelations of these doctors, produce a set of traditions and institutions that convey a very strong sense of authority to the judgments of doctors in the United States. They have a collective consciousness that is transmitted from generation to generation and that creates an open hostility to any perceived threat to this authority. Employing a concept of collective consciousness lets us explain this phenomenon in ways unavailable in explanatory schemes that focus only on individual consciousness.

The main goal of this chapter has been to give a sense of how collective consciousness can be understood in a way that takes into account both past work in continental social theory and current work in cognitive science and to give a sense of its importance in social and moral theory. An ancillary goal of this chapter has been to show that there can be fruitful exchanges between work in moral and social theory on the one hand and philosophical approaches to cognitive science on the other. I hope others more skilled in both of these areas will engage in similar explorations and that both groups of philosophers will begin the difficult task of developing a common language in which we can engage in dialogue about matters of common interest. I next turn to a more nuanced account of socialization that recognizes the problems for morality that result from certain forms of socialization.

4

SOCIALIZATION AND INSTITUTIONAL EVIL

In this chapter I wish to examine the nature and moral significance of the process of institutional socialization. The previous chapter discussed socialization as a positive influence that operates through cognitive and affective factors in collective consciousness to convey a sense of shared norms important for the maintenance of moral authority in a group. Now I wish to fill out that account and also to consider some of the negative effects of socialization, especially as it occurs in bureaucratic institutions. In later chapters I will examine how socialization practices in professional contexts have made it hard for individuals to do what is right, but also how changes in socialization could make it much easier.

In a series of writings, Hannah Arendt argued that certain institutions were able to instill in their members a willingness to do virtually anything, even to participate in great evil. She argued that "the nature of every bureaucracy, is to make functionaries and mere cogs in the administrative machinery out of men, and thus to dehumanize them."[1] The key component is the ability of bureaucratic institutions to instill in their members the idea that each member is completely replaceable and hence completely vulnerable to the whims of the institution. If, in addition, the individual has the idea that one should support family above all else, then the individual is in the unenviable position of feeling pressured to do virtually anything that the employing institution requests. Indeed, certain institutions are able to socialize their members to be more loyal to the institution than to city, nation, or humanity.

---

1. Arendt, *Eichmann in Jerusalem*, p. 289. One of the best discussions of Arendt's views of socialization is found in Margaret Canovan, *Hannah Arendt: A Reinterpretation of Her Political Thought* (Cambridge: Cambridge University Press, 1992), chap. 6.

Throughout this chapter, I try to draw some lessons from an analysis of bureaucratic socialization for other types of institutional socialization. In the first section, I reassess Arendt's claims about the role of bureaucratic institutions in the perpetration of the kind of dehumanization that sets the stage for great evil. In the second section, I will provide an account of institutional socialization, especially bureaucratic socialization, that draws on Arendt's work as well as work in anthropology and social theory. In the third section, I will confront recent models of institutional socialization in critical social theory, where such socialization is almost always seen as a positive contributor to the solidarity of communities. I will conclude by offering a cautionary note to critical theorists by advancing the thesis that some hierarchical or bureaucratic institutions may do more harm than good in terms of socialization of their members.

I. DEHUMANIZATION IN BUREAUCRACIES

In her provocative book *Eichmann in Jerusalem,* Hannah Arendt sets out, among other things, to explain how relatively "normal" people could come to participate in one of the world's greatest evils, the Nazi extermination of millions of Jews in the late 1930s and early 1940s.[2] Adolph Eichmann, Hitler's director of the Final Solution, was, as "everybody could see . . . not a monster."[3] Yet he was able to send thousands to their deaths and to administer a program that he boasted had been ultimately responsible for the deaths of millions of Jews. Arendt portrayed her inquiry as an exploration of Eichmann's conscience: how could a seemingly normal person come to believe that the right thing to do was to exterminate millions of innocent people? The answer to this inquiry was to be found in the institutional factors that socialized Eichmann, as well as so many other petty bureaucrats, into believing that their highest moral duty was to follow their superiors' orders. And more than this, the socialization was such that Eichmann and others felt driven to go beyond the call of duty to persevere with "painstaking thoroughness in the execution of the Final Solution."[4]

In this section, I will attempt to reconstruct Arendt's analysis of the role of bureaucratic socialization in the perpetration of the Holocaust. As I will describe it, this process of socialization, from which she attempts to generalize, involved four overlapping components. First, because of either societal or institutional factors, individuals came to feel increasingly vulnerable economically, especially vulnerable to losing their jobs. Second,

2. Arendt, p. 26.
3. Ibid., p. 54.
4. Ibid., p. 137.

these individuals experienced a loss of autonomy, or at least a loss of control over their lives within the institution. Third, loyalty to the institution was instilled as the chief moral value for these individuals. Fourth, the meaning of conscientiousness was transformed to the point where following orders scrupulously and then going beyond the call of institutional duty was the most virtuous behavior a person could engage in. I will examine each of these components below.

For Arendt, it is important that the bureaucracies in Nazi Germany were peopled by solid, respectable men who had shown their ability to develop strong habits, rather than by unreliable "Bohemians," fanatics, adventurers, sex maniacs, or sadists. Bureaucratic institutions need to be able to secure reliable people, but they also need to secure those who are not self-sufficient. In Nazi Germany, bureaucrats were recruited from the ranks of "job holders and good family-men"; the ideal candidate was the "devoted *paterfamilias*" determined "to make life easy for his wife and children." The first stage in the institutional socialization Arendt identified is the use of the economic insecurities of these individuals to redirect their single-minded devotion to family, turning this devotion into a drive to do whatever seems necessary to keep their jobs.[5] The "devoted *paterfamilias* worried about nothing so much as his security" and that of his family. As a result he was transformed into a very docile member of any organization or institution that would employ him.[6]

The economic climate puts pressure on these men, transforming them into people who will follow virtually any order. "It became clear that for the sake of his pension, his life insurance, the security of his wife and children, such a man was ready to sacrifice his beliefs, his honor, and his human dignity."[7] On this analysis it is important that the bureaucratic man identify his loyalty to family with his loyalty to institution, and that he transfer his strong respectable habits of always doing his duty to doing whatever the institution put forth as his professional duties, which he also saw as his familial duties. "When his occupation forces him to murder people, he does not regard himself as a murderer because he has not done it out of inclination but in his professional capacity."[8]

The second component in the dehumanization of the bureaucrat is the

---

5. Marilyn Friedman has been critical of the recent turn in moral theory toward an acceptance of the legitimacy of partiality. See her book *What Are Friends For?* (Ithaca, NY: Cornell University Press, 1993), especially chap. 2.

6. Hannah Arendt, "Organized Guilt and Universal Responsibility," in *Collective Responsibility*, ed. Larry May and Stacey Hoffman (Savage, MD: Rowman and Littlefield, 1991), p. 279.

7. Ibid., pp. 279–80.

8. Ibid., p. 281.

loss of autonomy. Each individual bureaucrat's action becomes merely a "tiny cog" in a machine so large that the bureaucrat cannot see what the eventual effects will be of the actions of the overall machine. As Arendt points out, "the political form known as bureau-cracy" is best described as "the Rule of nobody."[9] Most bureaucrats do not have control over the process by which decisions are made, or even over the way those decisions are to be carried out. And since the bureaucrats do not see themselves as in charge, their consciences are relieved of concern for the outcome of their actions.

In bureaucracies there is a diffusion of responsibility because of the collective nature of the enterprise. What is of crucial importance here is that the Nazi bureaucrats saw themselves as "fully exempted from responsibility" for their acts.[10] Most individual Nazi bureaucrats could not easily tell what their role was in the collective activity of the whole machine. The point of "bureaucracies" is that a certain kind of division of labor occurs in which work is compartmentalized to such an extent that individual human action is transformed into mere "behavior," that is, the activity of those who are, nearly unreflectively, responding to conditioning.[11] The members of a bureaucracy come to see themselves as not in control; indeed, they come to see that no one person is in control and thus to see the bureaucratic institution as somehow outside the human realm where they would normally have felt responsible for what occurred.

The third component in the dehumanization of bureaucracies is the rise of loyalty as the chief virtue. "The member of the Nazi hierarchy most gifted at solving problems of conscience was Himmler. He coined slogans like the famous watchword of the S.S., taken from a Hitler speech before the S.S. in 1931, 'My Honor is my Loyalty.'"[12] Once the individual Nazi bureaucrat had lost a sense of personal responsibility for his actions within the institution, normal moral scruples were thrown into chaos. To regain a sense of honor and virtuousness, the bureaucrat seized on the one moral concept left over from his previous set of norms: achieving honor and virtue through loyalty.

Eichmann was ultimately impressed that "not just the S.S. or the Party, but the elite of the good old Civil Service were vying and fighting with each other for the honor of taking the lead in these 'bloody matters.'"[13]

This loyalty is cemented in the understanding that the goals and norms

9. Arendt, *Eichmann in Jerusalem*, p. 289.

10. Arendt, "Organized Guilt," p. 280.

11. Arendt, *The Human Condition* (Chicago: The University of Chicago Press, 1958), p. 45.

12. Arendt, *Eichmann in Jerusalem*, p. 105.

13. Ibid., p. 114 (emphasis added).

of the institution are ultimately much more important than any individual goals or norms because "of being involved in something grandiose, unique ('a great task that occurs once in two thousand years'), which must therefore be difficult to bear."[14] The enormity of the importance of the institutional goals creates the feeling "Who am I to judge?" that the institution is pursuing these goals in the wrong way, let alone that these goals are themselves somehow wrongheaded.[15] And even for those individuals who still might raise such questions, the loyalty to family, which calls for doing all that one can to keep one's job, comes into play, and people come to identify loyalty to family with loyalty to institution.

The fourth component in bureaucratic dehumanization involves a thorough transformation of conscience. Here is how Arendt describes one of the most important elements of the socialization of Nazi bureaucrats.

> The problem was how to overcome not so much their conscience as the animal pity by which all normal men are affected in the presence of physical suffering. The trick used by Himmler . . . was very simple and probably very effective; it consisted in turning these instincts around, as it were, in directing them toward the self. So that instead of saying: What horrible things I did to people! the murderers would be able to say: What horrible things I had to watch in the pursuance of my duties, how heavily the task weighed upon my shoulders![16]

Once loyalty is regarded as the chief virtue, then a Nietzschean "transvaluation of values" occurs whereby what was previously thought to be morally wrong is now thought of as merely something that is difficult to bear. The more one could bear to do these previously immoral things, now seen as one's institutional duty, the more loyalty, and hence the more virtue, one displayed.

From here it is only a short jump to the idea that the most virtuous bureaucrat is the one who not only loyally follows orders but tries to do even more than that. Here "to be law-abiding means not merely to obey the laws but to act as though one were the legislator of the laws that one obeys. Hence the conviction is that nothing less than going beyond the call of duty will do."[17] Virtue comes to be associated with not only scrupulously doing one's institutional duty but going beyond that duty to do

14. Ibid., p. 105.

15. Ibid., p. 114 and elsewhere.

16. Ibid., p. 106.

17. Ibid., p. 137. Arendt notes the obvious parallels between the moral philosophy of Immanuel Kant and the views of duty taken by some Nazi bureaucrats. On this same point see A. Zvie Bar-on, "Measuring Responsibility," in May and Hoffman, eds., *Collective Responsibility*.

whatever one can to advance the goals of the institution. For Arendt, this transformation helps to explain why Nazi bureaucrats like Eichmann did more than merely follow what they were ordered to do; they acted with "horribly painstaking thoroughness in the execution of the Final Solution."[18] In this way, these bureaucrats were able to seize back a slight bit of the autonomy they had been forced to relinquish, and hence also to see their honor and virtue as again somewhat under their control.

We have now come to an understanding of how one very oppressive bureaucracy was able to transform normal people with regular consciences into people whose consciences urged them to outdistance one another by becoming extremely efficient murderers. It was not Arendt's intention, nor is it mine, for that matter, to argue that all bureaucracies, let alone all institutions, are analogous to the Nazi bureaucracy. Yet, while it is clear that Arendt's view of bureaucracy is greatly influenced by her examination of an admittedly extreme case, there are important general lessons to be learned from her understanding of this case. In the remainder of this section I will highlight two general lessons that Arendt draws from her examination of the Nazi bureaucrats.

For Arendt, bureaucracies are all manifestations of "the Rule of nobody."[19] In *The Origins of Totalitarianism,* she argues that the rise of bureaucracies in Western European countries brings about a replacement of the rule of law by bureaucratic rule and an ensuing "disregard for law and legal institutions" as well as a diminished sense of participation in politics in many members of the populace.[20] Bureaucratic institutions, in her view, impede people's sense of participation since the rule by decree characteristic of bureaucratic order causes people to feel cut off from the decision-making structures that affect their lives. Put in other terms, bureaucratic institutions socialize people to see themselves not as actors but as those acted upon. The ensuing feelings of powerlessness can give rise to the acceptance of, and even the participation in, harms these people one would never have found acceptable outside of the bureaucratic institution.

Arendt also draws the general conclusion that people could be socialized by bureaucratic institutions to be willing to do acts they would otherwise see as evil. In her essay "Thinking and Moral Considerations," she succinctly articulates the thesis on the "banality of evil" which she had first propounded in her book about Eichmann. Arendt says that the banality of evil refers to "something quite factual, the phenomenon of evil deeds, com-

18. Arendt, *Eichmann in Jerusalem,* p. 137.

19. A similar point is made by Iris Young in her book *Justice and the Politics of Difference* (Princeton: Princeton University Press, 1990), chap. 3.

20. Arendt, *The Origins of Totalitarianism* (New York: Harcourt Brace, 1951), p. 243.

mitted on a gigantic scale, which could not be traced to any particularity of wickedness, pathology, or ideological conviction in the doer, whose only personal distinction was a perhaps extraordinary shallowness."[21] The reason ordinary men and women can come to participate in great evil is that bureaucratic institutions socialize their members to be thoughtless, at least concerning what is right or wrong within the institution.

On Arendt's account, most people have a "need to think," but this can be erased by "more urgent needs of living."[22] Bureaucratic institutions are especially good at instilling in people a sense of this urgency and at pressing it in such a way that otherwise conscience-driven individuals are able to accept even a total reversal of their previous value scheme, so that at least some of what was previously wrong is now seen as right. Socialization in institutions can have this negative effect, in Arendt's view, and it is one of the most important things to be countered if evil is to be diminished in the world. But in countering this form of evil it remains important to remember that it is not intentional acts of evil but acts socialized by institutions that are to be combated.[23]

On my interpretation of Arendt, institutional socialization in bureaucracies transforms individuals into cogs, that is, these individuals come to think of themselves as anonymous. As anonymous cogs, they lack the face-to-face confrontation with one another, and with the consequences of their actions, that is necessary for a developed sense of responsibility. Lacking this personal dimension in their institutional lives, they are likely to lose their sense of responsibility in institutional settings as well. And on this construal of Arendt's position, the anonymity, not necessarily the top-down structure, is the key to the socialization that gives rise to what she called the banality of evil. As we shall see, anonymity is often a hallmark of many types of institutions. In this respect, then, Arendt's analysis of the negative side of bureaucracies can be extended to many forms of institutions.

II. RECONCEIVING INSTITUTIONAL SOCIALIZATION

In this section I wish to reconsider institutional socialization by analyzing in more detail the loss of autonomy and the sense of anonymity that are felt by many members of diverse institutions. But before beginning that enter-

---

21. Hannah Arendt, "Thinking and Moral Considerations," *Social Research* 38, no. 3 (autumn 1971): 417.

22. Ibid., p. 421.

23. See the postscript to *Eichmann in Jerusalem* for a thorough discussion of this issue, especially the failure of the current concepts in jurisprudence to comprehend this phenomenon.

prise, I will survey some of the more interesting recent accounts of how socialization operates to organize conventions in institutions. Both of these tasks will set the stage for a full understanding of institutional socialization. I will be guided by reflections on some ethnographic and sociological works, especially by Richard Titmuss and by Mary Douglas in her book *How Institutions Think*.[24]

Socialization is a form of learning, especially a development of attitudes, beliefs, and habits concerning one's role in a social group. A society is a social group that is bound together by certain common beliefs and organizational structures. For a society or institution to operate smoothly, the members of these social groups need to know, or to learn, how to coordinate their actions with the actions of others to achieve certain collective goals. It is useful, I believe, to begin to think of socialization as merely one of many possible forms of learning that occurs during the course of the development to maturity. Almost everyone is socialized into the ways of life of some institution or other. In the earliest years this socialization occurs in the institutions of family and school, as well as in the wider societies in which people live.

Institutions are mechanisms for organizing individuals by reference to various customs that assign roles to those who perform various tasks. Institutions may operate at a small-scale level, such as the institution of the handshake or of gift giving[25]; or they may operate at a large-scale level, such as the institution of the army or of General Motors. The organization of institutions can be hierarchical, such as that of a regiment or of a bureaucracy; or it can be egalitarian, such as that of the handshake. Importantly for our purposes, institutions have effects on their members: most significantly, the customs that govern the corresponding roles create expectations for individuals to conform their behaviors in various ways.

It is important to distinguish institutions that instill anonymity from those that instill other forms of impersonal behavior. Many institutions are designed to protect individuals from harms that are made more likely by closeness of association. The institution of marriage is supposed to protect both partners by providing relatively clear roles as well as corresponding duties and rights. The introduction of formal notions of duties and rights into a very personal relationship instills an element of impersonality into marriage. Another institution, blind review, is also supposed to protect both reviewers and those whose work is reviewed, by completely eliminat-

---

24. Syracuse: Syracuse University Press, 1986.

25. It is perhaps more common to refer to the handshake as a convention rather than an institution. But it seems to me, and to many sociologists, that there are roles and even a certain amount of social organization that occur here as well.

ing one of the most important markers of the personal, one's name. Such a practice often results in a reviewing process that is anonymous.[26]

In all cases of impersonality some peculiarities of the individual person are eliminated, diminished, or hidden. Anonymity is an extreme form of impersonality. Some less extreme forms of impersonality in institutions restrict a certain range of otherwise common emotional responses so that there is a greater likelihood that people will be able to respect each other as equals. The institution of free speech socializes people to be more tolerant of how they react to those whose speeches are disliked, and the reciprocal nature of this institution's enforced impersonality is often thought to breed a certain kind of distanced respect for those who are very different from oneself. Thus, some forms of impersonality in institutions can serve a positive moral purpose.

There are both positive and negative effects of the forms of socialization that occur within institutions (hereafter often "institutional socialization"). Anonymity can sometimes serve a positive moral purpose, as in the institution of blind refereeing, but it often serves negative moral purposes as well, as we saw in Arendt's account of the Nazi bureaucrats. In the previous section I surveyed some of the negative consequences that result from bureaucratic institutional socialization. I will examine some of the positive effects of certain forms of small-scale institutional socialization before turning back to large-scale (especially bureaucratic) institutional socialization. Throughout I will be guided by examples drawn from the rich literature in sociology and anthropology on these topics.

One of the best examples of small-scale socialization involves the institution of gift exchange: gift giving, gift receiving, and gift repaying. Ethnographic studies illustrate how in most societies there is an institution of gift exchange into which the members of the society are socialized from an early age. The socialization to give gifts and especially to accept and repay gifts is so strong that the members of many societies come to feel that they are under a set of strict obligations that are triggered whenever a gift is given to them.[27] Gift exchange is clearly an institution in the sense that there are customs governing this set of practices and the practices have organized a significant segment of social life in ancient societies as well as in contemporary ones.

---

26. This is not always true, for in very small subfields it is difficult to eliminate completely the possibility of identifying the persons involved because of markers such as idiosyncratic writing styles.

27. See Marcel Mauss's ground-breaking study of the ethnography of the gift relationship, *The Gift: Forms and Functions of Exchange in Archaic Societies,* trans. Ian Cunnison (London: Cohen and West, 1954).

The institution of gift exchange functions to organize social life in many different kinds of societies. The organization occurs in the realm of face-to-face interactions between members of these societies. In some ancient societies, the gift relationship was the basis of a rudimentary economy and was extremely important in governmental affairs as well. Richard Titmuss claims that quite a bit was lost "by the substitution of large-scale economic systems for systems in which exchange of goods was not an impersonal but a moral transaction, bringing about and maintaining personal relationships between individuals and groups."[28] A similar kind of point can be made about the substitution of large-scale, impersonal bureaucratic institutions for small-scale, face-to-face ones.

Institutions that accentuate the personal rather than the impersonal often can enhance humanistic impulses. This is well illustrated by Titmuss's argument that the institution of voluntary blood donation enhances altruism. Titmuss also claims, more controversially, that large-scale commercial institutions, such as those that buy and sell blood, diminish altruism.[29] A number of recent theorists, such as Jürgen Habermas, have claimed that institutions can play a positive mediating role in enhancing impulses to display solidarity with one's fellow citizens, or even with the members of the human race. Such claims appear to be consistent with the studies of gift giving. But, as I will argue, it is only personal, face-to-face institutions, such as the gift relationship, that clearly function in this way. The ethnographic evidence examined by Marcel Mauss and Richard Titmuss does not show that bureaucratic and other impersonal institutions enhance humanistic impulses. Indeed, their research appears to support the opposite result.

One work that is often cited to show the positive effects of large-scale institutions is Mary Douglas's *How Institutions Think*. In this study, Douglas argues that smallness of scale is not terribly important in ascertaining which institutions are likely to attain stability. Rather, the major factor here is whether or not the institution can attain solidarity. Douglas follows Durkheim in thinking that even very large-scale institutions can occasionally attain stability and enhance the moral sentiments of their members.[30] I agree with her that size of group alone is not the most important factor in determining whether an institution will be likely to attain

28. Richard M. Titmuss, *The Gift Relationship: From Human Blood to Social Policy* (New York: Pantheon Books, 1971), p. 72.

29. Titmuss, p. 245. See Kenneth Arrow's criticism of this result of Titmuss's study, "Gifts and Exchanges," *Philosophy and Public Affairs* 1, no. 4 (summer 1972). For a philosophical defense of Titmuss against Arrow's criticisms see Peter Singer, "Altruism and Commerce," *Philosophy and Public Affairs* 2, no. 3 (spring 1973).

30. Douglas, chap. 4.

stability and encourage altruistic impulses such as solidarity. She is right to think that collective belief formation and solidarity are the keys; but collective belief formation and solidarity are more difficult to achieve and sustain the larger the group gets.

Douglas rightly points out that there is a strong "political rhetoric" that romanticizes the small community based on mutual trust. Contrary to this rhetoric, many small communities are not loving environments but divisive and polarized environments. What distinguishes both successful small and large institutions, according to Douglas, is their members' "commitment to the given social order."[31] This is the factor which Emile Durkheim identified as solidarity and which, on Douglas's interpretation, chiefly involves a sharing of beliefs. And that factor is at least possible for large-scale institutions. So far, Douglas's position seems unexceptionable to me. But we need to ask further whether the impersonality of large institutions, especially bureaucratic ones, is likely to enhance or diminish the human impulses and attitudes, such as altruism, that would support solidarity.[32]

Douglas is quite unsure about the likelihood that solidarity will emerge in large-scale groups that are hierarchically structured. Coercion can also only go so far; it must be supplemented by what Douglas calls "extrarational principles" that produce and sustain a community.[33] These extrarational principles, such as habits and conventions, are both founded in analogy and reinforced by institutional socialization.[34] And while Douglas thinks that these principles can be extended to institutions of any size whatsoever, it is not at all clear from her work whether large, impersonal institutions will be likely to generate the sense of commonality needed for strong social bonds. Indeed, she criticizes Durkheim's own attempt to link strength of social bond with loss of individuality and autonomy.

Given the discussion in chapter 2, it is important to distinguish strong social bonds that contribute to evil from the kind of solidarity that can lead to the advancement of the common good. Loyalty to institution is not the same as solidarity in a community. The chief difference is that in some institutions, socialization will produce insensitivity to the needs of others, as the goals of the institution come to blot out the normal moral sentiments of individual members. On the other hand, in communities where solidarity exists, an enhancement of the normal moral sentiments occurs. What

31. Ibid., p. 28.
32. See chap. 2, "Solidarity and Moral Support," for a detailed discussion of solidarity and its applicability to large-scale groups.
33. Douglas, p. 29.
34. Ibid., p. 45.

seems to make the difference is whether the members of a community or institution feel supported in or alienated from their personal values. If the institution is alienating, then the strength of social bonds within the institution can intensify the alienation. If the community is supportive, then the strength of social bonds can intensify fellow feeling. Of course there is no necessity that sheer size of group will determine whether the members of the group feel alienated from or supported by the group. But there does seem to be a correlation, nonetheless, since face-to-face interaction stresses the uniqueness of each member. In some cases, though, it is possible for large groups to convey support for the uniqueness of each of their members, and for the strength of the bond felt by these members to result in moral good rather than evil.[35]

Following Hannah Arendt, I would argue that the strength of the social bond can contribute to the process of dehumanization, especially in bureaucratic institutions. Strong social bonds plus a diminished sense of personal autonomy are what create the "cogs in a machine" mentality of bureaucrats. Strong social bonds, especially in hierarchical institutions, often lead to a loss of autonomy and feelings of anonymity.[36] Certain institutions socialize most of their members to feel that decisions should be made by other, more knowledgeable and experienced members, the "experts." This is a theme that many, including Habermas, have discussed at length. But there have also been many recent writings, including some by Habermas, that have extolled the role of impersonal institutions in extending the realm of moral deliberation and discourse. I turn to some of these writings in hopes of showing that we should remain deeply suspicious of bureaucratic and other impersonal institutions, especially when we focus on the effects of the forms of socialization most often employed by these institutions.

III. ANONYMITY, INSTITUTIONS, AND CRITICAL THEORY

In some of his early writings, Jürgen Habermas expressed worries similar to those expressed by Hannah Arendt about institutional socialization in bureaucracies. Specifically, in *Legitimation Crisis* Habermas spoke of "the political anonymization of class rule." Such rule is characterized by "traditionalistic ties, fatalistic willingness to follow, lack of perspective and na-

---

35. I am indebted to William Rehg and Ralph Lindgren for making me aware of the importance of this point and for showing how it may undercut some of my doubts, expressed here and in chap. 2, that large-scale solidarity can act as a positive moral force in the world. I discuss this a bit more at the end of this chapter.

36. Some of the most persuasive evidence for this view can be found in Ervin Staub, *The Roots of Evil: The Origins of Genocide and Other Group Violence* (New York: Cambridge University Press, 1989), especially chaps. 2 and 5.

ked repression."[37] In this work, Habermas defines socialization as "the adapting of inner nature to society." Habermas here worries about the negative effects of the kind of socialization necessary for individuals to become individuated.[38] In his later works Habermas is seemingly so interested in pursuing the positive connections between socialization and individual maturation that he forgets the negative features of socialization he had also already described. Such a change parallels Habermas's change from showing strong support for participatory democracy to showing strong support for representative forms of government, where nonparticipatory political institutions are now seen as having mainly positive effects.

These changes manifest themselves quite clearly in the second volume of Habermas's book The Theory of Communicative Action. Habermas links socialization with learning role competences and with understanding authority in terms of the "generalized other."[39] Social control in institutions is understood intersubjectively, as it was for George Herbert Mead. Individuals mature to the extent that they can "assume the attitudes of others who are involved with them in common endeavor." Institutions are then nothing but bases for "normative consensus among group members." Importantly, "institutions claim a validity that rests on intersubjective recognition, on the consent of those affected by it."[40] But such consent is merely hypothetical, since it encompasses what individuals would agree to if they were to assume the standpoint of the generalized other, not what individuals have actually agreed to.

The strong emphasis on how consent is implicit in all institutions, and especially in institutional socialization, has brought Habermas to the point where he is an outspoken supporter of the role of institutions in mediating between the individual will and the collective will. In his most recent book to be translated into English, *Between Facts and Norms*,[41] Habermas continues to place more and more emphasis in his political philosophy on the role of institutions, with little corresponding attention to the possible negative effects of institutions.[42] Indeed, Habermas has come lately to glorify

37. Jürgen Habermas, *Legitimation Crisis,* trans. Thomas McCarthy (Boston: Beacon Press, 1975), p. 22.

38. Ibid., pp. 13–14.

39. Habermas, *The Theory of Communicative Action,* vol. 2, pp. 37–40.

40. Ibid., p. 39.

41. Habermas, *Between Facts and Norms: Contributions to a Discourse Theory of Law and Democracy,* trans. William Rehg (Cambridge, MA: MIT Press, in press). I will refer to the pagination of the penultimate typescript draft of Bill Rehg's translation.

42. In *Between Facts and Norms,* chap. 8, p. 31, Habermas does mention some negative effects of bureaucracy.

the anonymous, faceless member of a political institution as the embodiment of the perspective of universality and rights within a democracy. Such
a position is in stark contrast to his earlier, strong support—seemingly
now rejected—for participatory democracy.

Habermas has come to be critical of participatory democracy because
of his reasonable worries about the tyranny of the majority in popular political institutions that are unmediated by hierarchical institutions.[43] For
example, he worries that the voices of ethnic minorities have not been
heard in unmediated participatory democracies. But this is not comforting
to those like me who continue to follow Arendt in worrying about the dehumanization that occurs when hierarchical or bureaucratic institutions
mediate between individuals. In the remainder of this section I will advance the thesis that Habermas has moved too far away from his earlier
skepticism (inspired by Arendt) of bureaucratic and hierarchical institutions.

Habermas clearly recognizes the differences between his own view
and that of Arendt. After identifying Arendt with the republican tradition,
especially its emphasis on "decentralized self-governance," which takes
over and controls "the bureaucratically independent state power," Habermas maintains that his own view does not go this far.[44] He offers strong
support for governmental bureaucracies that guarantee that individuals
become anonymous rather than confront each other as unique selves. Indeed, though he echoes Arendt's own language in *The Origins of Totalitarianism* in describing the negative effects of bureaucracies, Habermas
nonetheless extolls the virtues of "subjectless forms of communication"
and "anonymous" "popular sovereignty."[45]

For Habermas, anonymity makes it more likely that people will form
judgments based on universalizable reasons rather than on considerations
of sentiment, emotion, or prejudice. So Habermas would agree that anonymity depersonalizes, but he would disagree that anonymity dehuman-
izes, since he follows Kant in seeing the appeal to universal reasons as, in

43. Habermas, *Between Facts and Norms,* chap. 7, p. 9.

44. Ibid., pp. 15–16.

45. These phrases are embedded in the following quotations: "Both within and outside the
parliamentary complex and its bodies programmed for deliberation, these subjectless forms
of communication comprise arenas in which a more or less rational opinion- and will-formation can take place in regard to the entire society and in need of regulation." "The 'self' of the
self-organized legal community disappears in the subjectless forms of communication that
regulate the flow of discursive opinion- and will-formation in such a way that their fallible
results enjoy the presumption of rationality. . . . Popular sovereignty, even if it becomes
anonymous, retreats into democratic procedures . . . only in order to make itself felt as com-
municatively generated power." Habermas, *Between Facts and Norms,* chap. 7, pp. 17 and
20.

principle, the most human of appeals.[46] Habermas also has a pragmatic response to my criticisms. The justification given to the admittedly problematic notions, such as "anonymity" and "subjectless communication," ultimately rests on Habermas's increasing frustration with unmediated forms of popular sovereignty.

While I am sympathetic to the practical difficulties of maintaining unmediated popular sovereignty at the national level, I do not wish to follow Habermas's headlong rush to support anonymous and impersonal institutions, such as various administrative agencies or parliamentary bodies, that mediate between and transform the face-to-face interactions and deliberations among citizens. My main reason is that a person's intuitions, upon which judgments are made, are much more problematic when they are based on impersonal and general considerations than they are when based on personal and particular ones. As Arendt herself shows so well in her later works (especially *Thinking*[47]), good judgment is based on the kind of intuitiveness or thoughtfulness that is vivid and intensely felt because it is thoroughly immersed in the particularities of one's life. When those particularities are absent, people often lack the sense of personal responsibility, another important ingredient in good moral judgment. Institutions, especially those that render their members anonymous, are likely to dehumanize their members in the sense that these members have less to base their autonomous moral judgments upon.[48]

Arendt distinguishes between those legal institutions that protect individual action and judgment and those that do not. As Margaret Canovan has noted, Arendt supports the idea of "laws as fences [which] limit and protect the spontaneous movements of individual[s]."[49] But legal institutions can become problematic when they reduce individuals to some common denominator and thereby eliminate any basis for uniqueness and spontaneity. What is lost in anonymity is the sense of personal responsibility that will counteract the possible willingness to contribute to harm or evil in the world. This point is as true in economically and socially oriented institutions as it is in politically oriented ones.

Let us consider the business corporation. This is an organized institu-

46. I am grateful to James Bohman for suggesting this formulation of Habermas's point to me.

47. Vol. 1 of *The Life of the Mind* (New York: Harcourt Brace Jovanovich, 1977).

48. Arendt differs from Habermas in considering that good judgment proceeds from, and remains tied to, particulars, "without any overall rules," whereas Habermas continues to follow Kant in thinking that good judgment proceeds by applying a universal rule to a particular case. See Arendt's fascinating discussion of this point in *Thinking*, pp. 69–70.

49. Canovan, *Hannah Arendt*, p. 88. Habermas does still somewhat recognize this point, as when he worries about the "suffocation of spontaneous public communication," in *Between Facts and Norms*, chap. 8, p. 54.

tion with its own rules, customs, and ethos. Businesses may be organized hierarchically or nonhierarchically. But it is commonly believed that only hierarchically organized businesses can achieve significant profitability. Business corporations are able to socialize their members to be highly motivated and loyal in the pursuit of corporate objectives and goals. The hierarchical structure mediates between individuals and makes their personal interaction much less important than it would be in a nonhierarchically organized business. Indeed, the hierarchical structure imposes an impersonality on the business corporation in that the individual members are concerned to satisfy the requirements of a particular role, first and foremost, rather than to act autonomously, as they would in a business that gave more independent authority to all of its members.

Institutional conventions that encouraged independent decision making could be established, and this could even be accomplished in a hierarchical institution if, for example, a supervisor identified a segment of the business of which an employee could be in charge, or if a supervisor regularly consulted with supervisees, recognizing them as equals, as seems to happen in some of the businesses set up on the "Japanese model." Perhaps based on this model, large-scale nonhierarchical institutions can be constructed. If they are, and remain, nonhierarchical, then they stand a chance of being more supportive of autonomy than of anonymity. If large-scale nonhierarchical businesses can operate efficiently, then perhaps the same can be true at the political level. So it is not the largeness of institutions, but rather their hierarchical nature, that increases the likelihood of dehumanization.

Autonomy and institutional socialization are not necessarily opposed to each other, but it often turns out that bureaucratic and hierarchical institutions socialize their members in such a way that autonomy (at least in terms of the choice of institutional ends) is diminished.[50] Autonomy involves the condition of being the ultimate source of authority in a certain realm of decision making. Hierarchical structures deny to some members of a group much if not all autonomy of judgment. But even within such institutions, autonomy is rarely extinguished completely. Some may rightly claim that autonomy is encouraged in those nonhierarchical components of hierarchical institutions.

Autonomy is also not necessarily incompatible with anonymity. Anonymity makes one less concerned about what others might say about one's conduct. In some situations this produces an increase in autonomy. When people live in very large cities, they often find that they are less concerned about the opinions of their neighbors and more likely to act on their own

---

50. See Irving Thalberg's provocative essay "Socialization and Autonomous Behavior," *Tulane Studies* 28 (1979).

principles. But in other situations, anonymity diminishes autonomy, as when one identifies too much with the role one plays (Arendt's conception of being a "cog") rather than with one's unique characteristics, and as a result sees oneself not as an agent but as a passive subject. Within most governmental and business institutions, socialization tends to work to the detriment of autonomy and in favor of "following orders."

The loss of autonomy and the increase in feelings of anonymity work to create the "dehumanization" that Arendt described. In my view, the feelings of shame or guilt at having contributed to a harm are chiefly what is diminished in this socialization process. In the remainder of this chapter I will address these features of humanistic sentiment the loss of which is risked by increasing institutional mediation and ensuing feelings of anonymity in economic, social, and political sectors of contemporary society.

IV. SHAME, GUILT, AND INSTITUTIONAL EVIL

One of Hannah Arendt's enduring legacies is her concept of the banality of evil. Arendt focused primarily on the way in which evil is often perpetrated because of thoughtlessness rather than intentional acts. I wish to take her point one step further by explaining how thoughtlessness leads to a diminution of feelings of shame and guilt and hence to a greater likelihood that people will participate in acts of great evil. Along the way I will also try to explain why Habermas has gone wrong in not recognizing the implications of his support for institutional mediation, especially in the domain of morality. Here I will employ his important conception of the "colonization of the lifeworld."

Shame is best understood as the response that people feel when they believe that others (an anticipated audience) would judge them to have a particular failing or character defect. Shame has its origins in the feeling of wanting to hide from someone whose gaze betrays some sort of disapproval of one's person. Guilt is best understood as the response that people feel when they believe that they have engaged in a transgression. Guilt has its origins in the feeling that one has broken the law and hence that one stands in a position to be punished. Both shame and guilt turn on various cognitive factors as well as on the affective factors I have just mentioned. In the case of shame, one believes that others would judge one to have a defect; in the case of guilt, one believes that there is a law or rule which one's conduct has violated.[51]

Institutional socialization can affect the cognitive dimensions of

---

51. See John Deigh's helpful discussion of the concepts of guilt and shame in "Shame and Self-Esteem: A Critique," in *Ethics and Personality,* ed. John Deigh (Chicago: University of Chicago Press, 1992).

shame and guilt in certain cases. Most importantly, the institutional audience may counteract one's normal anticipated audience, thus blocking shame from occurring. If none of those with whom one associates gives the slightest indication that one's behavior is defective and hence worthy of shame, then the normal, internalized sense of shame will also begin to change over time, perhaps resulting in the elimination of feelings of shame for certain kinds of institutionally approved acts. Indeed, there may be a reversal of the categories of behavior that trigger the feelings of shame such that a refusal to participate in harmful behavior may be seen as shameful. Guilt also may be blocked if institutional socialization causes one not to think that certain acts are indeed violative of legitimate laws or rules of conduct.

Institutional bureaucracies are especially well adapted to provide alternative bases of shame and guilt to that normally provided by family, church, or school. Two features are especially worthy of comment. First, institutional bureaucracies mimic institutions of family, church, and school in being top-down structures that rely on a group of easily known sources of authority to convey information about what is and is not acceptable conduct. Second, institutional bureaucracies connect self-interested motivations with normative motivations in significant ways, just as is true in family, church, and school. Few other institutions that adults encounter (with the exception of legal institutions) provide so strong an impetus to conform to the institutional norms as do bureaucratic institutions.

In her essay "Thinking and Moral Considerations," Arendt focuses on the internal dialogue between me and myself that may be extinguished if one does not think about what one is doing. This analysis is in line with my own, but it lacks a developed, positive explanation of how moral thinking works. I will try to provide a plausible account of how the thoughtlessness instilled by bureaucratic institutions will block moral thinking, but an account that is consistent with Arendt's conception of the banality of evil. Habermas provides a helpful concept in this respect when he discusses the notion of the colonization of the lifeworld. According to this notion, ideas or categories from an institution pervade an individual's conception of his or her life so that the individual conceives of his or her life in terms of the dominant categories of the institution. According to James Bohman, colonization occurs, for instance, "when the imperatives of the insurance industry and the defense bureaucracy begin to dictate the character of medical practice and the goals of scientific research."[52] Bureaucratic institutions are one example that Habermas employs to explicate the phenomenon of

---

52. James Bohman, *New Philosophy of Social Science* (Cambridge, MA: MIT Press, 1991), p. 176.

how a person's identity may be changed by institutional socialization, but he seems to downplay their effects.[53]

I think that Habermas's conception of the colonization of the life-world can be used effectively to fill out Arendt's story of how bureaucratic institutions perpetuate the banality of evil. This can be seen by further examining how a person's normal conceptions of shame and guilt become colonized by bureaucracies and other forms of hierarchical institutions. Such an analysis will also allow us to see where Habermas has gone wrong in attempting to downgrade the negative effects of institutional socialization.

Shame and guilt may be colonized by the institution in the sense that the institution imposes its own conception of what is to be done onto the existing conceptions of shame and guilt held by its members. Previously, people felt shame when they acted in a way that indicated deficiency in certain respects, for instance, not displaying sufficient sympathy toward fellow humans. Institutional socialization can transform this sense of shame by changing the anticipated audience before whom one would feel shame. The new audience, the people who are the authorities in an institutional hierarchy, imposes a new sense of deficiency, one drawn in terms of the specific normative goals of the institution. The moral sense of the individuals who belong to the institution is thus colonized by internal rules and roles of the institution. And the idea of what constitutes pride in oneself is also transformed so that one takes pride in satisfying the new audience, and the greatest pride in going beyond what this audience expects.

With guilt a similar transformation occurs. The social rules concerning what is a transgression and what is not, which constituted the moral bedrock of these individuals, are replaced by the rules of the institution. As a result, a member of an institution comes to feel guilty for violating the rules of the institution, even when those rules conflict with the rules of the society at large or of one's family. This helps us fill out the story that Arendt had begun to tell about institutional socialization. Indeed, at one point she discusses Eichmann as a kind of rule chameleon.

> He functioned in the role of prominent war criminal as well as he had under the Nazi regime; he had not the slightest difficulty in accepting an entirely new set of rules. He knew that what he had once considered his duty was now called a crime, and he accepted this new code of judgment as though it were nothing but another language rule.[54]

---

53. On p. 311 of vol. 2 of *Theory of Communicative Action*, Habermas discusses the effects of bureaucracies but says that these create serious problems for a person's identity "only if there is an *irresistible* tendency to an ever *expanding* bureaucratization."

54. Arendt, "Thinking and Moral Considerations," p. 417.

Eichmann differed from the rest of us only in the sense that it was seemingly easier for different institutions to colonize him in terms of guilt feelings.

One of the reasons Habermas seems to be blind to these results of his own conception of socialization is that he regards guilt and shame as mere "affective responses to violations" of rules or conventions. This affects what he calls the realm of ethical life, but not of morality proper.

> "Mere" conventions bind, so to speak, in a groundless fashion by custom alone; we do not associate a moral claim with them. Duties, by contrast, derive their binding force from the validity of norms of interaction that claim to rest on good reasons.[55]

To focus on shame is, according to Habermas, to focus merely on the responses to what lies much more deeply within the individual, namely, the sense of duty; or to focus on guilt is to focus on an illegitimate basis of morality, namely, the institutional rules of "mere" conventions.[56]

Habermas doesn't come to terms with the way his category of the colonization of the lifeworld applies to the moral domain because he denies that the ethical lifeworld has any connection to the moral domain in the first place. Habermas's sharp distinction between morality and ethical life has allowed him to ignore the negative effects of socialization on moral sentiments. But this should not be true even on his own terms. Duty is a cognitive concept, and anything that affects our cognitive capacities, especially in the moral domain, should be of great interest to Habermas. Yet his deontological conception of morality has rendered Habermas blind to the consequences of socialization for both moral sentiments and moral understanding. Our feelings of shame and guilt are often important sources of moral understanding.

As has been argued throughout this chapter, institutional socialization can have quite a negative impact on an individual's understanding of right and wrong. Especially in the case of bureaucracy, anonymity results from institutional socialization and can change the way that shame and guilt operate within an individual. Evil is made more likely, although it is not inten-

---

55. Habermas, *Justification and Application,* trans. Ciaran Cronin (Cambridge, MA: MIT Press, 1993), p. 41. It should be pointed out that earlier in this paragraph Habermas says that "*affective responses* to violations . . . constitute the *experiential basis* of obligations, though they do not exhaust their semantic meaning." But he also says, in the next paragraph, "Sanctions (however much they are internalized) are not constitutive of normative validity; they are symptoms of an already felt and thus antecedent, violation of a normatively regulated context of life" (pp. 41–2).

56. For a critique of this overall approach to the place of shame in morality, see Bernard Williams, *Shame and Necessity* (Berkeley: University of California Press, 1993).

tional evil that is at stake.[57] Perhaps this is the problem. Habermas, unlike Arendt, has been so focused on the intentional acts of individuals that he has failed to see that it is unintentional acts that need to be combated. In this respect, we should be very suspicious of the anonymity of institutions. For in anonymous interactions, the face of evil is not easy to identify. In the next chapter, in an attempt to address the concerns I have just expressed about Habermas's version of deontological moral theory, I will set out a model of moral responsibility that focuses on attentiveness and responsiveness.

57. For a good discussion of this point see John Kekes, *Facing Evil* (Princeton: Princeton University Press, 1990).

5

SOCIAL RESPONSIBILITY

In contemporary writing about ethics, a number of otherwise disparate philosophical schools of thought have come to endorse an ethic of responsibility. Some communitarians, feminists, virtue theorists, critical theorists, moral psychologists, and postmodernists have all embraced the centrality of responsibility in moral thinking and deemphasized the importance of obligation, duty, and abstract moral rules.[1] I will examine and build on some of this disparate literature, looking especially for the reasons why so many theorists are employing concepts of responsibility, especially social responsibility, instead of obligation or duty. My view is that there is a coherent and highly plausible theoretical perspective that unites many contemporary writings on responsibility, and that such a coherent conception of responsibility is well suited to discussions of social responsibility, especially in professional cases. Whether this constitutes a full-fledged movement to rival the other movements in contemporary ethics remains to be seen.

The term *social responsibility* has been a red flag waved by those who are opposed to the unbridled pursuit of self-interest and profit by businesses, hospitals, law firms, government agencies, and universities, as well as by their individual members. In its most popular form, social responsibility merely refers to the idea that one needs to take into account more

---

1. I will mention many of these theorists in what follows. It should be noted that the three major early existentialists, Martin Heidegger, Karl Jaspers, and Jean-Paul Sartre, all focused on the concept of responsibility in their writings as well. Of special interest is Jaspers's book-length treatment of the question of whether Germans are responsible for the Holocaust, *The Question of German Guilt*. Of more recent vintage is Hans Jonas's *The Imperative of Responsibility* (Chicago: University of Chicago Press, 1984). Jonas regards the parent-child relationship as "the archetype of responsibility" (p. 130).

than oneself when making decisions that affect the larger society. In this chapter I will pursue the philosophical task of providing a more developed conception of the larger ethic of responsibility of which social responsibility is a part.

In his 1918 essay, "Politics as a Vocation," Max Weber distinguished between "an ethic of responsibility" and "an ethic of conviction."[2] Weber clearly had Kantians in mind as those who epitomized the ethic of conviction. Weber criticized this ethic for being absolutist in its rejection of the relevance of context and consequences.

> If an action of good intent leads to bad results, then, in the actor's eyes, not he but the world, or the stupidity of other men, or God's will who made them thus, is responsible for the evil. However a man who believes in an ethic of responsibility takes account of precisely the average deficiencies of people.[3]

Weber used this distinction to argue for a consequentialist solution to the problem of dirty hands in politics, contending that good can often be achieved only through the otherwise immoral use of violence. Thus, Weber's argument is generally interpreted as merely juxtaposing a consequentialist ethic and a deontological one.

But as Gerth and Mills write in their introduction to Weber's essays, Weber developed an ethic of responsibility in response to his own experiences in dealing with his deeply religious and contentious siblings: "He became the confidant of almost everyone concerned, learning to appreciate and sympathize with their respective values."[4]

Weber's ethic of responsibility was a call for the individual to downplay the kind of conviction that is associated with rule-oriented theories of obligation or duty and instead concern himself or herself with how other people and relationships are likely to be affected by his or her actions. In this sense Weber foreshadowed the recent movement I am about to describe, which is perhaps why his work is often cited in this literature.

I begin this chapter by providing an outline of an ethic of responsibility. In the second section, I am concerned to fill in the outline with a view of responsibility that is especially useful for the professions. In the third section, I draw heavily on the most developed treatment of responsibility, namely, that found in feminist writings. In the fourth section, I respond to some of the objections to concepts of responsibility, especially

2. Reprinted in *From Max Weber*, trans. and ed. H. H. Gerth and C. Wright Mills (New York: Oxford University Press, 1946), p. 120.

3. Weber, p. 121.

4. Ibid., p. 9.

those by Jürgen Habermas. Finally, I provide a new approach to social responsibility and contrast it with an approach provided by Robert Goodin. Throughout, I will focus on the relation between *social* responsibility and *personal* responsibility. Such an approach has the added advantage of showing how morality is linked with social and political theory, something that is often not obvious in other theoretical approaches to morality.

I. TOWARD AN ETHIC OF RESPONSIBILITY

There are several interlocking aspects of an ethic of responsibility. I begin with a preliminary list of the elements of such an ethic most often noted in the literature:

1. a responsiveness to those whom we could help, especially those who are in relationships with us or toward whom we have taken on a certain role;
2. a sensitivity to the peculiarities of a person's concrete circumstances and contexts;
3. a motivation to respond to another that grows out of the needs of others, especially those who depend on us;
4. a wide discretion concerning what is required to be a responsible person, rather than an emphasis on keeping an abstract commandment or rule;
5. a respect for the legitimacy of emotions as a source of moral knowledge, and especially for the feelings of guilt, shame, and remorse that are central to people's actual moral experiences;
6. a sense of what it means to be a responsible person that is tied more to who we are, and what we can do, than to what we have done.[5]

These elements do not yet constitute an ethic in the way that the principle of utility or the categorical imperative do. But this is just the point.

An ethic is not merely, and not necessarily, a superrule or even a set of universal guidelines. To be sure, an ethic must give guidance for practical decision making. But that guidance need not be the sort that can be encapsulated in a simple commandment or algorithm. Indeed, an ethic of responsibility allows quite a bit of discretion to the agent. An ethic must be action-guiding, but to be action-guiding for a particular person it need not be so in terms of an abstract and universal rule. The portrayal of an ideal can be action-guiding in a way that does not involve the stipulation of an

---

5. In this sense an ethic of responsibility is most at home in a communitarian social and moral framework. See chap. 1, sec. 1, for a more detailed analysis of what this entails.

abstract rule. Indeed, a saintly life or a prototype can do this as well.[6] An ethic of responsibility is action-guiding in a way that is more akin to these latter examples. For this ethic speaks personally to each of us, but it may also speak differently to each.

How would an ethic of responsibility be different from other ethics concerning a particular case? Consider the case of a parent who must decide whether to go to the university to teach or stay home with a mildly sick child. One can imagine constructing an elaborate utility calculus or searching for the duty with the greater weight. But these strategies fail in two important ways. First, hardly anyone would make such a decision on the basis of these strategies. Second, it is not clear that happiness or duty are indeed the most relevant factors to consider. A responsive parent would think about the concrete needs and desires of the child, and the needs and desires of the students. While the child is not very sick, careful attention to the child's complaints may reveal an emotionally needy child at this moment. As a result, a responsive parent may opt to stay home even though the greatest happiness, or the most important duty, would be served by teaching the students. Some other parent, also attuned to these competing needs and desires, may decide differently and still be socially responsible. What is critical is the determination of whose needs most call out for our response, given who we are.

Morality is here conceived as much more "up to us" than some of the traditional perspectives, which emphasized ethics as a voice of moral authority external to the self. In contrast to some traditional approaches, it is thought that if we do not feel the weight of moral theorizing on our daily lives, it will not motivate us. Those who support an ethic of responsibility are concerned to reconnect our moral experiences with our moral theorizing. Some, like Owen Flanagan, claim that this is best done by paying closer attention to empirical work in psychology.[7] Others, like Martha Nussbaum, claim that this is best done by paying closer attention to the great works of literature.[8] And still others look to the everyday dilemmas that people talk about in work and home life.[9] What is rejected is the tradition in ethics of employing highly unrealistic hypothetical cases. Of course, in principle there is no reason why utilitarian or deontological ethi-

---

6. See Edith Wyschogrod, *Saints and Postmodernism* (Chicago: University of Chicago Press, 1990); and Johnson, *Moral Imagination,* for discusssions of saints and prototypes respectively.

7. See Flanagan, *Varieties of Moral Personality.*

8. See *The Fragility of Goodness* (Cambridge: Cambridge University Press, 1986).

9. See John Sabini and Maury Silver, *Moralities of Everyday Life* (Oxford: Oxford University Press, 1982).

cal theorists could not also reject the reliance on hypothetical cases. But throughout most of the recent history of these movements, hypothetical examples have been employed. Yet, as many of us have observed in our classrooms, students simply aren't motivated by such discussions that don't relate to them personally.

An ethic of responsibility differs considerably from the standard way that utilitarian and deontological ethics are often characterized. But if one looks at the actual discussion of these ethics by their most famous proponents, John Stuart Mill and Immanuel Kant respectively, the difference may not appear so great. For Mill is more concerned with what he calls "the theory of life on which this theory of morality is grounded" than he is with the articulation of a rule.[10] And Kant, while clearly focused on morality as a matter of law, does provide a principle of humanity and certainly recognizes that there are both perfect and imperfect duties, thereby opening the door for responsibility as well as obligation.[11] When one looks at the larger discussion within which rules are articulated in the writings of Mill and Kant, it turns out that they are far more aware of the diversity of the landscape of morality than was true, until quite recently, of their contemporary defenders.[12]

To get our main task under way, let me say something more precise about the distinction between an ethic that focuses on obligation or duty and an ethic that focuses on responsibility. I will cite two very helpful discussions, the first by Joel Feinberg:

> A responsibility, like a duty, is both a burden and a liability; but unlike a duty it carries a considerable discretion (sometimes called "authority") along with it. A goal is assigned and the means of achieving it are left to the independent judgment of the responsible party.[13]

For Feinberg, being the responsible party means that, for example, a particular ship's captain should have prevented a particular harm on shipboard, but it is not specified how the captain should have done that. The

---

10. John Stuart Mill, *Utilitarianism,* ed. George Sher (1861; Indianapolis: Hackett, 1979), p. 7.

11. Immanuel Kant, *Grounding for the Metaphysics of Morals,* trans. James Ellington (1785; Indianapolis: Hackett, 1981), p. 57.

12. Barbara Herman and Wayne Sumner could be cited as examples of recent defenders of Kantianism and utilitarianism, respectively, who reflect a new approach to these traditional ethical perspectives. See Barbara Herman, "Agency, Attachment, and Difference," in *The Practice of Moral Judgment;* and L. Wayne Sumner, "Aspects of a Theory of Rights," chap. 7 in *The Moral Foundations of Rights* (Oxford: Clarendon Press, 1987).

13. Joel Feinberg, "Duties, Rights, and Claims," in *Rights, Justice, and the Bounds of Liberty* (Princeton: Princeton University Press, 1980), p. 137.

discretionary nature of responsibility makes responsibility judgments sensitive to the specific details of each situation one confronts because how one satisfies one's responsibility varies from context to context much more than is true of a duty. At least on one level, a duty is fixed; either it applies or it doesn't, and if it doesn't apply, then there is normally one specific thing that one is required to do to satisfy the duty.[14]

Claudia Card has pointed out that there is a use of the term *responsibility* that is completely compatible with theories of obligation or duty, but there is also a use of the term that is not. When responsibility is assimilable to obligation or duty, responsibility can be expressed as a triadic relationship of the form "A is responsible to B for x."

> Responsibility, in this sense, is a correlative of rights. If A is responsible to B for x, then B has a corresponding right against A regarding x. So understood, responsibility is about controlling people, about the distribution of such control.[15]

Card distinguishes the triadic type of responsibility from the dyadic, where the form is simply "A is responsible for x," where there is no other person to whom the responsibility is owed. Here the object of responsibility is something that has a welfare and "the focus is on maintenance or caretaking" rather than on controlling people. These dyadic forms of responsibility are not easily captured by theories of obligation or duty, except in the nonstandard case of duties to oneself.

There are two possible roots of *responsibility* that Card and Feinberg are being influenced by. There is the root of "giving a response," or being accountable, to a particular person or group for what one has done; and there is the root of "being responsive for" someone in need in a particular situation. The former root is quite assimilable to the tradition of discussing ethics in terms of duties or obligations, whereas the latter is not easily construed in this discretionary way. Because of the discretionary aspect of responsibility, how people should be responsive for someone in need cannot be cast in terms of a simple abstract rule or formula. If there is a distinct "ethic of responsibility" that differs from both deontological and utilitarian ethics, such an ethic will not provide us with anything like a simple abstract rule or commandment that is to be impartially applied.

An ethic of responsibility calls for people to be sensitive and respon-

14. Barbara Herman has argued that conceptions of duty need to be much more sensitive to context as well. See her essay "The Practice of Moral Judgment," in *The Practice of Moral Judgment* (Cambridge, MA: Harvard University Press, 1993).

15. Claudia Card, "Intimacy and Responsibility: What Lesbians Do," in *At the Boundaries of Law,* ed. Martha Albertson Fineman and Nancy Sweet Thomadsen (New York: Routledge, 1991), p. 78.

sive for those whom they have harmed or those whom they could help. The call for sensitivity carries with it a call for attention to the details of one's own life and the lives of those with whom one comes in contact. Rather than paying attention to what it is that we all share in common, for instance our "humanity," an ethic of responsibility calls for us to pay attention to what is unique and even peculiar about one another. To gain this knowledge, we cannot be armchair theorists; rather, we must find out about the world, both the facts of the world that various people inhabit and the facts of how individuals respond to that changing world. This means that the social facts of how people in a certain situation relate to each other and affect each other, as well as how people's attitudes and desires are affected by such interactions, need to be taken quite seriously. An ethic of responsibility is thus deeply entwined with both sociology and psychology.

II. THE SOCIAL DIMENSION OF RESPONSIBILITY

The concept of responsibility seems especially well suited to problems in applied ethics (such as those in professional or business ethics) because it has an inherently social dimension, namely, that it is responsive to the way individuals relate to each other (as we have seen) and to the way individuals relate to groups (as we will see).

In addition, the concept of responsibility is also well suited to the social and political facts of life in a pluralistic society. Here there are many, often conflicting, norms and values, and except in extreme cases, what is called for is an ethic that allows for a fairly large range of "grays" between the "blacks" and "whites." Responsibility, with its roots firmly planted in responsiveness to difference, is much more likely to be adaptable to the changing moral landscape of pluralistic societies than would be true for most variations of deontological and consequentialist ethics.

Professional responsibility, for example, is best conceptualized as discretionary rather than rule-bound, because there are far too many avenues, many crossing each other, that a person could traverse that could lead to a morally legitimate life. An ethic that emphasized simple algorithms or rules would have a difficult time capturing this dimension of professional life. Implicit here is the idea that an ethic is better if it conforms to the contours of the type of life to which it is applied. Of course there are exceptions here, such as when an entire society or type of life is itself clearly immoral. But no one seriously argues that this is true of professional life. Professionals may occasionally do the morally wrong thing, but the enterprises that they are engaged in are not in and of themselves immoral. If for no other than motivational reasons, a professional ethic should somewhat conform to the peculiar features of social life that professionals experience. A failure of much work in professional ethics is that it speaks in absolute terms to people who see themselves as conflicted because of their multiple group affiliations.[16]

Responsibility is well situated to deal with ethical quandaries that arise out of one's multiple group affiliations. If one is a member of a group that has caused harm, even if one has not directly participated in the perpetration of the harm, there is a sense in which one can appropriately feel responsible for that harm. Since one did not participate, guilt is not appropriately felt. But shame is different.[17] One may feel ashamed that one did not do anything to stop the harm from occurring; or one may feel shame merely for being a group member, since one's group memberships form who one is. And in many cases something like a group failure or defect is the source of the feelings of shame. In such cases, community membership is the key to an expanded notion of the responsibilities people have. When members of a community share responsibility for harms perpetrated by or within communities, it is often inappropriate to speak of blame or guilt. Shame and moral taint are the categories of evaluation appropriate for many of the problems that arise in professional life. For membership in a community, or in any group that could have prevented harm, is normally a function of the kind of moral being one is rather than the kind of action one has taken. Within communities, the moral problems that people face are often best captured in terms of shared responsibility rather than personal obligation.[18]

Who one is, especially when one is different from the majority, is especially important in a pluralistic society. On the communitarian view of social and moral philosophy I sketched in chapter 1, understanding who one is means that one understand one's group affiliations. Identity is bound up with group membership. In this sense, responding to who one is may mean responding to the relationships one finds oneself in. This is the way that a concern for one's identity connects with a responsiveness to others. All of us achieve our identities through relationships with those who are in some respects similar to, and in other respect different from, us.

Recognizing one's group memberships also helps one see the importance of diversity and difference in determining who one is.

There is a sense of responsibility that is focused on the importance of

---

16. See chap. 6, "Professional Integrity."

17. There is a rich literature developing on the concept of shame. See Deigh, "Shame and Self-Esteem: A Critique"; Gabriele Taylor, *Pride, Shame, and Guilt;* and Bernard Williams, *Shame and Necessity.*

18. For more discussion of this point see May, *Sharing Responsibility.*

difference in a pluralistic society.[19] It sometimes appears that responding to otherness can be accomplished merely with a change in one's attitudes, and seemingly with no explicit change in one's behavior, either individually or collectively.[20] But individual or collective action is sometimes called for by persons who are responsive to who they are and who are responsive to those with whom they are in relationships.

The popular use of the term "social responsibility" connects in interesting ways with an ethic of responsibility. Popularly, social responsibility is opposed to selfish or self-interested behavior. This simplification of social responsibility connects the emphasis on "responsiveness" to the peculiar predicaments that others find themselves in. In this sense, an ethic of responsibility will emphasize such concepts as altruism, and by implication deemphasize egoism, in the domain of things considered to be valued behavior by an individual. Of course, there will be distinct limits to the emphasis on altruism, especially when acting altruistically is inappropriate to the situation at hand, as when the altruistic acts of men toward women further entrench the idea of the vulnerable and dependent female.

An ethic of responsibility sets limits on what is acceptable human conduct, but these limits are guides rather than harsh rules. Indeed, the promulgation of models of acceptable behavior, in which a high sensitivity to context and role is key, is preferred to a listing of rules or commandments. All in all, an ethic of responsibility seeks to provide an awareness of our relationships and a responsiveness to our surroundings that will accentuate what is good in human conduct. Such a view stresses that we are social in the best sense of this term: where it is important for how we view ourselves that we do what is reasonable, especially for those who count on us. Social reasonableness will be the key basis of the limits set by an ethic of responsibility. If there are multiple individuals or groups that one could be responsive to, an ethic of responsibility will favor that individual or group that it is reasonable to favor given the potential consequences for the society at large.[21]

An ethic of responsibility has a strong social dimension, and there is an identifiable ethic of *social* responsibility that emphasizes (as does the popular version of social responsibility) sensitivity, attentiveness, and respon-

19. See Stephen K. White, *Political Theory and Postmodernism* (Cambridge: Cambridge University Press, 1991). According to White, "Fostering otherness must become as important as tolerating otherness" (pp. 116–17).

20. For a postmodern defense of the importance of otherness in discussions of justice, see Young, *Justice and the Politics of Difference.*

21. As I will explain later, it is features such as this one that make me say that an ethic of responsibility is much closer to consequentialism than to deontology.

siveness to the larger community within which one acts and lives.[22] An ethic of responsibility tries to be responsive to otherness and to inspire people to act collectively to combat harm in their communities. This ethic is intimately connected to emotional and other affective states of people who find themselves in moral quandaries. Feelings of guilt and shame, remorse and regret, pride and embarrassment are appealed to as a source of moral knowledge and also as a source of inspiration. Feelings of respect, esteem, and worth are also appealed to normatively in an attempt to bring minority groups into the larger community on an equal footing with their majority counterparts.

III. FEMINISM AND THE PRIMACY OF RELATIONSHIPS

Some of the most developed philosophical work in an ethic of responsibility has come out of feminist ethics, especially from those feminists who have followed or criticized the psychological writings of Carol Gilligan.[23] Here is how Gilligan characterizes the differences between what she calls a justice orientation and her own care orientation:

> A justice perspective draws attention to problems of inequality and oppression and holds up an ideal of reciprocity and equal respect. A care perspective draws attention to problems of detachment or abandonment and holds up an ideal of attention and response to need. Two moral injunctions—not to treat others unfairly and not to turn away from someone in need—capture these different concerns.[24]

In Gilligan's landmark study *In a Different Voice,* she refers to the care orientation as part of "an ethic of responsibility."[25]

Diana Meyers has a very illuminating discussion of the kind of reasoning found in a feminist ethic of responsibility.

> In responsibility reasoning, the individual's moral sense gains expression through an exercise of imaginative introjection. Instead of asking what one would believe if one were not in a position to skew

22. In this respect, as well as several others, an ethic of responsibility is similar to the view of ethics espoused by John Dewey. See *Human Nature and Conduct.*

23. Nel Nodding's work is almost as important as that of Carol Gilligan. See *Caring* (Berkeley: University of California Press, 1984).

24. Carol Gilligan and Jane Attanucci, "Two Moral Orientations," in *Mapping the Moral Domain,* ed. Carol Gilligan, Janie Victoria Ward, and Jill McLean Taylor (Cambridge: Harvard University Press, 1988), p. 73.

25. Gilligan, *In a Different Voice* (Cambridge: Harvard University Press, 1982), p. 52 and elsewhere.

arrangements to one's own advantage, one asks what choices are compatible with or reinforce desirable aspects of one's personal identity. Questions like "What would it be like to have done that?" and "Could I bear to be the sort of person who can do that?" are foremost.[26]

As I indicated above, an ethic of responsibility is best understood in terms of exemplars and prototypes rather than rules. The question that a parent, for instance, asks himself or herself is not, What do the rules connected to parenthood tell me I should do? Rather, he or she asks, What does this context call for? For Meyers, the moral point of view, rather than involving an intellectual task, such as achieving reflective equlibrium, involves responsibility reasoning based in an understanding of the actually existing self, where the chief question is "whether she can take responsibility for this or that action."[27]

The concept of "taking responsibility" for one's actions or attitudes or more generally for oneself cannot be easily assimilated to the ethics of conviction. There is, of course, a literature on whether one has duties to oneself, for instance, the duty not to kill oneself. But such discussions fail to capture the idea that the unique characteristics of a particular self, and the unique contexts it faces, call for quite different understandings, from one person to the next, of what it means to take responsibility for oneself. In addition, as Feinberg has reminded us, responsibility, unlike duty, carries with it considerable discretion. If one has a duty to oneself, then there are very specific things that anyone must do to satisfy this duty. But there are countless ways to show that one takes responsibility for oneself. Many feminists, especially those concerned to affirm the importance of the differences among us, have found the language of responsibility much more suited to their concerns than the language of obligation or duty.

Feminists share with communitarians a concern for the self, especially, as Meyers puts it "for the person's sense of her own identity."[28] It is part of the feminist project to challenge the way that autonomy and the self have been construed in mainstream theorizing. In some mainstream work, women's dependency and inability to make impartial judgments has not been valued as highly as certain "male" values.[29] In response, feminists have sought to reconstrue autonomy and self-respect in a way that allows a

26. Diana Meyers, "The Socialized Individual and Individual Autonomy," in *Women and Moral Theory*, ed. Eva Feder Kittay and Diana T. Meyers (Totowa, NJ: Rowman & Littlefield, 1987), p. 151.

27. Ibid., p. 150 (emphasis added).

28. Ibid., p. 151. Meyers cites Charles Taylor at this point in her text.

29. The work of Lawrence Kohlberg is often cited by feminists for displaying this tendency.

mother's partialistic identification with the lives of her children, for instance, to be seen as a way for her to take responsibility for her particular life, based on a realistic assessment of her circumstances and on her own self-conception of who she wants to be.[30]

But many feminists have recently sounded a cautionary note about the ethic of responsibility, especially its seemingly uncritical acceptance of the value of caring, and rejection of considerations of justice, in family life. Gilligan has been criticized by some feminists for not taking seriously enough the pitfalls that women face when they come to identify too closely with their families. Self-sacrifice is surely not something to be encouraged, these feminist critics argue, especially when it contributes to the lack of self-respect. Here is where an ethic of responsibility and an ethic of conviction can come together to complement each other, and a number of feminists have recently urged that we proceed in just this direction.[31]

Several feminists have presented a more encompassing ethic of responsibility.[32] One fascinating attempt is presented by Margaret Walker in what she calls "an expressive/collaborative conception of ethics."[33] Walker thinks that the hallmark of this ethic is "mutual adjustment" and "moral negotiation" that is based on a "flexibility, rather than uniformity" and that is "constructed in actual dialogue, [with] sensitivity to alternatives, presuppositions and ambiguities."[34] This construal of the project of feminist ethics is deeply indebted to an approach to philosophy (epitomized in the writings of Stanley Cavell) that stresses the intersubjective attempt to understand what each of us is willing to take responsibility for, and how we thus come to live in the same moral universe. This approach is still "naturalistic" in that it is the actual mutual adjustments and compro-

---

30. See Meyers, *Self, Society and Personal Choice* (New York: Columbia University Press, 1989).

31. Marilyn Friedman and Sarah Hoagland can be cited as two of the most forceful critics in this group, who have urged that too much emphasis on care will make the critique of oppression difficult to mount. See Sarah Lucia Hoagland, "Some Thoughts about Caring," in Card, ed., *Feminist Ethics;* and Marilyn Friedman, "Beyond Caring: The Demoralization of Gender" in Friedman, *What Are Friends For?* Also see the excellent anthology *An Ethic of Care,* ed. Mary Jeanne Larrabee (New York: Routledge, 1993).

32. Of special note is Caroline Whitbeck's essay "A Different Reality: Feminist Ontology," in *Beyond Domination,* ed. Carol Gould (Totowa, NJ: Rowman & Allanheld, 1983). Whitbeck assigns a role to rights and obligations in her ethic of responsibility, but rights and obligations are subsidiary notions to that of responsibilities, which are thoroughly grounded in relationships among human persons.

33. Margaret Urban Walker, "Feminism, Ethics and the Question of Theory," *Hypatia* 7, no. 3 (summer 1992).

34. Ibid., pp. 32–33.

mises that people work out that form the basis of judgments of responsibility.

We are now in a better position than we were to understand Feinberg's point that responsibility, unlike duty, is discretionary. An ethic of responsibility is discretionary in that there are no fixed points that must, a priori, dictate certain results merely from the application of a moral calculus or algorithm. Since the very terms of the "algorithm" are up for constant negotiation and compromise, there will be few fixed points, at least before actual situations are examined in some detail. The term "discretionary" is a bit misleading, though, for an ethic of responsibility is not discretionary in the sense that it is literally up to the agent to decide what is morally appropriate. Rather, it is discretionary in the way that a judge's powers are often said to be, namely, that within the framework of the canons of law, the severity of sentence, although not whether to sentence at all, is left to the judge to decide on the basis of the particular characteristics of the case and of the convicted felon.[35]

Feminist ethics has set the stage for a rethinking of the role of morality. When people choose to act in a certain way out of concern or care for the other, they normally do not perceive themselves as acting on a rule or principle. Rather, they are acting on the basis of an emotional response to a particular person in a specific predicament or vulnerability. It is possible to reconstruct what these people are doing in terms of abstract rules or principles, but such reconstructions fail to capture anything like what these people were thinking at the time they acted. In addition, the failure of many people to act on abstract principles or rules, especially concerning those who are very distant from themselves, also points out that being responsive or sensitive to the plight of the other is a crucial component in getting people to act for the overall good. But, as we will next see, there has not been a unanimous acceptance of the turn toward an ethic of responsibility.

IV. CRITICS OF AN ETHIC OF RESPONSIBILITY

As we have seen, an ethic of responsibility is not primarily an ethic of claims and counterclaims but one of negotiated compromise. Though one of the main strengths of an ethic of responsibility, this characteristic is con-

---

35. Feminist ethics has made its most important contribution to the ethic of responsibility literature in the area of the ethics of personal relationships. But in my opinion the most interesting writings are about how such an ethic will work itself out in social or political terms. The work of Sara Ruddick is especially insightful in this respect. Ruddick defends a version of pacifism that begins from maternal experience in sustaining relationships. See Sara Ruddick, *Maternal Thinking: Toward a Politics of Peace* (New York: Ballantine, 1989).

sidered by some to be one of its main weaknesses. Unlike Kantian or utilitarian ethics, an ethic of responsibility will not speak unequivocally about injustice; indeed, one of the hallmarks of an ethic of responsibility is that all moral principles are contingent and revisable. Even such principles as those underlying a conception of human rights are, as it were, up for grabs, thus undermining one of the main tenets of human rights theory, namely, that a person's most basic rights are not subject to change or to compromise.

An ethic of responsibility is open to the objection that it is unable to provide a firm basis for such important concepts as human rights. Such an objection is difficult to counter since it is based on the correct view that such an ethic stresses compromise and conciliation. In the human rights camp, compromise and conciliation are what is often rejected. Dictators are notorious for suspending human rights so that supposed political or economic goals can be accomplished. In many parts of the world, citizens have been asked to give up such things as free speech and free press so that political and economic stability can be more easily sustained, or so that economic reform can occur in a more orderly fashion than would be true in the cacophony of competing claims. Human rights activists have rightly worried that such compromises were sometimes not in the interests ultimately of the people asked to engage in these compromises.[36]

To begin a response to this objection, it is instructive to point out that an orientation to human rights cannot ignore what differences in context would look like. It cannot be determined that basic economic rights are, or are not, being met without some reference to the diet, climate, soil fertility, annual gross national product, extent of class stratification and mobility, etc. One thing is certain, it is always a mistake to use what is considered subsistence in the United States as a measure of whether Third World peoples lack basic economic rights.[37] What counts as "subsistence" varies considerably from one part of the globe to another. And so too will the content of the right to economic subsistence.

Nonetheless, there are certain empirical facts of the matter, such as what a person's minimum nutritional needs are in order to be kept alive. If such minimum nutritive material were to be denied to a person, wouldn't this constitute a deprivation of basic human rights in all cases? Normally so, yes. But one need only consider the society where extreme scarcity ex-

36. See Abdullahi Ahmed An-Na'im, "Islam, Islamic Law and the Dilemma of Cultural Legitimacy for Universal Human Rights," in *Applied Ethics: A Multicultural Approach,* ed. Larry May and Shari Sharratt (Englewood Cliffs, NJ: Prentice-Hall, 1994).

37. See Claude Ake, "The African Context of Human Rights," in May and Sharratt, eds., *Applied Ethics: A Multicultural Approach.*

ists to understand that even the deprivation of basic minimum nutrition might not necessarily violate a basic human right. After all, if there simply is not enough food to go around to meet everyone's basic needs, then failing to meet one person's basic needs cannot be an a priori violation of his or her human rights. As in the rest of morality, the "Ought implies Can" proviso applies, and this proviso can only be fleshed out when people are responsive to differences in social context.

Rights are important to an ethic of responsibility since they are based largely on relationships that individuals have with one another. But rights are not given the priority that they are in deontological theory. This is true, if for no other reason, because rights and responsibilities often conflict with one another. The Heinz dilemma used in moral psychology illustrates well this point, since in order to respect the property rights of the pharmacist, Heinz must ignore the needs of his wife, who is dying of a disease that Heinz can only cure by stealing the necessary drug. But it is not a tragic flaw in an ethic of responsibility that rights and responsibilites will conflict, since rights and responsibilities are each important and complement each other in an overarching conception of morality. Indeed, it is sometimes possible to translate a claim of responsibility, such as the claim that Heinz should take responsibility for the needs of his spouse, into a claim about rights, such as the claim that Heinz should respect the right to life of his spouse.[38]

A second set of objections have been voiced by critical theorists who align themselves with the deontological tradition in ethics. Habermas has often referred to Weber's distinction between an ethic of conviction and an ethic of responsibility. In his 1990 book, *Moral Consciousness and Communicative Action*, Habermas is especially concerned to respond to Carol Gilligan's view of the ethic of responsibility. He contends that his own communicative or discourse ethic, while remaining within the Kantian tradition, does not fall prey to the problems identified by Gilligan and other feminist theorists.

> Every cognitivist morality will confront the actor with questions both of the situation-specific application and of the motivational anchoring of moral insights. And these two problems can be solved only when moral judgment is supplemented by something else: hermeneutic effort and the internalization of authority.[39]

Habermas argues that his version of deontological theory can embrace

38. I am grateful to Carl Wellman for pointing this out to me.

39. Jürgen Habermas, *Moral Consciousness and Communicative Action* (Cambridge, MA: MIT Press, 1990), p. 179.

"the principle of care and responsibility—insofar as these expressions designate *moral* principles—[as] already contained in the meaning of the term normative validity."[40] The "integration of cognitive operations and emotional dispositions and attitudes in justifying and applying norms characterizes the mature capacity for moral judgment."[41] An ethic of care or responsibility need not be opposed to an ethic of obligation or justice, on Habermas's view; rather, an ethic of care or responsibility is merely one part of Habermas's version of an ethic of conviction. Considerations of context and situation arise, says Habermas, whenever the *application* of a moral principle is in question. But such considerations are not relevant to the foundations of the *theory* of morality.[42] Understood in this way, an ethic of responsibility can be integrated into an ethic of conviction, thereby dissolving Weber's distinction.

Seyla Benhabib has tried to modify Habermas's discourse ethic to be more responsive to the concerns of feminists, communitarians, and postmodernists. She calls her approach an "interactive universalism" that is contextually sensitive and cognizant of difference. Benhabib finds fault with some of Habermas's writings for not recognizing that taking the other's point of view cannot be done "unless the identity of the other as distinct from the self, not merely in the sense of bodily otherness but as concrete other, is retained."[43] To accomplish this task she urges that traditional approaches to ethics be revised.

> The nerve of my reformulation of the universalist tradition in ethics is the construction of "the moral point of view" along the model of a moral conversation, exercising the art of "enlarged thinking." The goal of such conversation is not consensus or unanimity (*Einstimmigkeit* or *Konsens*) but the "anticipated communication with others with whom I know I must finally come to some agreement."[44]

Benhabib is quoting Hannah Arendt in this approach, which seeks to soften Habermasian critical theory in many of the same ways that other theorists have sought to soften approaches to ethics that are rule-bound and formalistic.

Critical theorists have generally been the deontological theorists who have shown the most sensitivity to the concerns of those who endorse an

40. Ibid., p. 181.

41. Ibid., p. 182.

42. See Habermas's latest attempt to make this point in *Justification and Application,* especially chap. 1.

43. Benhabib, *Situating the Self.* p. 10.

44. Ibid., p. 9.

ethic of responsibility. But the various attempts to reorient deontological theory or merge it with some of the central features of an ethic of responsibility have not been systematically pursued.

At the heart of the difficulty is the open-textured nature of moral discourse itself. Actual moral discourse is often based more on sensitivity to context than on the application of rules. It may be that the ethic of obligation and duty, which relies on abstract, impartial rules, is not incompatible with an ethic of responsibility that relies on partialistic sensitivity. In any event, whether the ethic of responsibility is merely one aspect of a contextually sensitive deontological ethics, or whether a deontological ethic and an ethic of responsibility are each aspects of a larger, more comprehensive, ethical perspective, greater attention needs to be paid to the ethic of responsibility than has previously been paid.

V. A NEW APPROACH TO SOCIAL RESPONSIBILITY

Those who display social responsibility are those who take responsibility for the facts about their societies over which they have at least some control. Socially responsible individuals are attentive and sensitive to the social conditions of their communities, large or small. Such individuals are not necessarily those who criticize corporate profit-maximizing behavior. But what would be subject to criticism from this perspective is the pursuit of profit that is conducted without any attention to the effects of such practices on the larger community. Socially responsible individuals may support maximization of profit, but only in those cases where it seems to be most responsive to those who need help and are most vulnerable in our society.

The main features of this conception of social responsibility are attentiveness, sensitivity, and responsiveness to the social world within which an agent resides. An ethic of *social* responsibility shares certain features with some consequentialist theories in forcing us to think about the social consequences of our actions, attitudes, and character traits. But social responsibility does not necessarily involve a maximization (or even an optimization) strategy. Attentiveness to social consequences is indeed one of the main parts of the social responsibility project, but one can be attentive to social consequences without seeking to maximize the best results. What is necessary is that the socially responsible person take responsibility for these consequences.

Robert Goodin has advanced a conception of social responsibility, somewhat similar to my own, in which he ties the notion of social responsibility to vulnerability. He maintains that what is crucial "is that others are depending upon us. They are particularly vulnerable to our actions and choices."[45] On such a view, consequences are terribly important, but what is important about them is whether they result from, or could have been prevented by, those upon whom the suffering depends. Here is why an ethic of social responsibility is not a maximizing view. When certain people depend on us, their vulnerability must be given greater weight than that of others whom we could help but who do not have a dependency relationship with us.

Goodin is wrong to think that all of our social responsibilities arise out of relationships of dependency and vulnerability. There are relationships among equals, or at least rough equals, in professional life and many other aspects of community life that can also give rise to social responsibilities. The voluntary acts that people engage in, such as the making of contracts, also create expectations that give rise to social responsibilities, even though the contracting parties may not be dependent upon each other in the sense that one is vulnerable to the other. Indeed, *mutual* (rather than unilateral) vulnerability and dependency is often the hallmark of social relationships, such as citizenship, that generate social responsibilities. But Goodin is definitely right to think that many of our social responsibilities grow out of relationships of vulnerability.

Let me return again to the idea that an ethic of responsibility is based on exemplars or prototypes rather than rules. An ethic of responsibility is deeply influenced by various communitarian theses, especially the idea that the self is socially embedded in the various communities of which it is a member, and that the self needs to be motivated to act in various ways to become better. Prototypes are models formed by extrapolations of those who represent the best conduct and character within a given community. Exemplars and prototypes are themselves aimed at motivating people to be better than they are, to improve so that they become more like the exemplars or prototypes, which themselves are admirable.[46] In this sense, an ethic of responsibility has as much to do with character as with behavior.

An ethic of social responsibility is meant to be inspirational in precisely the way that ethics of obligation have generally failed to be. Its motivational dimension comes from two sources: the close connection stressed between our conceptions of who we are and what we do, and the close connection sought between the insights of the ethic and the normal feelings of shame and guilt, remorse and regret, embarrassment and resentment. Such feelings are socialized in most people from an early age as a

45. Robert Goodin, *Protecting the Vulnerable: A Reanalysis of Our Social Responsibilities* (Chicago: University of Chicago Press, 1985), p. 11.

46. See Lawrence Blum, "Moral Exemplars," in *Moral Perception and Particularity* (Cambridge: Cambridge University Press, 1994).

means of advancing what are considered the highest values of a particular community. In this sense, the popular version of social responsibility, which I alluded to above, is correctly perceived to be a red flag that can·be waved to motivate people to act more sensitively, attentively, and responsively across a wide variety of professional and social contexts.

In this chapter I have tried to provide a theoretical model of an approach to ethics that stresses the social dimension. Such a model allows us to see the way that socialization and social identity influence morality. An ethic of responsibility, like other ethics, provides us with an understanding of what restraints we should place on our behavior. But, more importantly, it provides us with a vision or, as the college catalogues call it, a mission statement. The challenge of living among diversity is to construe morality in such a way that it is flexible enough to accommodate very diverse circumstances and life-styles, but not yet to give up on a vision of a shared conception of the good life. An ethic of responsibility challenges us to recognize that there are alternative visions of the good life that can coexist within a social web of relationships. Just as each self is a web rather than a solid core (as we saw in chapter 1), so too are societies. In the next five chapters I will spell out the implications of my views about integrity, solidarity, moral authority, socialization, and responsibility for various problems that have vexed professional communities.

II

PRACTICAL
APPLICATIONS

6

PROFESSIONAL INTEGRITY

In the previous chapter, I provided a model of moral responsibility that stressed the importance of negotiated compromise in ethics. An ethic of responsibility is deeply embedded in particular social practices, especially socialization and solidarity. For this reason it is very well suited to the realm of professional life, which is itself to a large extent constituted by bonds of solidarity and long-standing practices of socialization. Indeed, questions about the moral roles in professions are largely indistinguishable from questions about socialization. Contrary to what is often thought, the inquiry of professional ethics cannot be conducted without understanding the kinds of compromises that must be reached between personal and professional roles. There are genuine conflicts here that cannot be resolved once and for all.

By examining cases in professional ethics, I hope to show how plausible it is to think in terms of negotiated compromise. The reasonableness of some of the positions I defend is offset, though, by the fact that these positions are often quite restricted in scope and often hard to generalize from. The proposed solutions to problems arising from professional practice are unsettling in that they do not resolve the conflicts and make them go away. Rather, issues remain unsettled and conflictful, yet a temporary way out is found that is respectful of both sides to the conflict. These cases in professional ethics will illuminate what motivated the earlier abstract discussions of moral responsibility. The intractability of some of these conflicts points us toward the legitimacy of compromise, even though it leaves things much messier than rule-oriented solutions to applied ethics problems that are so common in the deontological and utilitarian literature.

The following discussion seeks to shift the emphasis in professional ethics away from the individualistic model of the isolated, autonomous

professional struggling to decide what is right. In its place, a communitarian, group-oriented picture of professional ethics is sketched that is
informed by the insight that professionals increasingly work for large organizations in which they often face a conflict between acting in an ethically principled way and being personally secure.[1] Professionals are
generally not isolated practitioners; they are not their own bosses and must
contend with various groups that have a significant impact on their professional lives. Issues of collective and shared responsibility need to be more
fully integrated into the educational and theoretical discussions of professional ethics.[2]

My initial remarks in this chapter will concern the nature of professional integrity and responsibility, emphasizing what has been left out of
the story generally told about professional integrity. In the second section,
I will turn, for illustrations, to specific ethical quandaries that arise in the
emerging profession of public relations. In the third section, I will explain
how organizational constraints can affect professional integrity. In the
fourth section, I will argue that professional groups that promulgate codes
of behavior also need to provide moral support for their members who try
to live up to the standards advanced in these codes. In the final section, I
will propose a dual standard of professional integrity that is oriented to
what it is reasonable to expect of professionals given the changing work
conditions in most professional lives.

I. HAVING INTEGRITY AS A PROFESSIONAL

Today, professionals are increasingly employed by large organizations.
Professionals are not predominantly self-employed individuals who have
nearly complete autonomy over their jobs. Almost twenty years ago, the
head of a Canadian professional institute recorded this fact in the following terms.

> We can all accept the pragmatic view that, whatever the public belief
> may be, in reality the typical professional . . . is unlikely to be a doc-
> tor in his office, a lawyer in his chambers or a parson in his pulpit. He
> is much more likely to be either one of twenty chemists in a quality
> control laboratory or one of five meteorologists in a federal govern-
> ment department or, perhaps, one of a thousand engineers in an aero-
> space plant. He is no longer, in fact, a self-employed practitioner . . .

1. I am certainly not the first to address this problem. One of the most widely cited articles on
the problem is Richard De George, "Ethical Responsibilities of Engineers in Large Organizations," *Business and Professional Ethics Journal* 1, no. 1 (fall 1981): 1–14.
2. I have begun this task in chap. 5 of *Sharing Responsibility*. Also see chap. 2 of *The Morality of Groups*.

but is an employee . . . often very uncomfortable about his role and his future in the overall pattern of things.[3]

In this and succeeding chapters, I wish to reflect philosophically on the changes in our conceptions of professional ethics that derive from this change in the facts of professional life.

Professional roles are generally conceived in an individualistic way.[4] Professional roles are thought to create responsibilities by virtue of the professional's agreement to take on a certain set of tasks in society, or perhaps by virtue of his or her agreement to be thrust into the position of assuming various tasks. Professional responsibility is generally seen as a subcategory of the role responsibilities an individual assumes explicitly. This characterization makes the most sense where there has been some explicit arrangement in which becoming a member of a group is understood to grant a person a certain amount of autonomy of judgment and also to commit the person to follow certain clearly delineated norms.[5] In most professional contexts, there is a code or some other source of information about the behavior that is required of those who assume a particular professional role. On the assumption that a person can avoid these requirements simply by leaving the profession, there is generally no reason for worrying that professional roles are often conceived quite rigidly.

From my communitarian, group-oriented perspective, it is important to note that a profession is a group of people who profess, collectively, to have attained a special body of knowledge. A professional is merely a member of one of these groups. The idea of professional integrity or professional responsibility is intimately connected with the way a group of people comes to regard itself, and the way that society comes to regard that group. The earliest professional association was the guild, which engaged in protective practices to establish and maintain the profession with a particular social status, excluding others and claiming for itself certain privileges within society. Professional codes of conduct attempt to portray each profession as a privileged group in the society, specifically with the ability to police the conduct of its own members (and to keep outsiders, such as government officials, from doing the policing).

Professional responsibility involves regarding oneself as personally ac-

3. L. W. C. S. Barnes, *The Changing Stance of the Professional Employee* (Kingston, Canada: Industrial Relations Centre, 1975), p. 2.

4. One major exception to this trend is Paul Camenisch, *Grounding Professional Ethics in a Pluralistic Society* (NY: Haven Publications, 1983). Camenische's approach is very different from my own, but we share a common interest in integrating professional norms with wider societal norms.

5. See H. L. A. Hart's very influential treatment of role responsibility in *Punishment and Responsibility* (Oxford: Oxford University Press, 1968), pp. 212–14.

countable for the effects of one's professional judgments and actions. Professional integrity is often similarly portrayed as having standards of professional responsibility that one is largely unwilling to violate. One cannot have integrity and merely follow orders. But, as I have argued in an earlier chapter, integrity does not necessarily conflict with self-interest.[6] This is especially true if one places personal security, or security of family, as one's highest value. Professional integrity is not a simple concept—it is not sufficient to view it, as many have, as doing what is right regardless of expected benefit or loss.[7] In most cases, self-sacrifice is not required to be an integrated person or an integrated professional. (I provide an argument for this claim in section 3.)

My view is that it is important that a professional not think that his or her goal is to submerge interests of the self, family, etc., into the professional role. Most people are members of multiple communities, and each community has a plurality of often overlapping roles. There are important relationships that exist for a person who is a professional that are not related to the professional community to which he or she belongs. The most significant of these relationships, and the greatest source of difficulties, comes from those organizations and institutions that employ most professionals. In what follows I will argue that these relationships create role responsibilities that often cannot be subjugated to the role responsibilities one has as a professional without serious risk of harm (to career, to status in society, or to one's finances) for the professional. There are also familial, civic, and national communities in which people who are professionals also assume various roles with corresponding responsibilities.

Professionals normally take their responsibilities seriously, but their professional lives are not conducted in a vacuum. The major stumbling block for professionals accepting full responsibility for the harms that result from their judgments and actions is that most professionals risk being retaliated against if they try to prevent their professional judgments and actions from being used by their employing organization in ways that may cause harm. Sometimes, if the harm is great enough, we have to recognize that a professional is indeed required to risk loss of job to prevent harm from occurring. But it would be quite unreasonable to expect professionals to jeopardize their own careers (or livelihoods) for the prevention of all harms connected to their professional judgments or actions, especially those harms that the professional neither initiated nor condoned.

---

6. See chap. 1, "Integrity, Self, and Value Plurality."

7. For one of the most recent attempts to oversimplify integrity see Ralph W. Clark and Alice Darnell Lattal, *Workplace Ethics: Winning the Integrity Revolution* (Lanham, MD: Rowman and Littlefield, 1993), p. 9: "Moral integrity in business is the strength of character needed to do what is right regardless of expected financial gain or loss."

Whenever a professional's judgment is confronted by profit-oriented constraints imposed by the organizations that employ professionals, then the integrity of the professional may be jeopardized. To ensure that professional judgment and integrity are not compromised, it may be necessary for professionals to act collectively to protect their fellow members from potential retaliation by their employing organizations when their principled behavior is indeed opposed to the goals of the organizations. Before turning to the group-oriented problems of professional ethics, I will present some examples from the emerging profession of public relations that will set the stage for the discussion of organizational constraints on professional ethics.

II. PUBLIC RELATIONS: AN INTEGRITY CASE STUDY

Often discussions of professional ethics of distinct professions center exclusively on the personal standards that every professional of a certain sort should hold to. Here honesty and fairness are the most widely discussed and most important. I will examine a few examples of honesty and fairness in the emerging profession of public relations in order to show how the standard analysis of professional ethics tends to run, and in order to set the stage for presentation of my communitarian, group-oriented approach to professional ethics. Let us look first at the principle that professionals should be honest in their dealings with their clients and with the general public.

When I teach professional ethics, I often ask my students to consider the claim that public relations is inherently deceptive.[8] The standard response by these students, many of whom are heading for jobs in public relations and marketing, is that public relations is merely involved in the conveyance of information. But, I will then argue, information can be conveyed in a deceptive manner, so this commonly expressed response is not particularly effective. Imagine that you are hired by R. J. Reynolds Tobacco Company to design a public relations campaign aimed at enhancing the positive image of smokers and of cigarettes. Obviously, because you want to keep this client, you will not start off with a balanced account of the pros and cons of smoking.[9] For, you may argue, full disclosure is not required in order to avoid the charge of deception or dishonesty. So be it. But as you put together the campaign, just how much "negative" information should you leave out? And how should you tell the positive story? Should it be told in a way that suggests that there is no negative story? Or

8. This is presented in a pedagogically inflamatory manner to elicit maximum response.
9. For a carefully argued account of why smoking is morally suspect see Keith Butler, "The Moral Status of Smoking," *Social Theory and Practice* 19, no. 1 (spring 1993).

should it be told in a way that implies that the negative story is not worth telling? Of course, none of this is yet deceptive, unless the public relations professional believes that the truth lies elsewhere and is intentionally misrepresenting the story.

I have heard it said that public relations professionals are like legal advocates: it is expected that they will tell only one side of the story. No one expects a defense attorney to give a balanced account of the pros and cons of convicting her client, and no one expects a balanced account from a public relations offical either. In a world where everyone expects only part of the story, it is not deceptive to leave out the other part of the story, even if this intentionally conveys a misleading picture of the truth. In criminal law, there are both prosecutors and defense attorneys. The other side of the story will be presented with force and vigor by the prosecutor—there is no need for the defense attorney to do so as well.

Does legal advocacy provide a good ethical analogy for public relations? I think not, and I think this for two reasons. First, it is not clear that we live in a world where people expect public relations professionals to fail to disclose negative information about their clients. Someone who is the spokesperson for Washington University is not expected to hide, or to fail to disclose, negative information about Washington University. My suspicion is that the only public expectation is that such a spokesperson will not *stress* the negative side of the story about Washington University. Second, public relations is disanalogous to law since there often is no one who is likely to provide the negative side of the story.[10]

Dishonesty or deception is not merely a matter of intending to tell an untruth. Instead, deception is often more subtle, involving the intentional distortion of the truth by exploiting the expectations of one's listening audience. Public relations often is, although it is not necessarily, a deceptive enterprise in this sense. What the public relations professional often tries to do is to make his or her audience positively disposed toward the client, regardless of the professional's own balanced assessment of the worth of that client. This has probably contributed quite a bit to the somewhat negative reputation that public relations professionals have. And for this reason, if no other, these professionals should be concerned about charges of deception and dishonesty.

In addition to honesty, fairness is also thought to play a large role in the guiding principles of public relations, as well as all other professions. The public relations professional is often in a position to exploit the differences in knowledge that exist between the professional and the public. For example, the Washington University public relations officer simply has ac-

---

10. This is not to imply that I accept the idea that zealous advocacy in law relieves lawyers of the normal obligation to be honest. See chap. 8, "Legal Advocacy."

cess to much more "information" about the university than do any of the members of the media to which information is conveyed. Also, differences in education, economic power, and social status, as well as the above-mentioned differences in knowledge, will inevitably result between professional and nonprofessional. Fairness is said to dictate that the special status of the professional not be used to manipulate those with whom the professional interacts.

Consider the use of provocative photographs in news reporting. A segment of video footage can be used in a highly unfair manner if the viewers of the footage are not able to assess the video in the same way that the television studio personnel can. Here in St. Louis, a local television station ran the same fifteen-second segment of video every night for more than two weeks. The video seemingly portrayed a woman named Christine Busalacci waving at the camera and smiling from her hospital bed. What was unusual was that Busalacci was said to be in a persistent vegetative state, and her father had petitioned to have life-support systems withdrawn to allow her to die. The video footage was presented in such a way as to make the audience think that Busalacci was recovering. What was not conveyed to the public, but was known by many members of the television station, was that the video camera had caught a moment of involuntary muscle spasm and that all of the rest of the footage not shown portrayed Busalacci to be indeed in a coma. To me, and to others, it seemed unfair for the television station to exploit this difference in knowledge. It was unfair precisely because the station was exploiting this knowledge difference so as to manipulate public opinion.

Honesty and fairness provide a good basis for beginning to assess the ethics of public relations professionals. But should we say that every time a public relations professional acts contrary to these moral principles, he or she has acted in a way that lacks professional integrity or is professionally irresponsible? Not necessarily. For we also have to examine the various pressures that the professional was exposed to, as well as the other values that were at stake—factors that may somewhat mitigate the claim that the professional acted unethically. I turn next to a consideration of some of the factors, especially group-oriented ones, that are implicated in judgments of professional ethics.

III. ORGANIZATIONAL CONSTRAINTS ON THE PROFESSIONAL

As I said above, it is important to recognize that most professionals hardly ever are their own bosses. Since professionals typically work for businesses, governmental agencies, professional firms, universities, hospitals, etc., they normally have many bosses. And in each of these cases, the organization will often have values and goals that are at odds, in certain situations, with the values which the professional, from the standpoint of the profession as expressed in its code, is supposed to uphold. Most public relations professionals, and most professionals in general, must rely on their employers for the continuance of their professional life (and for their very livelihoods), and this means that the values of the organization are taken very seriously by the professional. But should not the professional fight organizational attempts to submerge professional values in a sea of organizational values?

Part of the answer to this difficult question turns, I believe, on how serious the consequences are likely to be to the professional who puts professional values ahead of those of the organization that employs him or her. There is no general moral obligation for any of us to be heroes or saints or to sacrifice everything for our principles.[11] This is especially true if, as seems to be the case in public relations, professionals are not asked by their organizations to do things that would cause loss of life or serious harm to others. John Stuart Mill recognized the basis for this claim when he argued that if one engages in substantial self-sacrifice for a minor matter, the result will be that the world is now made worse, since the harm to the self-sacrificer is not outweighed by the harm prevented. On his view, and on most commonsense approaches to this issue, self-sacrifice has moral value only if the self-sacrificer prevents more harm to others than is done to himself or herself.[12]

Yet, many professional codes of conduct seemingly call for scrupulous honesty and fairness regardless of the personal consequences. For example, the International Association of Business Communicators' Code of Ethics, rule #1, calls for "the highest standards of professionalism" concerning "honest, candid and timely communication."[13] But when complete honesty virtually guarantees that one will lose one's job, how can it be morally required? The codes of conduct of many professional associations have been interpreted as having similarly strong standards about the obligations their members should conform to. But, as I will indicate later, there has been no corresponding attempt by these professional associations to come to the aid of members who follow the code and who are retaliated against by their employers.

Consider the following case. You work for a major university's communications office. For many years you struggled as a self-employed free-

11. See Susan Wolf's provocative essay "Moral Saints," *Journal of Philosophy* 79, no. 8 (August 1982): 419–39.

12. See Mill, *Utilitarianism*, p. 16.

13. See Mark R. McElreath's essay "Dealing with Ethical Dilemmas: Applying the IABC Code and the Potter Box to Solve Them," *IABC Communication World*, March 1993, 12.

lance public relations professional. From year to year you barely met your bills and never managed to save much at all. When your children entered high school, you decided it was time to get a stable job with good fringe benefits. The best thing to come along was a job at a university where your children would get a tuition break and you would earn enough finally to start saving money toward retirement. Over the past year and a half you have attained true peace of mind in your new university job. Then one day your supervisor, who is an associate provost with no knowledge of the field of public relations (and its code of ethics), calls you into his office. He tells you that the university is facing a serious image problem that will surely affect future enrollments and may affect the fiscal livelihood of the university. Various reports in the media have strongly suggested that your university does not take teaching seriously and is instead a glorified think tank with little regard for its students. You are asked to design a campaign to combat this negative image. After a few weeks of investigation, you discover that many faculty members at your university exemplify the negative image and appear to confirm it in conversation. You casually mention this to your supervisor and he says, "I don't want you to give a balanced assessment of our campus; I want you to combat the negative image, regardless of whether it's true.[14] If you can't do this, I'm sure I can find someone else who can." What would you do?

I think that one of the first things to note about this case is that if there are people who will be harmed by the proposed deception the supervisor is calling for, some of these people may not be harmed seriously. Yet if the public relations professional sticks to her principles, she will most likely be harmed quite a bit. Of course, if the result of giving in to organizational pressure is that very serious harm is likely to occur, then it is important for the individual to stick to her principles above all else. And it is extremely important for society to encourage such courageous activity by providing moral and economic support for such individuals. If we truly value acting on certain principles, then we should not ask professionals to have to choose between being ethically pure and being economically secure. In chapter 4, I discussed the way that hierarchical institutions can structure their socialization practices so as to put enormous pressure on members to conform to organizational goals and commands.

The problem of possible retaliation for those who put professional ethics codes above organizational goals is well illustrated in cases of professionals working for profit-making corporations. In the case of the Goodrich air-brake scandal, professional engineers were pressured with

---

14. I do not mean to suggest that this case is representative of the situation at universities in the United States, although such negative images are routinely portrayed in the media.

threatened loss of their jobs to falsify test data so that their company could successfully bid on an Air Force contract that was vitally needed to bring Goodrich back into a profitable mode.[15] I believe that such cases illustrate the moral relevance of the kind of pressure that can be put on professionals working for profit-making corporations. I am especially concerned to refute the following claim, made by Albert Flores and Deborah Johnson:

> One's decision to resign or stay on in a position will, of course, be pressured by various circumstances, for example, one's duty to support a family, one's duty to pay debts, one's commitments to the persons he works with, etc. Though these circumstances may make quitting undesirable, they never coerce a person to stay in a position that requires the person to contribute to immoral or illegal activities.[16]

Flores and Johnson misunderstand the nature of coercion as well as the extent of the pressure that large corporations can bring against their professional employees.[17]

Flores and Johnson employ far too narrow a notion of coercion, seemingly holding that threats are coercive only if they completely force someone to do something that he or she does not want to do. But coercion is a more subtle and far-reaching practice than that. For many professionals, organizational threats of retaliation, especially loss of job, are coercive and can seriously undermine professional integrity. They are coercive in the sense that they reduce greatly or eliminate options that existed previously for the professional. In this sense they force upon a person a worse menu of choices than existed prior to the organizational threat, and one worse than the person would want. Insofar as one's choices are adversely changed against one's will, one is coerced.[18] The reason many people do not think that organizational pressure against professionals is very serious is that these people continue to think of the professional as largely self-employed or as an independent contractor. On this view, it may be undesirable to lose

15. See the discussion of this case in Kermit Vandivier, "Case Study: The Aircraft Brake Scandal," in *Ethical Issues in Business,* 3d ed., ed. Thomas Donaldson and Patricia Werhane (Englewood Cliffs, NJ: Prentice-Hall, 1988), pp. 290–303.

16. Albert Flores and Deborah Johnson, "Collective Responsibility and Professional Roles," *Ethics* 93 (April 1983): 542.

17. For an analysis of a case based on an expanded conception of coercion see Larry May and John C. Hughes, "Is Sexual Harassment Coercive?" in *Moral Rights in the Workplace,* ed. Gertrude Ezorsky (Albany: State University of New York Press, 1987).

18. For more details of my view of the nature of coercion and why certain threats and offers are coercive, see Larry May and John C. Hughes, "Sexual Harassment," *Social Theory and Practice* 6, no. 3 (fall 1980).

a particular job but, given the status of professionals, it is not as important as when an unskilled or semiskilled worker loses his or her job. Besides, since professionals are generally paid so much better than nonprofessionals, it is thought, professionals are not as dependent on retaining a job as are nonprofessionals. This line of reasoning makes the most sense in the case of doctors and lawyers of the past, since they were, by and large, self-employed. It makes much less sense for accountants, social workers, public relations professionals, and even engineers—as well as doctors and lawyers—today.[19]

IV. PROFESSIONAL SOLIDARITY

At a conference on engineering ethics, several heads of leading engineering associations called for professional protection by engineering associations of their members in light of the kind of profit-oriented pressures that can act as countervailing pressures to the ethical motivations of professional engineers.[20] They cited various cases, including the Goodrich air-brake scandal, as examples of how engineers could be subtly coerced by upper management to falsify safety test results, contrary to the most deeply held principles of their profession.[21] Only when the autonomy of the judgments of professionals is protected does it make sense to speak, as the engineering codes do, about the highest standards of professional responsibility, especially when the pressures of personal security and loyalty to company are so strong.

Professionals who work for large organizations will continue to have trouble meeting their professional standards concerning honesty and integrity. Until protection can be established for them against possible retaliation by these organizations for doing what they think is right, it is a mistake to continue to talk as if these professionals should blindly conform to these professional standards. It seems relatively uncontroversial that group membership often does affect an individual's values. Professional associations, as well as the organizations that employ professionals, can

19. A friend of mine who is an engineer recently lost his job. He was informed of his dismissal one morning and within the hour security guards came to escort him from the premises. He was given only two weeks' severance pay even though he had worked with the company for three years.

20. See Normand Laurendeau, "Engineering Professionalism: The Case for Corporate Ombudsmen," *Business and Professional Ethics Journal* 2, no. 1 (1982).

21. See May and Curd, *Professional Responsibility for Harmful Actions,* for more extensive elaboration on this point.

have a profound impact on how professionals understand their moral responsibilities.[22]

Professional associations should be as willing to step in and protect their members against organizational retaliation as they are to issue codes and guidelines about the appropriate conduct of these professionals. When a supervisor threatens to fire a professional unless that professional acts against his or her professional code, there is a threat to the moral integrity not only of the individual professional but also of the profession. Every successful, and publicly known, threat against an individual professional of this sort weakens the moral solidarity of the profession as a whole. Once professions recognize this point, they should make it their chief task not only to promulgate codes of conduct and police their members but also to issue specific sanctions against those organizations that violate the moral integrity of their members. Until this becomes a reality, it is disingenuous for professional associations to pontificate to their members with unbending codes that are enforced only against the members themselves and not against those employing organizations that threaten these members.

But, it might be asked, how can a professional group enforce its code against organizations that employ its members? There are many ways this can be done, but all of them involve some sort of collective action—for example, the strike, the boycott, and public censure—and all implicitly recognize that the members of a profession have various collective responsibilities to their fellow members.[23] There have been successful strikes by university faculty members, government scientists, and medical personnel in hospitals over salaries and working conditions in a number of countries in recent years.[24] Even the American Bar Association has recognized that collective bargaining of its members may be appropriate in certain cases.[25]

A good example of a professional group with a long record of acting to

22. See May, "Professional Actions and The Liabilities of Professional Associations: ASME vs. Hydrolevel Corp."

23. See James Muyskens, "Collective Responsibility and the Nursing Profession," in May and Hoffman, eds., *Collective Responsibility.*

24. On nurses' strikes in Britain see Sarah Haywood and Elizabeth Fee, "More in Sorrow Than in Anger: The British Nurses' Strike of 1988," *International Journal of Health Services* 22, no. 3 (1992); Lesley Fisher and Sally Colter, "Should Nurses Strike?" Nursing Times 84, no. 5 (3 February 1988). On physicians' strikes in Israel and New Zealand see P. S. Sachdev, "Doctors' Strike—An Ethical Justification," *New Zealand Medical Journal* 99 (11 June 1986). On Canadian strikes of government scientists and of faculty members see Barnes, "Changing Stance of the Professional Employee."

25. Sar A. Levitan and Frank Gallo, "Collective Bargaining and Private Sector Professionals," *Monthly Labor Review,* September 1989, 25.

support its members is the American Association of University Professors. For many years the AAUP has maintained a committee that is especially concerned to protect the free-speech rights of its members, especially when the members try to uphold the highest standards of truthfulness in teaching. There have been successful cases of censure of universities that have retaliated against AAUP members for violating the rules governing tenure and for doing what the faculty members thought was right.[26] There is no reason to think that similar collective actions could not be taken to support members of other professions who find their integrity undermined by their organizational employers.

One of the implications of the foregoing discussion is that issues of collective and shared responsibility need to be more central to our deliberations about professional ethics. Professionals have been reluctant to use the strike option against, or even to censure, an organization that threatens or retaliates against a professional who is trying to do what he or she thinks is right. This is perhaps because professionals have continued to think of themselves as autonomous practitioners, or at least as privileged members of society who should be able to resist pressures that are merely economic. But the cases I have asked us to consider point up the fact that many professionals are quite vulnerable and are much more like other employees of a large organization than they are like sole practitioners.[27] What professionals need is an increased sense of solidarity with which to meet the challenges to their professional integrity posed by some organizations.

V. A DUAL STANDARD OF PROFESSIONAL INTEGRITY

I have claimed that it is a mistake to set the standards of professional ethics too high, especially if the professional does not have strong moral support from his or her profession when trying to live up to those standards. This claim is consistent with claims by various communitarians and critical theorists who have argued that moral integrity and community solidarity need to be linked and that it is generally a mistake to demand that people

26. The American Association of University Professors publishes a bimonthly journal called *Academe*. In its March/April 1993 issue there were forty-eight colleges or universities listed as censured for "not observing the generally recognized principles of academic freedom endorsed by this Association." The AAUP urges its members to "refrain from accepting appointment to an institution so long as it remains on the censure list" (p. 93).

27. See Mary E. Guy, *Professionals in Organizations* (New York: Praeger, 1985). Guy contends that her studies show that disparate health care workers in large hospital settings have at least as much, if not more, in common with each other as with members of their professions who work outside the hospital context.

sacrifice greatly for principle. In this final section I will briefly sketch some of the arguments in support of these views that I find most persuasive, and indicate how these considerations should cause us to reconceptualize the notion of professional integrity.

In general, my view is that the ethical standards in professions should be based on reasonable expectations for individual behavior. Such a consideration will get us a dual standard. When moral support is not provided, what is reasonable is not to demand that professionals risk their careers (or livelihoods) unless great harm is likely to occur.[28] When moral support is provided, professional associations can enforce standards more stringently, perhaps demanding that professionals refuse to compromise their professional principles in most cases. In order to ascertain whether professional standards are set at what it is reasonable to expect of people, it becomes important to know how much support the profession will offer to the individual professional.

Much has been written lately about whether moral integrity requires that people never compromise their moral principles. Bernard Williams and Jürgen Habermas have both argued, from very different premises, that compromising one's moral principles does not necessarily mean that one cannot lead an ethical life. Williams argues that an ethical life must seek to balance many things that are valued by the individual, where questions of life-style and aesthetics need to be weighed alongside moral values.[29] This line has been echoed in recent discussions in professional ethics.[30] The life plans one has invested in cannot easily be overridden by considerations of moral principle since these life plans are often constitutive of the self. This also seems evident when the livelihood of one's family is at stake.

Professional responsibility should not be characterized in such a way that social interaction is seen as a battlefield between isolated, irreconcilable interests. Critical theorists have articulated a model of social interaction, called "communicative action," that places a premium on participatory modes of discourse. Of crucial importance to a critical theoretic approach to professional ethics will be the idea that as members of various groups, people participate in forms of life that change their responsibilities, making these responsibilities as much communal as individual. It is also important, from this perspective, that there be an ongoing public dialogue about what principles should form the core of a

28. See chap. 2, "Solidarity and Moral Support."

29. Bernard Williams, "Persons, Character and Morality," in *Moral Luck* (Cambridge: Cambridge University Press, 1981).

30. See, for example, Betty J. Winslow and Gerald R. Winslow, "Integrity and Compromise in Nursing Ethics," *The Journal of Medicine and Philosophy* 16 (1991).

profession's code of conduct, as well as how much self-sacrifice is expected of a given professional and how much moral support the profession should provide.

While the main focus of this chapter has been on what professional integrity does not require, a number of themes have emerged that make it easier to see what the positive account of professional integrity should look like. In the previous chapter, our sketch of an ethics of responsibility stressed a responsiveness to the way that people can come to the aid of those who are in need. Professional integrity should be based on this model rather than on the sort of rule following that has been characteristic of many discussions of professional responsibility. And according to this model, what an individual can do to aid others is based, at least in part, on the kind of support that individual receives from others in one's community. As I have argued, if the moral support of one's community is high, then it may be appropriate to demand of professionals quite a high standard of care for those who can be helped, especially those who have raised expectations for our assistance based on our publicly proclaimed roles.

Professional integrity is a call for individual professionals to look to their social responsibilities. Here the responsiveness to the needs of others, especially those who depend upon us, is extremely important, but so is the personal security of the individual professional. The socially responsive professional is one who understands that only in the most extreme situations should he or she feel compelled to sacrifice personal security for the common good. When an individual professional is strongly supported by his or her professional community, it will be less likely that doing what is socially responsible will conflict with personal security. When professions display solidarity, the various aspects of the professional self will more readily cohere.

Fledgling professionals need to be provided with a more realistic picture of professional life. In addition, professional norms and rules need to be reconceptualized so that they are consonant with the realities of professional life, especially the reality that many professionals in American society are employed by large organizations. As we have seen, this will produce a group-oriented understanding of professional roles and responsibilities that is responsive to the actual social dilemmas professionals are increasingly experiencing.[31] We should not lose sight of the concrete realities involved in professional life. Professional associations, and society at large, should not demand more of its members than those groups are willing to

31. For more discussion of this point see chap. 10, "Scientific Whistle-Blowing and Professional Solidarity."

support. In this sense, communitarians and critical theorists are quite correct to link integrity with solidarity.[32]

Professional integrity is a complex concept. The integrated professional must be true to himself or herself in several different ways. On the standard understanding of professional integrity, the professional needs to be true to the principles of his or her profession. But matters do not end there. The integrated professional must also be true to the principles that are important for the rest of her or his life, including the principles of his or her society and family. In addition, the integrated professional must be true to the life plans he or she considers to be important. All of this requires, sometimes, a difficult balancing act, rather than slavish conformity to one principle or to a narrow set of principles. The chief reason for this is that professional life is a part of larger personal and societal life, not a realm in which an individual is alone with his or her conscience.

32. I have in mind statements such as the following made by Jürgen Habermas that "moralities are supposed to compensate for the vulnerability of living creatures who through socialization are individuated in such a way that they can never assert their identity for themselves. . . . solidarity concerns the welfare of consociates who are intimately linked in an intersubjectively shared form of life—and thus also to the maintenance of the integrity of this form of life itself" ("Justice and Solidarity: On the Discussion Concerning 'Stage Six,' " pp. 46-7).

7

CONFLICT OF INTEREST

The classic clash between personal interests and professional principles occurs in cases of conflict of interest. The paradigm of a responsible professional, so it is often said, is that person who can scrupulously avoid conflicts of interest by keeping personal considerations completely out of his or her professional judgments.

Conflicts of interest are to be avoided, so the prevailing wisdom has it, because the professional's objective judgment is compromised, making it less likely that he or she can act in a principled way. When a professional has a conflict of interest, the professional's self is divided, with one part of the self pulled toward serving the interests of his or her client, and the other part of the self pulled toward personal gain (or some other interest) at the expense of serving the client's interests. *Black's Law Dictionary* defines such conflicts in terms of "a clash between public interest and the private pecuniary interest of the individual concerned."[1]

Most codes of professional conduct urge people to avoid conflicts of interest in order to be more integrated professionals and to be more likely to avoid the violation of their professional duties. Generally, the literature on conflict of interest is in agreement with the codes. For example, in their monograph, *Conflicts of Interest in Engineering,* Wells, Jones, and Davis write that "most conflicts of interest can be avoided. We can take care not to put ourselves in a position where contrary influences or divided interests might undermine our ability to do what we are supposed to do."[2] I will challenge this view in light of my earlier discussions of integrity and responsibility.

1. *Black's Law Dictionary,* 5th ed. (St. Paul, MN: West Publishing Co., 1979), p. 271.
2. Paula Wells, Hardy Jones, and Michael Davis, *Conflicts of Interest in Engineering* (Dubuque, IA: Kendall/Hunt Publishing Co., 1986), p. 21.

In this chapter I will draw on some very recent work in postmodern social philosophy[3] that challenges the view that conflicts within the self are to be avoided or minimized. The postmodern approach to the world is generally to celebrate conflicts, to think of them as part of what constitutes the self. The self just is the diversity of conflicting interests that are constantly operating over the course of a life, if indeed there is such a thing as a stable and coherent concept of a single self at all. While some postmodernists think of the self as an incoherent notion, a view which I do not endorse,[4] postmodernism has important insights nonetheless, which moral philosophers would do well to take seriously.

Postmodernism contains at least two divergent strains. Some postmodernists think of the self as a fiction, or even as an incoherent notion. Jacques Derrida is the best-known defender of such a view. Derrida and his followers have largely eschewed talk of morality and politics, opting instead for a version of nihilism. But there is another postmodern strain that, though highly critical of the modernist conception of the self, still thinks that there is enough coherence to the self to provide a basis for moral and political obligation. Jean-François Lyotard is the best example of a postmodernist of this sort. In what follows I will work with the latter rather than the former strain in postmodern social theory. At the end I suggest where I part company with postmodernism.

Most modernist discussions of conflict of interest merely assume that they are bad things to be avoided, especially when they adversely affect the independent judgment of the professional. But there are some exceptions. Charles Wolfram, for instance, begins his hornbook, *Modern Legal Ethics,* by noting that

> conflicts of interest are part of the world around us, always have been and inevitably must be. . . . In a sense, every representation begins with a lawyer-client conflict. If the representation is for a fee, the lawyer's economic interest will be to maximize the amount of the fee and the client's will be to minimize it.[5]

---

3. By "postmodern social theory" I mean roughly what Lyotard means by "the postmodern perspective" on social bonds. Among other things, Lyotard says that there are irreconcilable voices in society but that "the self does not amount to much" in trying to resolve these conflicts, adding: "Consensus is an outmoded and suspect value. But justice as a value is neither outmoded nor suspect. We must thus arrive at an idea and practice of justice that is not linked to that of consensus." *The Postmodern Condition,* trans. Geoff Bennington and Brian Massumi (Minneapolis: University of Minnesota Press, 1984), pp. 15 and 66.

4. See my discussion of the self in chap. 1.

5. Charles Wolfram, *Modern Legal Ethics* (St. Paul, MN: West Publishing Co., 1986), pp. 312–13.

I wish to argue that we will seriously misunderstand the moral difficulties of conflicts of interest if we do not realize the extent to which some conflicts of interest are "inevitable" or at least not necessarily problematic in professional settings.

The inevitability of some conflicts of interest in professional settings should not lead us to think that all conflicts are morally permissible. Indeed, I will attempt to explain which conflicts can and should be avoided. But the thesis of this chapter is that conflicts of interest per se are not morally problematic. What makes some conflicts of interest morally problematic is that they involve deception or they infringe client autonomy, but not all conflicts of interest are of this sort and hence not all conflicts are morally problematic. In presenting this thesis I will consider and reject the standard accounts of what is wrong with conflicts of interest. Let us first turn to some cases that will begin to illustrate why the extreme view, namely, that all conflicts of interest are morally problematic, should be rejected.

I. REAL ESTATE BROKERS: CONSTANT CONFLICTS?

Recently I had the unhappy task of selling one house and buying another. I was struck by the fact that the real estate brokers with whom I worked in buying my St. Louis home were involved in what would standardly be called a conflict of interest. Most of such brokers' work involves showing houses to a prospective buyer and advising the buyer whether to place a bid on a certain piece of property and at what price. These real estate brokers, who claim to work for the buyer, will actually be paid by the seller. In addition, assuming a zero-sum game, every potential decrease in price offered by the buyer clashes with the pecuniary interests of the buyer's broker, since the broker's commission is determined as a percentage of the selling price. There is indeed a conflict of interest here since there will surely be situations in which it is in the buyer's best interest to offer a lower price or back out of a sale, whereas it is clearly in the personal interest of the buyer's broker to advise the buyer to accept a higher counteroffer and go through with the sale. Yet these brokers see nothing wrong in these situations. My view is that their claims should not be lightly dismissed.

The identity of real estate brokers is conflicted. On the one hand, because of the sheer amount of time they spend with the buyer, guiding him or her through house after house, they clearly work for, or at least with, the buyer. But on the other hand, it is quite clear that their business and personal interests coincide with the seller's interests. As long as real estate brokers are paid by the seller, it is in a sense inevitable that there will be a conflict of interest between brokers' personal interests and the interests of their buyer-client; and even if they weren't paid by the seller, they would have a very strong interest in the buyer's paying more rather than less for a piece of property. The brokers I met, however, continued to talk as if they worked for the buyer. Nevertheless, it was clear that they did not take an adversarial role toward the seller, nor did they have any desire to do so. It was as if they assumed that everyone knew, or at least should have known, that brokers have a personal interest in being paid as high a commission as possible, and that this common knowledge meant that it was not problematic to maintain nonadversarial relations with both parties. Such an arrangement places brokers into a different category than some other professionals.

Real estate brokers who work with buyers could reasonably claim that their main professional duty is to facilitate housing market transactions rather than to serve in an adversarial process in which they "represent" one person's interests against another's. If facilitation and cooperation are indeed the goals they seek to serve, and if it is assumed that both buyer and seller have a primary interest in houses being sold rather than not, then the brokers' interest in their own greater monetary gain is not necessarily (even though it is traditionally thought to be) in conflict with their buyer-client's primary interests. In a sense, real estate brokers can take a communitarian rather than a contractarian view of the world, and this may at least partially explain why they are less troubled by their potential or actual conflicts of interest. The problem is that many real estate brokers continue to talk as if they "represented" the interests of the buyer and often claim explicitly to do so. Because of this fact, these professionals remain entangled in conflicts of interest.

There is a sense in which many other professionals are caught in conflicts of interest from the beginning of their relationships with their clients. Lawyers, doctors, engineers, accountants, etc., generally do not work for free and are therefore, as Charles Wolfram points out, already in a conflict of interest the minute they begin work for a client, since their interest in making a larger income clashes with the client's interest in paying as little as possible to solve his or her legal, medical, safety, or financial problems. More importantly though, many professional lawyers, doctors, engineers, accountants, etc., work for large organizations and corporations. Their salaries are not paid directly by a client, and so their relationship to their client is often one which involves another conflict of interest since the interest in serving the organization or corporation, which pays the professional, is often at odds with serving the interests of the client. This is evident, for instance, in the case of doctors who work for health maintenance organizations (HMOs) that put pressure on these doctors to minimize expensive diagnostic testing, even though such testing may be in the interests of their patients.

In addition, engineers, for instance, are supposed to serve not only their clients' interests but also the larger societal interest in public safety. This latter interest often comes into conflict with the former interest, when, for example, an engineer is urged by her company to use the least costly, and weaker, material in a product even though public safety would dictate a stronger and more costly material. Similarly, lawyers sometimes forget that they are supposed to be serving the interest of justice, a paramount societal interest, while also serving their client's interests. Yet they are paid by those whose interests are often at odds with the societal interests these professionals are supposed to be serving, as is true when criminal lawyers are told by their clients of the location of missing bodies, for instance. If I am right about there being rampant conflicts of interest in most professions, should we advise our students not to become professionals at all, so as not to risk entering into morally problematic behavior?

Several strategies could be employed to avoid these difficulties. The American Bar Association's code of professional responsibility stipulates that lawyers need to concern themselves only with conflicts that have a "reasonable probability" of interfering "with a lawyer's professional judgment" by compromising the lawyer's chief professional duties of loyalty and confidentiality.[6] Michael Davis sees the ABA standard as a way to capture what it is about some conflicts of interest that is morally problematic.[7] We could formulate a general rule, namely, that professionals should be concerned only with those conflicts of interest that are likely to have a material effect on their professional judgments. But even if the inherent ambiguity of the word "material" is overlooked, would such a strategy substantially limit the cases of conflict of interest that professionals should worry about?[8]

Such a strategy runs into the following difficulty: one's professional judgment can be materially affected by almost any personal monetary incentive. If real estate brokers working for buyers are being paid by the sellers, then their professional judgment is always at risk of being clouded and they are often in such a compromised position that, from the perspective of the way conflicts have been viewed, they should not continue in their profession. And yet it is worth considering whether or not there is any insight to be gained from the moral intuitions of these brokers, which clearly tell them that they are not being morally compromised.

Lawyers have long recognized that not all conflicts of interest are mor-

---

6. See Canon 5 of the American Bar Association's *Code of Professional Responsibility and Code of Judicial Conduct,* 1976; and Wolfram, pp. 316 and 324.

7. Michael Davis, "Conflict of Interest," *Business and Professional Ethics Journal* 1, no. 4 (summer 1982): 17–27.

8. I here pursue the line of thought developed in chap. 5, where I offered criticisms of rule-based approaches to social responsibility.

ally problematic. Not only has their code distinguished between conflicts that are likely to affect professional judgment and conflicts that are not, but the judges who interpret the lawyers' obligations have recognized that in many cases the informed consent of the client to a conflict relieves the conflict of interest of its morally problematic character.[9] In the following sections, I will build on this insight in conjunction with some insights gained from the standpoint of postmodernism.

II. POSTMODERNISM AND THE INTERESTS OF THE SELF

My view is that what makes conflicts morally problematic is not merely that judgments are compromised but in addition that the professionals continue to assert that they are able to serve the interests of their clients unambiguously, even though they know, or should know, that their judgments are likely to be clouded. As I will argue, it is deception or the infringement of client autonomy that is morally problematic, not merely the compromised judgment. The alternative I advocate, informed by the postmodern perspective, is to accept rather than decry such potential conflicts, worrying only about the possible deceptions or infringements of client autonomy that might result.

Instead of engaging in the often futile attempt to eliminate conflicts, I follow Lyotard, who calls for a "metalepsis," a change in the "level of one's take." From my own perspective, the change in the way we respond to conflicts should allow clients to become fully informed about them through a full and open disclosure of the conflict of interest.

Professionals should feel the need to avoid a conflict of interest only if those who have been made aware of these conflicts, and who are likely to be adversely affected by the judgments rendered in such conflict situations, are not willing to accept or for some other reason cannot consent to the situation. In such cases, the professional should either remove the cause of the conflict or terminate his or her relationship with the person whose interests the professional is supposed to serve. Otherwise, the chief professional duty will be that of full and open disclosure of potential and actual conflicts (along with a correspondingly diminished fiduciary duty—to be explained later), rather than the more strenuous and sometimes impossible task of eliminating or evading all possible or actual conflicts.

From a postmodern perspective, selves are always multiply interested and they are also often involved in conflicts concerning those multiple interests. Lawyers, for example, are so often involved in various conflicts of interest that they should discontinue the practice of advertising themselves

9. Wolfram, pp. 337–49.

as persons who act only in the interest of a client. And the American ideal of professional life, which is modeled on the way the lawyers in our society have conceived of themselves, should no longer be the single-minded pursuer of a client's or patient's interest. Rather, there should be a great deal more honesty in the way professionals present themselves to their clients and patients.

Lyotard and other postmodern theorists argue that modernists make the mistake of assuming that the self can be objective and unconflicted in its judgments and can blind itself to, or remove, all of its egoistic motivations. For Lyotard and other postmodernists, the self is always seen as "in progress," pulled toward several different poles at once.[10] It is never fixed or settled, and if one were to take away all of the various poles, or interests, to which it is attracted or repelled, the self would be lost altogether. Similarly, if one were to try to make of the self something that is not drawn in several directions at once, the lack of tension would often destroy the self.[11] It is characteristic of the modern point of view, which Lyotard wholeheartedly rejects, to think that the self or mind can attain an objective, universal, and hence unconflicted standpoint. The postmodernist's target is well presented by Wells, Jones, and Davis when they write:

> A conflict of interest is like dirt in a sensitive gauge. For the same reason rational persons want reliable gauges, they want those upon whose judgment they rely to avoid conflict of interest (insofar as practical). . . . though conflicts of interest cannot always be avoided, they can always be escaped. We can end the association, divest ourselves of the interest, or otherwise get beyond the influence that might otherwise compromise our judgment.[12]

The postmodernist would deny that the self is indeed like "a sensitive gauge" that, with the proper care, can be kept clean insofar as it is unconflicted.

Lyotard uses the term *differend* to refer to an impasse or unresolvable conflict that often characterizes social interactions.[13] Occasionally, a self is able to communicate with another self in such a way that conflicts are resolved. But in most cases, it is "not possible to evade the differend by antic-

---

10. Jean-François Lyotard, *Peregrinations: Law, Form, Event* (New York: Columbia University Press, 1988), p. 6.

11. Ibid., p. 5.

12. Wells, Jones, and Davis, pp. 20–21.

13. Lyotard, *The Differend,* trans. Georges Van Den Abbeele (Minneapolis: University of Minnesota Press, 1988), pp. 9 and 13.

ipating it."[14] While Lyotard's analysis of differends is meant to concern all forms of conflict involving some sort of stated claim by two parties, I find it especially useful in understanding why conflicts of interest are often inevitable and, contrary to prevailing sentiment, why they are not things which professionals can or should always avoid.

Lyotard, in a mode characteristic of postmodern thinkers, seriously considers the proposal that since we have such intractable problems with conflicts of interest, we should dispense with the idea of professional obligations and duties altogether in such cases:

> Instead, obligation should be described as a scandal for the one who is obligated: deprived of the "free" use of oneself, abandoned by one's narcissistic image, opposed in this, inhibited in that, worried over not being able to be oneself without further ado.—But these are phenomenological or psychoanalytic descriptions of a dispossessed or cloven consciousness. . . . They maintain the self even in the very acknowledgement of its dispersion.[15]

Lyotard does not follow the nihilistic postmodernists. He does propose that we give up our "nostalgia for the self," that is, our nostalgia for an unconflicted self that knows its obligations absolutely. Nonetheless, Lyotard urges that we retain the notion of obligation, although it is a more time-bound notion of obligation, indeed a notion very similar to the contextually sensitive view of responsibility I proposed in chapter 5.

Lyotard argues that we should reject modernist conceptions of universal moral obligation.[16] But he also contends that obligations are like the rules of a language game, binding on those who choose to play the game. While I don't agree that we should reject all univeral moral obligations, as I indicated at the end of chapter 5, a more limited construal of Lyotard's view fits nicely with the notion of professional duties and responsibilities.[17] Professionals take on special duties by agreeing to project themselves to the world as persons having unique expertise.[18] But there is no reason to think that these duties should involve unrealistic self-sacrifice on the professional's part. In keeping somewhat with Lyotard's brand of postmodernism, I will argue for a revised understanding of the fiduciary relationship between professional and client. First, let me say a bit more

14. Ibid., p. 19.

15. Ibid., pp. 109–10.

16. Ibid., p. 127.

17. Dorothy Emmet ably argues for the conclusion that professional codes are matters of role morality and not universal morality. See *Rules, Roles and Relations* (Boston: Beacon Press, 1966), pp. 158–63.

18. For a more detailed analysis of the moral basis of a professional's duties, especially concerning negligence, see chap. 5 of *Sharing Responsibility*.

about the core problem in conflict-of-interest cases: deception and the infringement of client autonomy.

III. DECEPTION AND CLIENT AUTONOMY

Michael Davis correctly states the major moral difficulty with conflicts of interest:

> If a lawyer does not at least warn his client of the conflict, he does more than weaken a guarantee worth preserving. He presents himself as having a judgment more reliable than in fact it is. He invites a trust the invitation itself betrays.[19]

As I shall argue in this section, Davis is largely correct, but for the wrong reasons. Davis goes wrong, as do most modern theorists, in believing that there is a type of professional judgment that is trustworthy and reliable in that it is completely uninfluenced by the material considerations of one's other interests.

Lawyers have perpetuated the view that professionals can and should be expected to serve absolutely the interests of their clients, a view stated well by Wolfram:

> Whatever may be the models that obtain in other legal cultures, the client-lawyer relationship in the United States is founded on the lawyer's *virtually total* loyalty to the client and the client's interests. . . . The entrenched lawyerly conception is that the client-lawyer relationship is the embodiment of centuries of established and stable tradition.[20] (emphasis added)

Other professionals have come to model themselves on this ideal of the Anglo-American legal profession.

The idea that professionals should serve "virtually total[ly]" the interests of their clients is at best unrealistic and at worst deceptive. It is unrealistic, as we will see, because it asks lawyers to blind themselves to their own interests in ways that are nearly impossible, and because it ignores the fact that there is often no objectively right way to conceive of someone's interests. It is deceptive because it creates false expectations of loyalty on the part of clients, expectations that when thwarted lead clients to a position where they lose control over their cases. The clients unknowingly render themselves vulnerable to possible abuses of trust that they would otherwise remain vigilantly on guard against. Lawyers betray the trust they have solicited when they act as if they were capable of rendering judg-

19. Davis, p. 21.
20. Wolfram, p. 146.

ments in their clients' interests that are unaffected by their other interests.[21]

Many factors intrude upon a professional's judgment, rendering the notion of a "virtually total loyalty" in serving the client's interest itself quite suspicious. Consider again the case of lawyers. Lawyers who are in private practice must be constantly concerned about paying the rent—indeed, many lawyers find themselves spending so much time getting, keeping, and billing clients that they come to regard the practice of law as a type of business. Yet rarely is this the picture of lawyers that lawyers themselves present to the public. In addition, the lawyers I have known are often highly ambitious individuals who see the pursuit of a particular client's case as a means of furthering their own careers. Furthermore, lawyers also have political agendas. As Wolfram and others have pointed out, "Even in pro bono representations, the ideological or altruistic motives that induce a lawyer to offer legal services" can often obscure the pursuit of the client's interests.[22] All of these factors make it unrealistic to think that lawyers can offer "virtually total loyalty" to their client's interests, a loyalty lawyers nonetheless continue to claim to be the hallmark of their profession.

It is an infringement of client autonomy for professionals to deny clients the knowledge they need to decide whether to entrust themselves to a particular professional. It is deceptive of professionals to present themselves as capable of rendering objective judgments when they are aware of conflicts that will make it even more likely than normal that their "objective" judgments are compromised. This is why some conflicts of interest are morally problematic. But if a professional is quite open about the interests he or she has, or is likely to have, that are at odds with the client's interest, and secures from the client an understanding and consent to the lawyer's continued service under these circumstances, many conflicts of interest are no more troubling, from the moral point of view, than other cases of consensual client services.

It may be objected that in order for possible conflicts to be disclosed, my proposal calls for professionals to be able to identify what all of their interests are, a feat sometimes not feasible. On my view, professionals need to be, or to become, self-reflective concerning their interests. But this is no more troublesome for my view than it is for any other view of conflicts of interest. The traditional view, for instance, which calls for professionals to *avoid* all conflicts of interest surely must also call for professionals to be, or to become, aware of what their interests are that may conflict with the client's interests. My view is no worse off than the traditional view.

It may be further objected that I have misidentified the morally sus-

21. For more discussion of my views on lawyers' roles, see chap. 8, "Legal Advocacy."
22. Wolfram, p. 313.

picious feature of conflicts of interest. Some might claim that the difficulty with all conflicts of interest is that they create temptation for wrongdoing. There are two things to be said about such a view. First, my consideration of the postmodern conception of the self leads me to think that at least some conflicts of interest are not occasions for wrongdoing at all but manifestations of the perfectly legitimate situation in which one has multiple and conflicting motivations. Second, the wrongdoing occurs, when it does, because of a presumed promise that all of the professional's other interests have been subordinated to the client's interests. But when professionals stop claiming that they can subordinate all of their other interests, the basis of the wrongdoing also begins to disappear. Disclosed conflicts that are consented to are not temptations for wrongdoing because the client has waived the right that would otherwise be the basis of a claim of wrongdoing due to the conflict of interest.

From the standpoint of deception and client autonomy, real estate brokers are better off than lawyers. Real estate brokers make it quite well known that they are working toward the consummation of real estate sales and that their income depends on securing higher rather than lower prices for these pieces of real estate. While they sometimes claim to represent the interests of the buyer, and in this sense perpetuate a deception, they do not claim to serve these interests absolutely. Those who are in the market for real estate are made much more aware of the conflicted nature of the brokers they encounter than is true of those who find themselves in need of legal counsel. In contrast, lawyers make it very difficult for a client to see the possible ways in which the client's interests will not necessarily be served. In this way, lawyers infringe client autonomy especially when they continue to assert so strongly that they are uniquely situated to devote themselves to the client's interests.

At this point it may be useful to consider a case of conflict of interest that I would find morally problematic. A scientist forms a corporation to support the research he is doing to find a cure for a certain disease. Many people who have this disease contribute money to the corporation. It is clear that the scientist's future research is now driven by a desire for personal monetary gain. But he contends that he has relieved himself of any problematic conflicts of interest by clearly disclosing to potential investors and to the university that is his primary employer that he has a strong personal monetary interest in the research he is conducting. Is there a morally problematic aspect to this case?

In my assessment, the people who have the disease in question and who contribute to the scientist's research corporation are not likely to be able to make informed decisions about what is best for themselves because their hopes for a cure for their own disease will cloud their judgments. In such cases it may not be possible for the scientist to rely on the consent given by those to whom he has disclosed a conflict of interest. For this reason, in similar kinds of cases, professionals should avoid such conflicts even when disclosure and consent are present. While these cases need to be addressed one by one, a general guideline could be that whenever an affected party is unlikely to be able to give fully informed consent, the professional should withdraw when conflicts of interest arise.[23]

Next, consider a different kind of case taken from engineering. A mechanical engineer is asked to give an informal opinion about a matter which the company he works for is planning to bring before the product standards committee of his profession at large. This engineer helps his work associates draft a letter of inquiry that is then submitted to his profession's product standards committee for review. As it turns out, this very engineer serves on the relevant product standards committee and is assigned the task of responding to the inquiry (which he had helped draft) in behalf of the professional committee. The engineer gives a ruling favorable to the drafters of the inquiry, who also happen to be his associates at the company for which he works. A competing company is placed in a disadvantageous position as a result of the ruling and eventually goes into bankruptcy. Needless to say, the ruling also works to the advantage of the engineer's own company. In 1982 the United States Supreme Court reviewed a similar case and held that the professional association had acted wrongly in allowing the engineer to review an inquiry he himself had helped to draft.[24]

Since it is true that professional engineers must staff such committees as the professional product standards committee discussed above, and since most engineers are employed by private organizations that will need to get rulings from such committees, conflicts of interest will almost inevitably manifest themselves in such contexts. In my view it was not initially wrong for the engineer in question to consult with his work associates and also to draft a response to the inquiry made by his work associates. Surely it is a mistake to think that professionals must never assume those roles that will possibly conflict with other roles they *may* play. In the case at issue, the engineer needed to inform the professional organization as well as the parties who would possibly be affected by the professional organization's ruling, and resign from the committee if any of those potentially affected objected to his remaining on the committee.

---

23. I am grateful to Carl Wellman for urging me to see that this refinement of my view was called for.

24. See *American Society of Mechanical Engineers v. Hydrolevel Corporation* (72 L Ed 2d 330) 1982. For an extended discussion of this case see May, "Professional Actions and the Liabilities of Professional Associations: ASME vs. Hydrolevel Corp." Also see Wells, Jones, and Davis, pp. 1–24.

Deception and infringement of client autonomy are the key moral problems when personal interest conflicts with client interest. If the engineer in the case discussed above had informed all relevant parties that he had a special, work-related interest in the outcome of the product standards review he was preparing, and if these people had consented to let him remain on the committee, and if he had continued to notify others who might come to rely on the report, then the writing of this report would have posed no special moral problems. As it was, though, the people who relied on the report did not have sufficient knowledge of the writer's interests to be able to assess it properly; their autonomy was infringed through the lack of such disclosure. They were put into a vulnerable position which they would otherwise have wanted to guard against. In what follows, I attempt to set out a new model for understanding the fiduciary duties that have traditionally been seen as the basis for requiring professionals to avoid potential and actual conflicts of interest.

IV. FIDUCIARY DUTIES AND PROFESSIONAL RESPONSIBILITY

The above-described postmodern critique of the unified but also isolated professional self has merit, but it is too extreme in dissolving the coherence of professional identity. In this final section I will propose a more moderate position that builds on some of the postmodern insights but mediates them in light of the discussion of communitarianism and critical theory that permeated the previous chapters of this book. A socially responsive professional will both be influenced by the socialization of his or her environment and take responsibility for a fair amount of this socialization. Most importantly, the socially responsive self will not merely withdraw into the self-indulgence that often characterizes postmodern conceptions of the self.

In law and other professional contexts, there is thought to be a fiduciary relationship between professional and client. *Black's Law Dictionary* defines *fiduciary* as follows:

> The term is derived from the Roman law, and means (as a noun) a person holding the character of a trustee, or a character analogous to that of a trustee, in respect to the trust and confidence involved in it and the scrupulous good faith and candor which it requires.[25]

A "fiduciary relation" establishes a situation in which various professionals "in equity and good conscience" are "bound to act in good faith and with due regard to interests of one reposing the confidence."[26] When

25. *Black's Law Dictionary,* p. 563.
26. Ibid., p. 564.

professionals are viewed as fiduciaries, they are thought to be bound to act as if their interests were those of their client and hence to sacrifice their own interests for the sake of their client's interests.

It is instructive to contrast this situation with that of the standard way that two parties are viewed if they are not in a fiduciary relationship. In his book *The Critical Legal Studies Movement,* Roberto Unger rightly points out that in law, nonfiduciary relations are ones in which neither party is thought to owe anything to the other: "the other party's interests can be treated as of no account as long as the rightholder remains within his zone of discretionary action."[27] The contrast between normal commercial relations and fiduciary relations is quite striking—surely there is a middle position that would more appropriately apply to conflict-of-interest cases. Like Unger, in this section I will strive for a view of fiduciary relations that takes account of the reality of professional life.

Unger proposes a fiduciary standard that "requires each party to give some force to the other party's interests, though less than to his own."[28] This proposal is a compromise between the overly minimalistic notion of simple contractual obligation, which some might apply to professional-client relationships, and the unrealistic selflessness of the legal model of fiduciary duty. Unger goes too far here. Surely it is not too much to require professionals to place the interests of their client at least on a par with their most strongly held personal interests. The special status afforded professionals calls for some serious attempt to serve the client's interest. In order to give proper care to the client, the client's interest must be given serious weight, and this means that it should be at least *equal to* the professional's most strongly held personal interests.

Those who have voluntarily placed themselves in positions of trust concerning the interests of others must give careful consideration to those interests. But it is simply a mistake to demand selfless service to the client's interest. Since "virtually total loyalty" is not a realistic possibility in professional life, the chief duty of professionals cannot be absolute service to their client's interests. The chief professional duty concerning conflicts of interest should be merely the duty of full disclosure, along with the duty to withdraw from serving the client if the client finds the disclosed conflict objectionable. It is too much to expect professionals to have a duty to be totally loyal or to place the interests of their client significantly above their own interests. As I have indicated, the perpetuation of the myth that pro-

27. Roberto Mangabeira Unger, *The Critical Legal Studies Movement* (Cambridge, MA: Harvard University Press, 1983), p. 83.
28. Ibid., p. 83.

fessionals have these more strenuous duties is both unrealistic and deceptive.

It is important to note that many of the most serious harms that occur in conflict-of-interest cases result from one party's becoming less vigilant on the assumption that another party is serving absolutely the first party's interests. When the professional raises expectations of total loyalty and trustworthiness, he or she is indeed implicated in whatever harms result from the ensuing diminished vigilance of the client. This is also true of those expectations raised by the profession of which a given professional is a member. But as with other collective responsibilities, an individual can diminish or possibly extinguish his or her personal responsibility by taking steps to overcome the expectations raised by the profession at large. By explicitly stating the interests the professional has that are likely to conflict with the interests of the client, the professional at least partially distances himself or herself from the expectations of objectivity that the rest of the profession may raise. This heightens the vigilance of the client and makes him or her less likely to be harmed.

Professional responsibility is not merely a matter of conforming to the fiduciary duties one has, even if we understand these duties in the way in which I have suggested. Rather, it is important that elements of shame exist alongside the guilt that is associated with the direct violation of a professional duty. Even when a professional has done all he or she can do to avoid harm to a client, the professional should deeply regret whatever harms nonetheless occur, and when harms result from actions taken by the profession as a whole, shame is often not at all misplaced.[29] But the appropriateness of such shame should not lead us to think that professionals have a *duty* to serve absolutely the interests of their client, such that they should feel guilt whenever they let personal interest interfere with the pursuit of the client's interest. As I have argued, such guilt is appropriate only in certain cases involving deception or infringement of client autonomy.

I have tried to provide a new basis for understanding what is morally problematic about some conflicts of interest in professional life. In arguing that the deceptiveness and infringement of client autonomy of certain conflicts of interest are their undoing, I have indicated a straightforward strategy for rendering many conflicts of interest morally unproblematic, namely, full and open disclosure of potential conflicts by the professional. This strategy is an example of the negotiated compromising I spoke of in chapter 5. In general, professionals have for too long mistakenly thought that they can and should avoid all conflicts of interest, as if it were possible for

---

29. See May, "Metaphysical Guilt and Moral Taint," in May and Hoffman, eds., *Collective Responsibility.*

the professional thereby to provide objective judgments and absolutely loyal service for the client. I have provided a challenge to this assumption that has drawn on a postmodern perspective of social and personal conflicts. At least in this case, reliance on some postmodern ideas has not thrown us into a moral abyss[30] but rather has clarified the picture of a certain part of the moral landscape we call professional life.

30. See Edith Wyschogrod's *Saints and Postmodernism* for another attempt at arguing that postmodernism can be conceived as a nonrelativistic standpoint. Also see my review of Wyschogrod's book in *Ethics* 103, no. 1 (October 1992).

8

LEGAL ADVOCACY

Another pillar of traditional conceptions of professional ethics is that the professional should be loyal to the client and pursue the client's interests in a zealous manner, fighting for the client's interests above all else. The model of the fierce adversarial approach taken by lawyers in defending their clients has been carried over into many other domains. It is regarded as a violation of professional responsibility for professionals not to fight for the interests of their client, and against the interests of nonclients. A communitarian and group-oriented approach to professional ethics will oppose this traditional approach by stressing conciliation, compromise, and cooperation rather than confrontation and adversity. I will defend a nonadversarial conception of client advocacy that is in keeping with the earlier construals of the socially responsive self.

The standard law texts, including texts in legal ethics, assume that the adversarial role and the advocacy role are virtually the same.[1] Legal advocates are said to have the duty to be zealous and aggressive in promoting the interests of their client over the interests of others. Lurking here is the assumption that advocacy is a zero-sum game. But advocacy merely means that one argues for and promotes the cause of another. In many instances, it may be more effective to be conciliatory or cooperative rather than adversarial. Lawyers have known this for quite a long time, as is seen in the tremendously effective and common practice of plea bargaining. Yet the model of law in the Anglo-American tradition continues to be portrayed as one in which advocacy and the adversarial role are synonymous, and the socialization of lawyers rarely stresses nonadversarial advocacy.

The adversarial legal model is often unnecessarily coercive and insuffi-

1. See Wolfram, *Modern Legal Ethics,* p. 593.

ciently attentive to what is best for the client or for the shared values in a co:nmunity. In this chapter I wish to give serious consideration to alternative models of advocacy and dispute resolution. I will begin by discussing the ideas of a prominent early Soviet legal theorist, E. B. Pashukanis, who advocated a nonadversarial approach to law. I will next examine some criticisms of Pashukanis offered by Hans Kelsen in an attempt to discern the limits of nonadversarial approaches to advocacy and dispute resolution. Then I will provide some additional argumentation from the standpoint of contemporary critical theory against the exclusive reliance on the adversarial model. Finally I will explore a model of empathic advocacy based on a consideration of divorce mediation cases.

Contemporary American law has increasingly been taken up with disputes to be settled through rules already recognized as regulating conduct within governmental or organizational structures. Owen Fiss has argued: "Courts exist to give meaning to our public values, not to resolve disputes. Constitutional adjudication is the most vivid manifestation of this function, but it also seems true of most civil and criminal law."[2] Fiss believes that allocation of public resources, rather than resolution of private disputes, will be a dominant strain of law in the near future. If Fiss is right, professional lawyers will have to become as concerned about facilitating pluralistic dialogue as they previously were concerned about pitting one person's interest against another's. And this change will also mean that lawyers will have to emphasize cooperative interaction rather than adversarial interaction in certain cases. Law schools will have to change the way lawyers are socialized so as to reflect these changes in the lawyer's role.

I. A MODEL OF NONADVERSARIAL ADVOCACY

The early Soviet legal theorist E. B. Pashukanis tried to make practical sense of the Marxist contention that both the state and the law would wither away in postcapitalist societies. Pashukanis took as his point of departure Friedrich Engels's contention that in Communist society there would be a replacement of the "rule of law" by the "administration of things."[3] A system of technical rules was to provide a noncoercive way to allocate disputed resources and services in order to achieve ends already accepted by the members of a society. A system of law had traditionally been conceived as providing a coercive way to settle conflicts among essentially private parties who could not otherwise agree about either the means

---

2. Owen Fiss, "Foreword: The Forms of Justice, the Supreme Court 1978 Term," *Harvard Law Review* 93, no. 1 (November 1979): 29.

3. See E. B. Pashukanis, "The General Theory of Law and Marxism" (1924), trans. H. W. Babb, in *Soviet Legal Philosophy,* ed. H. W. Babb and John N. Hazard (Cambridge, MA: Harvard University Press, 1951).

or ends of proper conduct. For Pashukanis, the Marxist concept of law first and foremost demanded a decline in the threat of state coercion as a means of regulating social relationships.

Pashukanis proposed a theory of law that stressed the cooperative rather than the adversarial dimension of "dispute" resolution. In this regard he relied on an analogy to the rules embodied in a standard train timetable. The timetable tells prospective train passengers when and where they need to arrive in order to be admitted into a passenger train headed toward a particular destination.[4] Just as in the case of the rules regulating wills, the timetable "rules" are noncoercive, for the only penalty that follows upon nonconformity to the "rules" (for instance, arriving five minutes late) is that the train crew will not wait for you. But this "penalty" need only be conceived as a penalty if you wanted to catch that train. Train timetables are rules for cooperation. If someone wants to catch a train to a particular destination on a particular day, then that person is told what is required of her. These "rules" facilitate the accomplishment of common goals. H. L. A. Hart points out that a large part of contemporary practices governed by law are, at least in part, of this sort rather than of the sort for which individuals are in dispute or disagreement about goals.[5]

With the change in economic relations that was supposed to occur under communism, the conflicts of interest that made traditional law indispensable for maintaining social order in pre-Communist societies were to have diminished. In their place there was to arise a greater unity of interests that would usher in the two major changes in law in postcapitalist society: state coercion would be less and less needed; and legal rules would not concern adversarial adjudications among private isolated subjects.

> The form of law—with its aspect of a subjective investiture with rights—is born in a society, which consists of isolated possessors of private, egoistic interests. When the entire economic life is built upon the principle of accord of independent wills, then—as if reflected in a mirror—every sort of social function takes on a legal character—that is to say, it becomes more than a social function; it becomes also the right of the person who is carrying out the function. . . . A characteristic feature of bourgeoise society is specifically the fact that general interests are segregated from—and are opposed to—private interests; but in this antithesis they themselves involuntarily take on the form of private interests—that is to say, the form of law.[6]

4. Ibid., p. 137.

5. H. L. A. Hart, *The Concept of Law* (Oxford: The Clarendon Press, 1961), especially chaps. 3 and 4.

6. Pashukanis, pp. 155–6.

Yet these general interests will not always be best characterized as merely private interests to be weighed against other private interests, with each given roughly equal weight. Only because of the fact that legal socialization causes lawyers to conceive of disputes in terms of conflicts of private interests must this juxtaposition be maintained. Only because it is assumed that discord is essential to human relationships is it necessary to conceive of justice as requiring adversarial adjudications.

But is it not utopian to posit harmony of interests and unity of purpose given what we see around us today? I will try to render this position more plausible but not without being critical of some of Pashukanis's contentions. Consider another of Pashukanis's examples, the "rules" which doctors give patients to follow.[7] These rules apply to a group of persons—patients—who share with their doctors a common interest in the promotion of health. Patients are not seen as isolated organisms with unrelated medical problems. One does not start from the premise that each sick person, in pursuing his of her health interests, will be in an adversarial relationship to his or her doctor or to each other sick person. Rather, these interests do not necessarily compete with each other: it is through cooperation in the sharing of medical records and research that the common goal of health can be achieved.

In the example of the rules of train regulation, the two main elements of law are both missing. The egoistic subjective element, which is, for Pashukanis, the hallmark of law, is replaced by a normative element that is rooted in cooperation. The objective coercive element, which makes the rules reasonably inflexible and extends their application to all cases of a similar sort regardless of the results that will be achieved by this inflexibility, is replaced by a conditional formulation: if you want x you must do y (but where it is not dictated that you must want x, or that you will be penalized for not doing y). The only potentially coercive element here, as we saw, occurs in the following scenario. If you want to catch the train but arrive five minutes late, the train crew will not wait for you, thereby "penalizing" you for failing to conform to the rule. But this penalty is again merely conditional: it only affects you if you wanted that which was governed by the technical rule. This is clearly a type of social constraint rather than the kind of explicit display of political coercion that occurs when one is threatened with imprisonment for violating a law. (Pashukanis chooses to characterize the difference as that between state power and social constraint.) Indeed, if this is coercion at all, it is coercion to do that which a

---

7. I do not necessarily agree with Pashukanis that doctors impose rules on their patients. I am here merely reporting what he says, although in the next chapter I do offer some reasons to think that doctors believe they have authority over their patients.

person already considers to be best for herself or himself. While this position has rather dangerous implications, as we will see from Hans Kelsen's criticisms, it is clearly different from the model of adversarial law.[8]

II. PROBLEMS WITH NONADVERSARIAL ADVOCACY

Administrative law, according to a nonadversarial model of law, may be conceived as a set of rules concerned with the allocation of resources, services, and positions within a social organization characterized by the fact that the members accept the *general* goals and purposes of that organization, although they may disagree about certain specifics. Think of unemployment compensation proceedings. In such proceedings there need not be an antagonistic relationship between employer and former employee; indeed, both parties may wish to cooperate to obtain the agreed-upon compensation from the state fund into which the employer has been dutifully paying. Some legal theorists such as Owen Fiss have contended that it will be best to regard each of the parties as representing an entire class or group of individuals, all similarly situated. And the state does not need to be conceived of as an adversary either, especially if there is a compensation "table" that has already been decided upon as a matter of public policy. Emphasizing such cases will set the stage for a cooperative approach to law.

Some family-law courts in a number of societies operate on a cooperative model in the sense that the judge tries to get all of the parties to reach agreement about what is in the best interest of the whole family. But in order for an agreement to be reached, often a judge will have to impose a settlement on the parties which none of the parties favors. Alice Ehr-Soon Tay has extensively criticized these family courts for being what she calls the "new forms of star chamber" proceedings. She claims that these courts become a "scandalous law unto themselves" "because they are exposed neither to public scrutiny nor to the full rigor of proper judicial appeal."[9] Those who are least powerful, such as children, are not given adequate protection against judges who often have no interest in protecting the children's rights. This is a standard criticism of communistic or communitarian views, and it is a criticism I take quite seriously. Procedural due process should be an important concept in a cooperative, as well as in an

8. Charles Wolfram rightly points out that the adversarial model of law did not literally evolve from such models of dispute resolution as trial by combat. See his discussion of this point in *Modern Legal Ethics,* p. 567.

9. Alice Ehr-Soon Tay, "The Law, the Citizen, and the State," in *Law and Society: The Crisis in Legal Ideas,* ed. Eugene Kamenka, Robert Brown, and Alice Ehr-Soon Tay (New York: St. Martin's Press, 1978), p. 8.

adversarial, model of law, for without it abuses of power are too likely to occur, even where many values are shared by a community.

Tay's criticism can best be applied to Pashukanis concerning another of his examples, the rules of the military.[10] Pashukanis contended that the members of a company of soldiers are not in adversarial relations with each other or with their sergeant. Indeed, the soldiers cooperate with one another and with the sergeant by following rules to achieve a common, mutually accepted goal. Yet, it must be admitted, abuses that arise in these military relations have been notoriously difficult to end, precisely because the soldiers have little procedural recourse if they disagree with what the sergeant has ordered them to do. Especially in settings where force is likely to occur, a nonadversarial model should not be left unrestrained by an absence of procedural due process. To the extent that a nonadversarial model of law fails to take such factors into account, it is vulnerable to obvious counterarguments.

Hans Kelsen points us toward another major objection to views such as those of Pashukanis. Kelsen claims that Pashukanis failed to show why the "technical rules" that will regulate Communist society are not themselves properly legal rules. By downplaying the fact that technical rules must also often be coercive, Pashukanis failed to show that the supposed "unity of purpose" underpinning technical rules actually exists.

> The assumption that there exists a "unity of purpose" in any case whatever where constraint is exercised by one individual against another, is an obvious fiction. The very fact that one individual must be forced to comply with the will of another shows clearly that the purpose of the one, and that means his immediate purpose, is not the purpose of the other, and it is the immediate purpose which alone comes into consideration when "unity" is in question. Otherwise, there would be unity where there exists the greatest antagonism.[11]

The mere fact that there might be agreement about the long-run end is not sufficient to establish the kind of unity of purpose that would distinguish technical from legal rules. According to Kelsen, law is essentially bound up with the settlement of disputes about means, and rather immediate means at that. To show that technical rules are significantly different from legal rules, Pashukanis or a contemporary defender of nonadversarial approaches to law would have to show that even the immediate means are not in dispute. Otherwise, we will again be faced with a situation in which

10. Pashukanis's two other major examples, discussed earlier, are railway timetables and medical orders.

11. Hans Kelsen, "Pashukanis's Theory of Law," in *The Communist Theory of Law* (New York: Praeger, 1955), p. 104.

one party employs socially sanctioned coercion to compel another to follow his or her will—the paradigm of the adversarial model of advocacy.

In Pashukanis's example of the doctor-patient relationship, says Kelsen, the doctor is merely forcing the patient to do what is clearly in that
patient's interest. Since the patient, according to this early-twentieth-cen-
tury understanding of things, does not often comprehend what is good for
him or her, the doctor must exercise force to bring about the purpose
which the patient wants. The doctor-patient relationship is noncoercive
only if the patient agrees to undergo each and every application of a rule of
medicine to his or her own case which the doctor mandates. This is quite
unlikely, says Kelsen, and it is even more unlikely in criminal matters than
in medical matters.

Kelsen's main point is that coercion will be smuggled into the system
of technical rules whether Pashukanis wants it or not. This coercion is, at
the very least, necessary to cause people to act according to the general set
of technical rules rather than in an anarchic fashion to the detriment of
others within society. The social coercion in medicine or the military is still
coercion, and differs from state coercion only in that it is not officially le-
gitimated by the society at large. Even administrative agency proceedings
are ultimately backed by the coercive power of the state, for it they were
not, why would anyone trust that the agreed distribution of resources or
services would indeed be provided? If there were literally no state power
above the administrative agency, and similarly no level of legal appeal
above the administrative ruling, then the administrative agency would be
sovereign unto itself. And, as Tay argues, when these agencies approach
the point of sovereignty, those who must rely on these agencies are placed
in an increasingly vulnerable predicament.

III. COOPERATION AND PARTICIPATION

Two distinct issues are at stake in the preceding discussion. First, we have
been discussing whether law as practiced should conform to the adversarial model of advocacy and dispute resolution or to a nonadversarial
model of administration through 'technical rules.' Second, we have been
discussing whether law must, at some deeper motivational level, be coercive or whether a system of rules can operate effectively without coercion.
Law can be understood to be cooperative at each of these levels, that is, at
the level of how people, especially through their lawyers, resolve their conflicts or at the level of what motivates people ultimately to resolve their
disputes nonviolently. I am inclined to agree with Kelsen about the second
level, that is, I think that even in the most close-knit community there will
be disagreements about how best to pursue the community's commonly
accepted goals. And such disagreements will require some sort of coercion

as at least a background threat to bring people to the bargaining table. But I am also inclined to agree (at least partially) with Pashukanis about the first level, that is, I do not believe that all legal advocacy is best conceptualized according to an adversarial model.

According to the adversarial model of advocacy, lawyers are supposed to act as if the interests of two parties could not be reconciled by appeal to shared values, and hence their clients' interests are always best served when these interests are pitted against each other, ignoring what they agree upon. Adversarial advocacy comes to resemble trial by ordeal, where the least objectionable alternative will win the day so as to guard against the worst. Lawyers and their clients are often trapped, unable to embrace alternatives that often would be best for all concerned. The larger community's interest in justice, which lawyers are supposed to uphold, is not necessarily best served when lawyers provide the most diligent adversarial representation of a client's case.

I propose that we limit the adversarial aspect of dispute resolution to those areas of law where there is a demonstrable inability to resolve disputes by appeals to shared values. But in those areas of law where there is a history of success in obtaining out-of-court settlements, we should not insist that lawyers operate as adversaries. Indeed, it may be better, given that lawyers have been socialized to be combative, that we not have lawyers present at all—relying instead on mediators who have been socialized to seek consensus.[12] In any event, in those areas of law where there is no history of irreconcilable differences between parties, we should embrace a more cooperative approach to dispute resolution while still allowing for some adversarial protection of procedural due process.

Which types of dispute in law seem most conducive to the cooperative approach? Family law is currently one of the least adversarial branches of American law; but many critics have claimed that this distinction has led to many problems, especially for women. Because of the emphasis on cooperation in many family-law courts, battered wives, for instance, are pressured to settle for conflict resolutions that provide less than adequate protection of their rights.[13] It is my view that certain aspects of real estate law, as well as most aspects of administrative law, may be better suited to a

12. For an interesting discussion of the German "inquisitorial" system, which places much more emphasis on the role of judge-mediators than on lawyer-adversaries, see David Luban, *Lawyers and Justice* (Princeton: Princeton University Press, 1988), pp. 93–103.

13. For a good discussion of the difficulties facing battered women in American legal contexts see Deborah Rhode, *Gender and Justice* (Cambridge, MA: Harvard University Press, 1989), pp. 237–44. Also see Dories Klein, "The Dark Side of Marriage: Battered Wives and the Domination of Women," in *Judge, Lawyer, Victim, Thief,* ed. Nicole Hahn Rafter and Elizabeth A. Stanko (Boston: Northeastern University Press, 1982).

cooperative model than family law, although uncontested divorces, custody cases, and adoptions are often also better off seen as nonadversarial matters. It appears that cooperative negotiating already occurs in these domains, and in many cases the parties are already on more of an equal footing than is true in some family-law cases. Indeed, in many states it is common for real estate brokers and mortgage company agents rather than lawyers to represent buyer and seller at closing.[14] In general, civil law is easier to conceptualize as cooperative than is criminal law, although some legal scholars are exploring nonadversarial models in criminal matters.[15]

Critical theorists such as Jürgen Habermas have articulated a model of social interaction, called "communicative action," that places a premium on participatory modes of discourse that are noncoercive and that facilitate reaching consensus about shared values.[16] They have been highly critical of the intrusion of coercive state structures into all aspects of social life. I am very sympathetic to critical theory on these issues. Critical theory, itself a descendant of Marxism and left-Hegelianism, has provided an alternative between traditional liberal and Communist models of politics and law. I wish to draw on critical theory's insights in arguing for a model of advocacy that includes elements of the cooperative and the adversarial models.

Habermas has consistently stressed that a cooperative or consensus approach to shared values is not a call for forced compromise.[17] The worry expressed by Alice Ehr-Soon Tay concerning the "star chamber" atmosphere in some family courts is really a worry about the kind of forced compromises that are also anathema to those of us who favor a cooperative and consensus-oriented approach to certain areas of law.[18] Law must operate to offset the consolidation of power in the hands of the powerful,

14. See chap. 7, "Conflict of Interest," where I address at some length the roles and conflicts in real estate settlements.

15. See Kit Kinports, "Evidence Engendered," *University of Illinois Law Review,* 1991, no. 2: 413–56.

16. For the most accessible work on this topic see Habermas, *Moral Consciousness and Communicative Action.*

17. Jürgen Habermas, "Law and Morality," in *The Tanner Lectures on Human Values,* vol. 8, ed. Sterling M. McMurrin (Salt Lake City: University of Utah Press, 1988), especially p. 231. For a revealing discussion of this issue in the context of analytical jurisprudence see David Ingram, "Dworkin, Habermas and the CLS Movement on Moral Criticism in Law," *Philosophy and Social Criticism* 16 (1992), especially pp. 255–6.

18. Thomas McCarthy has argued that Habermas and others have misunderstood the importance of nonargumentative forms of compromise. See his essay, "Practical Discourse: On the Relation of Morality to Politics," in *Ideals and Illusions: On Reconstruction and Deconstruction in Contemporary Critical Theory* (Cambridge, MA: MIT Press, 1991), especially p. 198.

not to enhance the ability of the powerful to force their wills upon the powerless in the uncritical rush to achieve compromise.

Throughout this chapter I have been motivated by a desire to find a model of advocacy that does not conceptualize social interaction as a battlefield between irreconcilable interests. What I have been exploring is a model of advocacy that is "more appropriate to these [various] contexts of interaction,"[19] namely, a model that is sensitive to context and that does not mandate that in all contexts people see themselves as adversaries, but in which there will still be a place for some adversarial advocacy. This is a piece of the larger struggle Habermas described as the struggle against the "colonization of the lifeworld," the tendency of state processes of legalization to take over customary forms of organization.[20] The adversarial model of advocacy is held in such high esteem that it has been much harder for alternative forms of advocacy to get their day in court.

There is a stronger criticism of the adversarial method of advocacy and dispute resolution that is inspired by critical theory. When the adversarial method colonizes the political domain, it may jeopardize the participatory system of democracy. A participatory system of government depends on a certain degree of solidarity and communal sympathy among the citizenry. The adversarial model of advocacy and dispute resolution, when extended into the political domain, breaks down solidarity and community. As the Founding Fathers were well aware, the greatest threat to democracy is factionalism; and factionalism is often inspired by a group acting as if its interests were always at odds with a competing interest group. The adversarial model calls for people to think of their own interests in just this way, as irreconcilably pitted against the interests of another party. This model, which stresses conflict rather than cooperation, drives a wedge between parties who are, in most instances, more alike than different. This situation disrupts solidarity and community and makes participatory democracy all the more difficult to achieve.

I should say once more that I am aware that minorities within some societies should continue to have a basis from which they can challenge an oppressive majority. In certain situations, an adversarial response to that majority may be the best way to protect minority rights. It would be contrary to my own progressive and liberationist goals to deny this possibility.[21] Rather, what I am claiming is that when each interest group sees

19. Kenneth Baynes, *The Normative Grounds of Social Criticism* (Albany: SUNY Press, 1992), p. 166.

20. See Habermas, *The Theory of Communicative Action,* vol. 2.

21. See the final chapter of *Sharing Responsibility,* where I defend a view I have labeled "liberationist communitarianism." In that chapter I am specifically concerned to show how procedural rights can have a place in communitarian social theory.

itself as irreconcilably at odds with each other one—a position our society seems to be approaching—community breaks down. What we need is a sensitivity to context that will allow for a more reasonable appraisal of whether a particular group should feel driven to regard other groups as adversaries. I have suggested that contextual and historical considerations will often provide a reasonable basis for making such determinations. What I find suspect, though, is the colonization of social life by legal adversarialism, which makes us insensitive to these matters of context and history.

IV. EMPATHY, SENSITIVITY, AND ADVOCACY

In the remainder of this chapter I wish to use the example of divorce mediation to explain how the role of advocate should change in certain situations in which two parties have at least some interests and values in common. The problem with adversarial advocacy in divorce cases is well known, as Charles Wolfram notes.

> Mediation has received particular attention recently in divorce. For some time observers have complained that the presence of adversary lawyers in a divorce can exacerbate rather than solve problems, principally because some lawyers, habituated to the milieu of litigation, act as provocateurs rather than conciliators.[22]

In divorce mediation, a mediator sees himself or herself as a facilitator and an advocate for a couple, rather than for a single individual. In this sense there is advocacy (advocacy for the couple) without individual representation. The best way for the mediator to aid the couple in reaching an amicable and reasonable solution to custody and property problems is to keep both sides talking in a productive way toward the goal of reaching consensus. To do this, it is absolutely required that the mediator not take sides, or feel that the interests of either or both people must be zealously pursued.

While discussing virtue, Aristotle says that it is very difficult to hit the mean (where true virtue lies) rather than one or the other extreme. Divorce mediation is involved in just such an attempt to find the reasonable mean between the initially often extreme positions of two people who have decided to get a divorce. In attempting to hit the mean, mediators come to see two related facts. First, resolution of a problem is made easier if someone, normally the mediator, already has a solution in mind. And second, resolutions are easier to achieve when one of the parties is willing to be the first to compromise. In both cases, problems of autonomy arise, since the mediator, knowing these facts, is likely to put pressure on one or the other party to compromise rather than to hold his or her ground.

It might initially seem that divorce mediation is better than the adversarial model in terms of autonomy preservation. After all, the mediator is only helping the couple to facilitate the details of a solution they've already reached. But what often takes place is that two lawyers doing battle for the two parties are replaced by a lawyer/mediator who acts more like a judge than a facilitator. In such a situation there may be even less autonomy for the parties in mediation than there was under the adversarial model, where it is assumed that both parties have distinct interests and have no reason to want to agree to a settlement that is not completely acceptable to themselves. To avoid these various problems, in addition to procedural safeguards a high premium needs to be placed on instilling empathy and sensitivity in mediators.[23] I will end by exploring what it means to be, and what the advantages are of being, an empathic and sensitive advocate.

In many divorce cases, two individuals are struggling to extricate themselves from a legal relationship with an equitable property and custody settlement. But in some cases, they are also struggling to retain a less formal relationship, even in the face of strong emotions of anger, regret, frustration, and even retribution. This is especially true when young children are involved. It would be important, in most divorce cases, for the parents to retain enough of a relationship so that the day-to-day parenting decisions could be negotiated amicably. As Wolfram and many others have pointed out, lawyers often exacerbate the strongly negative feelings two divorcing individuals feel.

A socially responsive lawyer would worry that the zealous, aggressive, and single-minded promotion of the rights of parties to a divorce could make things worse for them as well as for the society at large. But given standard legal socialization, it is not clear that lawyers have much choice. If they try to be nonadversarial, they discover that very little of what they learned in law school provides them with resources to be good counselors. This is why it is important for legal socialization to be changed so that lawyers are trained to be empathic to the uniquely situated persons who are their clients, and to be sensitive to the feelings of these parties as well as to the history and context of their present predicament. Some have suggested that this would best be done by training lawyers to be therapists.[24] While I find this suggestion potentially problematic, there is some merit to its spirit.

23. I am grateful to Ralph Lindgren for first making me aware of the practical importance of empathy in mediation.

24. See Michael Joseph Rosanova, "Divorce-Related Mediation," *Perspectives on the Professions* 2, nos. 3–4 (September/December 1982): 2–6 (newsletter published by the Center for the Study of Ethics in the Professions, Illinois Institute of Technology).

Lawyers need to develop some of the same skills as therapists if they are to deal with their increasingly important roles as counselor, mediator, conciliator, and bargainer, which often require cooperation more than competition among people. The reason the skills of the therapist are valuable is that the focus is on understanding the person's interests in his or her own terms given a world where many interests are not in competition with one another. Here, facilitating a person's interests, especially when his or her interests are somewhat dependent on the fulfillment of the interests of others, will be harmed by an overly zealous and aggressive adversarial approach. Of course, as I suggested above, there are certainly other cases in which the adversarial approach is warranted.

Indeed, there have been a number of problems with divorce mediation, at least some of which can be traced to the complete lack of adversarialism in these proceedings. The lack of procedures aimed at protecting the rights of the divorcing individuals often means that the structure works to the advantage of the more powerful and sophisticated of the two parties. Given current circumstances in the United States, this means that the woman's rights are not nearly so well protected as the man's in divorce mediation. In addition, when mediators try to correct for this potential imbalance, paternalism on the part of the mediator occasionally surfaces as the mediator tries to do what he or she thinks is best for the woman, even though it may be against the woman's explicitly stated wishes.

It is important to recognize the possible pitfalls of nonadversarial arrangements. As I said earlier, some types of cases, especially where differences of interest and power would make it likely that one party would be systematically disadvantaged, are best handled through adversarial advocacy. But the pitfalls of nonadversarial advocacy can be minimized in certain types of cases, especially where there is significant agreement about common goals, making it true that nonadversarial advocacy is best for this type of case. What we need is a new model of legal socialization that stresses both adversarial and cooperative advocacy, based on which kind of case is involved. Lawyers should be free to act as conciliators when there appears to be a common interest for the parties concerned. But unlike some more radical proponents of mediation, I believe that there will remain cases in which lawyers should be adversarial advocates, that is, where common interest is not evident.

The debate about adversarial advocacy parallels the debate between liberals and communitarians about the role of mediating institutions in the democratic political process.[25] In that debate, it seems to me that the truth lies somewhere between liberalism and communitarianism. And it sim-

25. See the discussion of this point at the end of chap. 4, "Socialization and Institutional Evil."

ilarly seems to me that we do not have to choose between adversarial and nonadversarial advocacy. Rather, the best society may be one in which lawyers are trained to be able to perform both forms of advocacy. Liberalism, with its traditional championing of adversarial advocacy, and communitarianism, with its championing of cooperative advocacy, can coexist, as is beginning to be true in actual legal practice in the United States. Here, plea bargaining, labor negotiation, and divorce mediation take place in the same system in which highly adversarial litigation is conducted.

Throughout this chapter I have been exploring the problems and advantages of an adversarial approach as well as a nonadversarial approach to advocacy and dispute resolution. I have argued that a nonadversarial approach makes more sense than an adversarial one when there is a history of agreement about matters of shared value. But also this claim is modified in full recognition that there remain many areas of contemporary life that are not marked by consensus about goals. And I have been critical of some proponents of nonadversarial advocacy for failing to recognize that even when there is consensus, procedural due process needs to be safeguarded. In addition, I have pointed out that an uncritical reliance on the adversarial model, especially when that is extended into other areas of social and political life, runs contrary to the spirit of participatory democracy. This last point, which clearly could be the subject of an essay in its own right, will, I hope, help to break the stranglehold of the adversarial model, especially in the socialization of lawyers, which has made life so hard for those who favor alternative forms of advocacy and of dispute resolution, especially concerning social groups.[26] As our society begins to see the value of nonadversarial legal advocacy, we may also see ways of increasing the sense of community in our pluralistic society. This is one of the main topics of the next chapter.

---

26. See Larry May and Marie Failinger, "Litigating against Poverty: Legal Services and Group Representation," *Ohio State Law Journal* 45/1 (1984): 1–56. I discuss the question of justice for groups in the final chapter of *The Morality of Groups*.

9

CHALLENGING MEDICAL AUTHORITY

As a member of a hospital ethics committee in a city with a very large Christian Science population, I have seen firsthand the stalemate that exists between Christian Scientists and physicians, especially concerning the treatment of Christian Science children.[1] Physicians claim that it is a violation of their professional duties to allow those children to suffer who could be prevented from suffering by medical treatment. Christian Scientists claim that it is a violaton of their religious freedom to be forced to subject their children to medical treatment in violation of their religious beliefs. The stalemate is made more tragic since neither physicians nor Christian Scientists want children to suffer or die, yet Christian Scientists refuse even to have their sick children diagnosed for fear that the physicians will try to force them to accept medical treatment. In contrast to most discussion of this topic, in this chapter the Christian Science refusal cases will be considered as an example of a conflict of groups over authority within a plural istic society. I will offer a temporary solution to this stalemate that exemplifies the notion of a communitarian negotiated compromise discussed in previous chapters.

In the first section, I will present two contrasting cases of Christian Scientists who have refused medical treatment for their children. In the second section, I will rehearse some of the main doctrines and arguments espoused by Christian Scientists who refuse medical treatment. In the third section, I will attempt to explain why physicians in the United States are so strongly committed to the belief that they must be the exclusive authorities in matters of health. In the fourth section, I will discuss the problem of

---

1. My interest in this topic was fueled by many discussions with my fellow members of the St. Louis Children's Hospital Medical Ethics Subcommittee.

conflicts of belief in a pluralistic society and will apply such a framework to the Christian Science refusal cases. In the final section, I will suggest briefly how medical socialization should be changed so that doctors come to recognize the legitimacy of other forms of authority. And I suggest how this change, when conjoined with a corresponding change in the socialization of Christian Science commmunity members, might resolve the current stalemate over the Christian Science refusal cases.

I. TWO CHRISTIAN SCIENCE REFUSAL CASES

Let us consider a case that appears to most doctors and lawyers as a good illustration of why we should not give equal respect and treatment to the Christian Science community. On a Thursday evening in early April of 1986, two-year-old Robyn Twitchell ate a normal dinner but experienced severe pain and vomiting shortly after dinner. The pain and vomiting continued into Friday and Robyn's parents, both committed Christian Scientists, consulted several church officials, who determined that his pain was in his lower abdomen. After another day of intense pain and vomiting, on Saturday a Christian Science practitioner, Nancy Calkins, came to the Twitchell house to pray for Robyn. Robyn was still unable to hold food or liquids down, so on Monday a Christian Science nurse was called, who also ministered to Robyn. By Tuesday evening Robyn Twitchell had died. An autopsy was conducted and it was determined that Robyn had a bowel obstruction, which, in the opinion of one physician, "could have been readily corrected by surgery with an almost 100 percent chance of success."[2]

The mainstream position in medicine and law is that even in a pluralistic society a line needs to be drawn at the point where respecting a religious minority culture clearly jeopardizes the well-being of children. Indeed, what makes the case of Robyn Twitchell so tragic is that a relatively simple operation could have saved his life. The fact that his parents refused even to secure a medical diagnosis meant that they were completely unaware of how seriously ill their son was. Indeed, in another highly publicized case, the parents whose failure to secure a medical diagnosis and simple treatment resulted in the death of their child have subsequently left the Chris-

---

2. This is a paraphrase of the opinion voiced by the emergency room physican on call at the hospital where Robyn was taken after death. Most of the details here are taken from Paula Monopoli, "Allocating the Costs of Parental Free Exercise: Striking a New Balance between Sincere Religious Belief and a Child's Right to Medical Treatment," *Pepperdine Law Review* 18 (1991): 323–4.

tian Science Church and lobbied against statutory religious exemptions to the child abuse and neglect laws.[3]

From the legal and medical perspective, the Christian Science community simply cannot be respected by the dominant community to do what is best for their children without serious threats to the fundamental rights of these children. In the case of Robyn Twitchell, it seems clear to most physicians that respecting the beliefs and choices of Christian Scientists meant that Robyn's right to life and Robyn's right to minimally adequate health care were jeopardized. In a sense, respecting the wishes of these Christian Science parents meant that Robyn Twitchell was the subject of child neglect.[4] From the medical perspective, he may as well have been left alone by his parents to die, given what little his parents did to save his life. When the Twitchell case is used as a model, Christian Science seems to be the kind of community that cannot and should not be given equal respect with the other communities in our pluralistic society.

Consider another case of Christian Science refusal that is perhaps more representative of the clash between medical and Christian Science perspectives. In 1990 Colin Newmark's parents began to worry. The health of this three-year-old son of Christian Science parents had been deteriorating rapidly. The parents reluctantly took Colin to a hospital in Delaware near their home. The physicians could not immediately tell what was wrong with Colin and they recommended extensive X rays and blood testing. The parents refused and took Colin home. Colin's condition continued to deteriorate, and his parents returned to the hospital. X rays indicated that Colin suffered from an intestinal blockage. His parents agreed to surgery to remove the blockage since they considered the procedure to be purely "mechanical."[5] "A pathological report on tissue taken from Colin's intestines during the surgery revealed that Colin was suffering from non-Hodgkin's lymphoma. Five pathologists confirmed this diagnosis."[6]

---

3. See Rita Swan, "Faith Healing, Christian Science and the Medical Care of Children," *New England Journal of Medicine* 309, no. 26 (1983).

4. Yet even in this case the conviction of the Twitchells for involuntary manslaughter was overturned by the Supreme Judicial Court of the Commonwealth of Massachusetts in 1993, seven years after Robyn's death.

5. There is some dispute about this fact. The brief filed by Colin's parents when this case went to the Delaware Supreme Court asserts that the parents consented to this initial operation, at least in part, because of undue pressure to which their doctor had subjected them.

6. The facts of this case are taken from a case note on *Newmark v. Williams*, 588 A2d 1108 (Del. 1991), written by Patrick Bouldin, which appeared in the *Journal of Family Law* 30 (1991–2): 673–81; see especially p. 674. "Colin Newmark" is a pseudonym used by the Delaware courts to protect the privacy of the child and his parents.

The doctors in charge of Colin's case recommended chemotherapy and radiation, which would give Colin a 40 percent chance of recovery. Without chemotherapy, the doctors argued that Colin would be dead in six to eight months. The form of chemotherapy proposed can result in kidney failure, hair loss, immunological and neurological problems, and, as a result of multiple blood transfusions, increased risk of infection. One of the doctors, Dr. Meek, "predicted that chemotherapy would bring Colin near death and that the radiation treatments required would presumably render him sterile."[7] The Newmarks rejected the chemotherapy and attempted to remove Colin from the hospital to be placed in the care of a Christian Science practitioner. The hospital sued to obtain custody of Colin so as to authorize the chemotherapy, and the hospital tried to have Colin placed into a foster home where his caretakers would cooperate with the medical treatment regimen. The Delaware Supreme Court sided with the Newmarks.

In many such cases it is not so clear that medical science can save the life of a child or that the side effects of saving the life are themselves not worse than the saving. We get a very different result if we use the model of Colin instead of that of Robyn in assessing the Christian Science refusal cases. The model of Colin is also consistent with the many children of Christian Scientists who seem to be quite healthy even though their parents don't accept medical authority. What is especially important about the case of Colin Newmark is that his parents did not blindly refuse to seek all forms of medical diagnosis and help. In the end they refused one form of proposed therapy, but such a refusal cannot seriously be said clearly to jeopardize Colin's fundamental rights. The facts are such that it is not clear what would be best for Colin. Indeed, if this case had not concerned Christian Scientists, the medical profession would probably have been undivided in supporting, or at least not challenging, the parents's decision.

II. CHRISTIAN SCIENCE

Since the First Church of Christ Scientist was founded more than a century ago by Mary Baker Eddy, Christian Scientists have been locked in a struggle with the medical profession. In her major book, *Science and Health,* Eddy argues that "Mind," not matter, constitutes what is real. Each person should be able to be his or her "own physician, and Truth will be the universal panacea."[8] The power of prayer was thought to be an antidote to any ailment since the ailments themselves were really mental in

7. Ibid., p. 675.
8. Mary Baker Eddy, *Science and Health* (1875; reprint, Boston: First Church of Christ Scientist, 1971), p. 144.

origin in the first place. In some cases, Eddy suggested that people may need help in bringing their minds into alignment with "Mind." Such aid, in the form of reliance on certain others, was meant only to help the individual to help himself or herself.

Eddy formed a group of practitioners who were to assist individuals in finding mental or spiritual solutions to their problems. In the early years of the church, these practitioners were in direct competition with medical physicians. One recent writer on the history of these developments concludes:

> Whereas osteopathy and chiropractic [the other dominant challengers to medical physicians at the turn of the century] followed the strategy of getting legislation passed that would govern their practices, Christian Science pursued the policy of obtaining amendments to the existing medical practice acts that specifically exempted its practitioners from their provisions. Thus, unlike the others who were regulated by the state, Christian Science was able to maintain complete administrative control over its practitioners.[9]

From the early years of the development of both the Christian Science and the medical communities, struggles between the two groups have been common.

According to Christian Science doctrine, children sometimes suffer material discomfort because of the mental beliefs of their parents. So the parents are sometimes in the best position to affect their children's health by bringing their own spiritual lives into order through prayer before the children's health will return.[10] Such a position does not seem to be at odds with seeking medical care for these children while the parents work on their spiritual well-being. But such is not the case—for Mary Baker Eddy warns that "hypocrisy is fatal to religion."[11] When Christian Scientists put their faith in spiritual healing, they consider it hypocritical also to put their faith in medicine. Some Christian Scientists fervently believe that the power of spiritual healing is greatly diminished if the faith of the person praying is so weak that medical help is sought at the same time that prayer is being made. Indeed, Eddy admonishes, it "is a grave mistake to suppose . . . that Spirit and matter . . . can commune together,"[12] and "If we trust matter, we distrust Spirit."[13]

---

9. Norman Gevitz, "Christian Science Healing and the Health Care of Children," *Perspectives in Biology and Medicine* 34, no. 3 (spring 1991): 425.

10. See Eddy, p. 154.

11. Ibid., p. 7.

12. Ibid., p. 73.

13. Ibid., p. 234.

Yet Christian Science doctrine about the medical treatment of children is not so clear-cut as is sometimes supposed. There is no room in Christian Science for a blind faith in spiritual healing in all cases. According to Eddy, "Nothing is more antagonistic to Christian Science than a blind belief without understanding."[14] And there is nothing in the doctrine to forbid anyone from seeking medical healing. Rather, there is a strong sense that when one does seek medical healing one has turned one's back on the power of spiritual healing. But even Eddy herself came at the end of her life to advocate seeking medical care during delivery, and in *Science and Health* she allowed that surgery could be used to set broken bones.[15] Recently, the Christian Science Board of Directors has issued a restatement of church policy affirming that

> although it is entirely natural for students of Christian Science to rely on prayer, it is also important, when it comes to the care of children, that Scientists consider well their individual spiritual readiness, their own past experience and record, and the mental climate in which they live. . . . When circumstances result in a child's being brought under medical care, members of our Church would surely continue to cherish such a family and give them their full love and support during a challenging time. . . . To look upon another's progress with anything less than loving encouragement would not be Christian.[16]

Yet this restatement reaffirms that seeking medical care "clearly departs from the practice of Christian Science."[17]

These various nuances in the Christian Science doctrine, especially toward children, have resulted in a wide variety of Christian Science practices concerning sick children. The most interesting question from my perspective is why Christian Scientists have had such trouble seeing medical science as a diagnostic aid to their own attempts to remove disease through prayer. One reason may be that many Christian Scientists seem to take literally several passages in *Science and Health* (effectively the bible of Christian Science[18]) that say that little children should not be exposed to false belief and superstition, that is, to medical science. Even to use medical science as a diagnostic tool would mean to give it credibility in the eyes of a

14. Ibid., p. 83.

15. See Gevitz, pp. 427–8.

16. Christian Science Board of Directors, "Christian Scientists and the Practice of Spiritual Healing," *Christian Science Sentinel* 93 (7 October 1991): 25.

17. Ibid., p. 25.

18. This is not to suggest that Christian Scientists don't also rely on the authority of the Old and New Testaments.

child, which would diminish the authority of Christian Science and ultimately adversely affect the child, his or her family, and even the whole Christian Science community.

Yet, since even Mary Baker Eddy is willing to allow that Christian Science practices are not able to effectuate cures in all cases, and some "mechanical" forms of medical science should be relied on (as in the cases of childbirth, broken limbs, and dentistry), it seems odd indeed, even on the very principles of Christian Science and its emphasis on never accepting anything on blind faith, not to remain open to the possibility that more illnesses than those related to obstetrics, orthopedics, and oral surgery can be helped by medical diagnosis. At the very least, it would seem to make sense to know something about the physical condition of the body (even given that it is only effect and not cause of the illness) in order to be better able to direct one's spiritual resources.[19]

The Christian Science response is to insist that medical diagnosis is potentially pernicious in two important ways. First, according to the metaphysical doctrine that undergirds Christian Science, illness is caused by such "mental," rather than physical, factors as how the person thinks about his or her bodily states. Since medical diagnosis is aimed at identifying what is wrong with the physical body, acceptance of such diagnoses could make it harder for the person to change his or her conception of the health of the body. Second, once a medical diagnosis has been rendered, it will be much harder for the Christian Scientist to retain control over the decisions concerning his or her own health or the health of his or her children. Past experience has shown, as in the case of Colin Newmark, that once physicians get a Christian Scientist patient under their influence, they will try to force him or her to follow the medical regimen rather than the Christian Science one.[20] Medical diagnosis, so it is believed, can make things worse rather than better.

The official doctrine of the Christian Science Church is to be opposed to medical diagnosis,[21] but as I have been arguing, even Mary Baker Eddy found value in medical diagnosis in some cases. It is true, though, that Eddy distinguished between those conditions that could be corrected by mechanical means and those conditions, namely diseases, that could not. And she remained opposed to diagnosis for disease, as has remained true

19. It should be noted that Mary Baker Eddy several times decried medical diagnosis for causing the very disease it seemingly diagnoses. See *Science and Health*, pp. 161 and 370.

20. I am grateful to Peggy DesAutels for helping me to see why some Christian Scientists have such a strong reaction against medical diagnosis.

21. I base this claim on various communications I have had with staff members of the central office of the Christian Science Church in Boston.

of the official Christian Science doctrine. It seems to me, though, that until diagnosis is performed, it isn't clear whether mechanical correction or medication or something even more invasive is called for medically. If removing a bowel obstruction is mechanical, as some Christian Scientists seem to believe, then it would make sense to allow, even to encourage, diagnosis when symptoms of possible bowel obstruction manifest themselves, as well as in several other cases. But Christian Scientists have by and large remained committed to refusing any form of medical practice.

III. MEDICAL AUTHORITY

Cases that involve the refusal of Christian Scientists to accept medical authority fall into two important groups: where an adult refuses treatment for himself or herself, and where a parent refuses treatment for his or her child. In both cases, the medical establishment in the United States has opposed the refusal of medical care by Christian Scientists, and individual doctors have often responded with contempt and outrage to the public position of the Christian Science Church, namely, that the power of prayer is more effective than the power of surgery and medicine. It is clear that the medical establishment has seen the refusal cases not simply as a matter of conflicting beliefs but as a struggle for authority.

In the early part of the twentieth century, medical doctors consolidated their power and tried to enlist legal authorities in enforcing some of their decisions about what was best for patients, especially in life-threatening situations. Most adult Christian Scientists, especially in recent times, have managed to avoid what they perceive as the interventionist strategies of medical doctors by simply staying clear of doctors and hospitals. Many of those who work in medical ethics have recently broken ranks with their colleagues in medicine by arguing that adult Christian Scientists should be allowed to pursue matters of health on their own terms. Indeed, three well-known medical ethicists end a recent article on this subject with these words: "The right of patients to forgo life-sustaining treatment has been well established in health law and medical ethics."[22] This change in consensus has been due to the rejection of the doctrine of paternalism over the last twenty years.[23]

Many medical doctors continue to have strong objections to those Christian Scientists who refuse treatment for themselves, but the strongest

22. Stephen H. Miles, Peter A. Singer, and Mark Siegler, "Conflicts between Patients' Wishes to Forgo Treatment and the Policies of Health Care Facilities," *New England Journal of Medicine*, 6 July 1989, 48.

23. See my essay, "Paternalism and Self-Interest," *Journal of Value Inquiry* 14, no. 4 (fall/winter 1980).

criticisms have been directed at those Christian Scientists who refuse treatment for their children. Here the issue cannot easily be settled by reference to the doctrine of paternalism, for children cannot generally consent because of their lack of autonomy.[24] The general consensus among physicians is well stated by Norman Fost: "We're interested not just in the kids who die. What we're concerned about are the hundreds and hundreds more who suffer from inadequate medical treatment."[25] Unlike the case of Christian Scientists who refuse medical care for themselves, the reaction in the medical community to the case of Christian Scientists' refusal of treatment for their children has been nearly unanimously negative.[26]

The American Academy of Pediatrics has recently been spearheading a movement to remove the religious exemption provisos to the child neglect statutes throughout the United States.[27] This campaign is fueled by the belief that Christian Scientists and Jehovah's Witnesses should be forced to subject their children to the full range of curative powers at the disposal of modern medicine. The growing involvement in these legislative matters by the AAP has come as a result of the belief that child neglect and abuse are on the rise in the United States and need to be confronted.[28] The religious exemption is seen as a major impediment to the provision of the best of health care to all American children.[29]

Medicine in the United States is a profession in at least two senses of this term.[30] It embodies better than any other profession the idea of a group of people who all profess to be bound by a commitment to a particular ideal, roughly that which is found in the Hippocratic oath. And medicine is a profession in the sense that it is an organized institution that

---

24. Of course, children vary greatly in their maturity and ability to understand complex issues, even children of roughly the same age. In any event, it is a mistake to lump all children together, treating the two-year-old in the same manner as the twelve-year-old.

25. Quoted in Ronald Munson's popular textbook *Intervention and Reflection: Basic Issues in Medical Ethics,* 4th ed. (Belmont, CA: Wadsworth Publishing Co., 1992), p. 262.

26. In surveying recent work on this topic, I found only a couple of exceptions to this statement among the dozens of essays I read. The most notable exception was Norman Gevitz's article "Christian Science Healing and the Health Care of Children."

27. See Monopoli, "Allocating the Costs of Parental Free Exercise," p. 331.

28. See Gevitz, p. 429.

29. By the end of 1993 three states, Hawaii, South Dakota, and Massachusetts, had changed their "state laws to remove language that allowed people to deny their children medical care for religious reasons. . . . the majority of states [had] language that makes criminal prosecution dificult." *New York Times,* 19 December 1993, 16.

30. For a fascinating discussion of this view see the first chapter of Eliot Freidson's excellent study *Profession of Medicine: A Study of the Sociology of Applied Knowledge* (New York: Dodd, Mead and Company, 1970).

claims a considerable amount of authority for the judgments of its members. In addition, over the last century, the medical profession in the United States has achieved the status of a virtual state-sanctioned monopoly. This has meant that the already enormous power and influence of medicine has been augmented by alliances with the legal profession.[31] This alliance is nowhere more apparent than in the Christian Science refusal cases. Nearly every medical or legal discussion of these cases has been critical of the Christian Science position.

The nearly unanimous voice of the medical profession in rejecting the Christian Science position stems from the commmon socialization of medical students in the United States. The Hippocratic oath and its "do no harm" dictum, as well as the general principle of beneficence, have been interpreted in such a way that medical students are trained to be quite aggressive in pursuing what they believe will be least harmful and most beneficial for their patients. Once a determination, or diagnosis, has been made, it is considered harmful for the patient not to acquiesce in the regimen prescribed to overcome the diagnosed illness or disease. A patient's refusal to follow the prescribed regimen is seen as a failure of the doctor, indeed a failure specifically in the sense that the aggressive pursuit of "do no harm" and patient benefit has not been fulfilled.

But there is another tradition in medicine that apparently has not been discussed as much in medical school, at least until quite recently, as has the dominant tradition I have just set out. This tradition can be traced back to Maimonides, who declared that "the physician should not treat the disease but the patient suffering from it."[32] This tradition has also found expression in the idea that physicians should treat their patients as persons.[33] At the moment I merely note that there is this alternative, which, when made part of the common medical socialization, might produce a set of attitudes and practices different from those currently dominant in modern medicine.

Nonetheless, when patients challenge the authority of their physicians, this is perceived by their physicians as an affront to their medical expertise and ultimately to their status as authorities. And at least since medicine achieved a near monopoly over matters of health in the United States, the idea that there could be multiple authorities over matters of health has been simply rejected out of hand. Medical science is conceived

31. We should not ignore the other major alignment, namely, that between medical science and the enormous segment of the economy that is connected to medicine. Hospitals, drug companies, nursing homes, hospital suppliers, etc., constitute one of the largest sources of employment and economic activity in the U.S.

32. As quoted in Emanuel Goldberger, *How Physicians Think* (Springfield, IL: Charles C. Thomas Publisher, 1965), p. ix.

33. See Paul Ramsey, *The Patient as Person* (New Haven, CT: Yale University Press, 1970).

by physicians and lawyers alike to be the only legitimate way of promoting the health of the patient. Especially when the health of children is at stake, the medical and legal communities unite to preserve the authority of medicine in matters of health, even when the members of a religious minority challenge this authority.

IV. AUTHORITY IN A PLURALISTIC WORLD

There has been a serious debate recently about the role of moral and political authority in a pluralistic world.[34] The term *authority* can be used in its "representation" sense as referring to someone who is given the ability to act or speak in behalf of another, or in its "expert" sense as referring to someone who is recognized simply to be more knowledgeable than most others in a certain domain of inquiry. One of the most important questions in the recent debate concerns whether these two senses should be merged so that those who have the most knowledge are, by that very fact, more legitimately able to act or speak in behalf of the rest of the population. In contemporary medicine, the physcian's authority in terms of expertise is often transmuted into the physician's authority in terms of legitimacy to represent the community in determining how people should behave. One variation of this transmutation occurs when a medical doctor declares that he or she should have the right to decide what is in the best interest of a patient and to mandate that the patient follow the doctor's regimen toward securing that interest.

The exercise of authority by one person over another can restrict the freedom of the other. If the person over whom authority is exercised is a mature adult human being, then such exercise of authority may be illegitimate insofar as it restricts this person's autonomy.[35] The case of authority exercised over children does not normally raise the same problems since children generally are not thought to have autonomy. Parents must be able to exercise some authority over their children in order to properly instruct and protect them. Until quite recently this parental authority was assumed to be nearly inviolable. This is a questionable assumption since not all parents have the best interest of their children at heart, and some parents are quite mistaken about what is best for their children, or are even positively malicious, just as is true of certain members of nearly every group.

Liberalism has traditionally placed very strong emphasis on individual rights to the exclusion of concern for the collective good of various groups. Various liberal theorists have talked of the rights of children, rights that are

34. For a good general discussion of the various issues involved in this debate see Richard De George, *The Nature and Limits of Authority* (Lawrence: University of Kansas Press, 1985).
35. See De George's helpful discussion of this issue in ibid., chap. 9.

somewhat weaker than those of mature adults but that are nonetheless strong enough to override the claims of various parents, families, or communities to act toward their children in ways that seem likely to lead to harm to these children.[36] Communitarians have been the most vociferous in arguing that traditional liberalism entrenches divisiveness and separateness, thereby making it difficult for groups, especially families, to achieve coherence and stability.

In pluralistic societies, there are multiple and overlapping social groups, indeed often so many groups with conflicting goals that it seems impossible to reconcile the claims of each. In such times it seems quite reasonable to focus on the individual rather than the group. But this is a mistake since often with the increase in isolation comes a loss of solidarity and an increase in the individual's sense of rootlessness and alienation, especially among members of minority groups.[37] Ethnic, linguistic, and religious groups, when they exist as minority groups within a strongly dominant culture, need some protection from the larger community, which may engulf the minority culture at any time. Even in liberal societies, minority rights—especially the rights of religious minorities—have sometimes been trampled.

Charles Taylor has recently argued that there is a version of liberalism that would not so greatly risk harm to the collective goods and identity of minority groups.

> A society with strong collective goals can be liberal, on this view, provided it is also capable of respecting diversity, especially when dealing with those who do not share its common goals; and provided that it can offer adequate safeguards for fundamental rights.[38]

The Christian Science refusal cases offer a very good testing ground of Taylor's version of liberalism since, it is often claimed, the right of children to basic levels of health is precisely what is threatened by the collective goals of the Christian Science community. In addition, the Christian Science community's cohesiveness is thought to be threatened by the possibility that the medical community could force Christian Scientists to surrender to the power of the scalpel instead of the power of prayer.

The Christian Science refusal cases are best understood mainly as involving a conflict between two communities (Christian Science and medical) rather than a conflict between two individuals (Christian Scientist

---

36. For a good selection of positions on this issue see William Aiken and Hugh LaFollette, *Whose Child? Children's Rights, Parental Authority, and State Power* (Totowa, NJ: Littlefield, Adams, 1980).

37. See my discussion of this point in chap. 2, sec. 3.

38. Charles Taylor et al., *Multiculturalism and the Politics of Recognition* (Princeton: Princeton University Press, 1992), p. 59.

parent and medical physician). The seemingly irreconcilable positions in these cases are due to conflicting worldviews and conflicting conceptions of what counts as authoritative in matters of health rather than mere disagreement about what should be done for a particular child. Physicians and Christian Scientists act as if much more were at stake than merely the health of a particular child. Indeed, Christian Scientists often talk as if the very future of their church were hanging in the balance; and physicians often talk as if the very future of medical progress were at stake. This is why I think the issue is best addressed as a conflict of groups rather than as a conflict of individuals.[39]

The key question here is not only whether the physical health of a child is a fundamental right that should be given priority over such community goods as group cohesiveness, but also whether the medical community should be given exclusive purview in determining what is best for securing that right. The difficulty is that the Christian Science and medical communities give very different, and seemingly incompatible, accounts of what is the best method to secure health. Is this sociopolitical clash of communities subject to compromise, or must one community "win out," even in a pluralistic society? Taylor has claimed that "liberalism is not a possible meeting ground for all cultures, but is the political expression of one range of cultures, and quite incompatible with other ranges."[40]

Taylor is worried that even in a very diverse pluralistic society, some groups may act in such a disruptive manner that they jeopardize the stability and coherence of the larger community. On this view, not all forms of authority can be open to challenge. Some limits must be placed, especially where the overall community's survival is at stake or where fundamental rights of individuals are threatened. His view is that only a certain range of cultural diversity can be sustained, and hence only certain minority cultures can be tolerated, in a particular political society. The range of toleration should be determined by whether any fundamental rights of individuals or groups are likely to be violated by a minority culture that is seeking full recognition and respect within the larger community.

I have argued in a similar vein that some sort of compromise between liberalism and communitarianism is needed.[41] I draw a distinction not only between fundamental and nonfundamental individual rights but also between systematic and occasional violation of these rights. Such a distinction is necessary since there are many actions that could jeopardize the

---

39. Indeed, if one looks to the rank and file of these groups, quite a bit of sympathy is voiced for the other. But when one looks to the leadership of these groups, that is, to those who speak for the groups themselves, the situation looks hopeless.

40. Taylor et al., p. 62.

41. See the last chapter of May, *Sharing Responsibility*.

fundamental rights of individuals which hardly anyone would think constituted grounds for excluding the group that so jeopardized these rights.
Consider, for example, the suspension of fundamental rights during a state
of emergency. Arguably, the curtailment of a person's rights to free speech
or press, for instance, would normally be seen as a violation of fundamental individual rights. But this would not be sufficient to preclude this action
if the emergency were severe enough.

It must be kept in mind that most cultures risk the occasional violation
of some fundamental rights. What normally cannot be tolerated is the systematic violation by a minority culture of a fundamental right of the members of the larger community. The Christian Science refusal cases do not
show such systematic violation of fundamental rights. In any event, the
religious liberty of the members of these groups is of very high value and in
a pluralistic society should be given strong weight. Of course, this is not to
say, as some Christian Scientists have argued, that this issue can be decided
on grounds of religious freedom alone.

V. SEEKING A COMPROMISE

Today the medical community and the Christian Science community continue to argue that all Christian Science refusal cases be treated alike. According to the American Academy of Pediatrics, neither Robyn Twitchell's
nor Colin Newmark's parents should be allowed to refuse to accept medical authority. The position expressed by the AAP is hard to reconcile with
the features of a pluralistic society. While it is important to protect fundamental rights, Christian Science is not alone in occasionally jeopardizing
the fundamental rights of individuals. But it is relatively alone in discouraging its members from seeking medical diagnoses. Such a stance may be a
systematic risk to the fundamental rights of children. But it is not clear that
Christian Scientists as a group should, on their own principles, discourage
diagnosis. Indeed, the bylaws of the Christian Science Church state rather
clearly that if "a member of this Church has a patient whom he does not
heal, and whose case he cannot fully diagnose, he may consult with an
M.D. on the anatomy involved."[42]

The compromise I propose involves the following elements. Medical
science should be more attuned to the whole person who is the patient,
especially in non-life-threatening situations, and hence should be open to
nonstandard approaches to health. Christian Science should be more open
to the diagnostic services of medical science, so that it can be ascertained

42. In Mary Baker Eddy, *Church Manual of the First Church of Christ Scientist, in Boston,
Mass.* (1895; reprint, Boston: First Church of Christ Scientist, 1936), p. 47. Some Christian
Scientists also cite *Science and Health,* p. 444, where Mary Baker Eddy says that one may
temporarily take a medical approach to healing.

what type of spiritual healing is needed, and so that informed decisions can be made about when to consider medical help, especially in life-threatening situations. For both of these to occur, the socialization practices of the medical and Christian Science communities must be changed so that their members do not see themselves to be in opposition to each other. Medical professionals should be more open to the possibility that there are at least some aspects of health that are not their sole purview. Christian Scientists should be more open to the possibility (seemingly admitted by Mary Baker Eddy) that there are aspects of health that are best dealt with by material (at least "mechanical") means.

This approach to resolving, at least temporarily, the stalemate between the Christian Science community and the medical community is more communitarian than liberal, since I remain committed to maintaining the coherence of these two communities.[43] The compromise I propose is meant to be respectful to both communities. This is not to say that all of the members of the Christian Science and medical communities will find my approach acceptable. Indeed, I suspect that many will reject it. But this just points out to what extent this is a compromise and not a consensus.

One standard way to think about the divide between liberalism and communitarianism is to think that liberals believe in compromise and communitarians believe in consensus. One of the paradigms of communitarianism is the Quaker meeting, and one of the paradigms of liberalism is deliberations in Congress. Yet for consensus to be achieved in the Quaker meeting, many people will have to accept a compromise; and in Congress, the deliberative compromises often center on the common good. In light of these paradigms, I wish to propose that in pluralistic societies the move toward consensus sometimes denies or submerges differences among groups, and in this sense consensus runs contrary to communitarianism. Some compromises, on the other hand, really do leave group identities intact, since here both parties to a dispute temporarily must give a bit so as to achieve some higher social good.

The Christian Science refusal cases illustrate well the need to think in terms of compromise as well as consensus when conflicts arise between multiple authorities in a pluralistic society.[44] The rights of children, the authority of medicine, and the religious freedom of Christian Scientists must all be considered and balanced against each other. None of these factors should be

43. One may dispute my use of the term "medical community." It is not completely clear that there is a coherent community here, especially when one reflects on recent disputes between nurses and physicians about the future of health care. I am grateful to Bill McBride for pointing this out to me. I have in mind the community of physicians, who have, as I have said, shown a surprising coherence on this issue.

44. See Martin Benjamin, *Splitting the Difference: Compromise and Integrity in Ethics and Politics* (Lawrence: University of Kansas Press, 1990).

considered overriding. Even a temporary solution to this problem will only occur when the Christian Science and medical communities recognize that there are both Colin Newmarks, who may do better without medical intervention, and Robyn Twitchells, who may do better with that intervention.

My proposed compromise is likely to occur only when the medical community becomes willing to give Christian Scientists some room to consider the results of diagnostic testing without worrying that some doctor has already contacted a public prosecutor to force the Christian Scientists to accept proposed medical care. In addition, this change is likely to occur only when the Christian Science community stops discouraging its members from seeking medical diagnoses and, in life-threatening cases, medical care. Just as the socialization practices of the medical community need to change so that its members are more open to the Christian Science community, so the socialization practices of the Christian Science community need to change so that its members are more open to the medical community. In the remainder of this chapter I will consider three objections that could be raised against my view. In so doing I will try to make more explicit the philosophical assumptions and reasonings that led me to propose the compromise.

Let us first consider the most serious problem with my proposed compromise. If there really is a metaphysical dispute separating the medical and Christian science communities, then neither side will be able to compromise without somehow giving in to the other side. If Christian Scientists really believe that metaphysically medicine cannot cure disease and that diagnosis somehow makes disease worse, then acknowledging that diagnosis is a good thing, or at least not something to be condemned, would cause Christian Scientists to give up on a major part of their worldview. And if medical scientists really believe that prayer can never cure and that failure to diagnose and treat medically is tantamount to child neglect, then acknowledging that Christian Scientists should be allowed to pursue prayer rather than medical treatment would cause medical scientists to give up on a major part of their worldview.[45]

This first objection strikes at the very heart of my proposal, for it was my intent to show that neither party to this dispute would have to give up on its worldview in reaching a compromise. I argued that Christian Scientists as far back as their founder, Mary Baker Eddy, have acknowledged the legitimacy of certain forms of medical treatment. And I argued that medical scientists have not been committed to pursuing physical health at the expense of the mental well-being of the patient. If I am right about this, then the

45. I am grateful to Hamner Hill for forcefully pushing this objection in a commentary he presented on an earlier version of this chapter at the 1994 AMINTAPHIL meetings in Charleston.

worldviews, while conflicting on many points, are not completely at odds with each other. The key philosophical assumption that I make throughout this chapter is that we should be respectful of the integrity of these communities. But being respectful does not mean allowing each community to set unreasonable demands on its members or on nonmembers. In deeply pluralistic settings, it is important not to let one community hold the members of another hostage over issues that are not of central concern.

This brings me to a second objection. It could be objected that Christian Scientists are not being reasonable about any of this since they refuse to discuss the evidence upon which their claims for the power of prayer are based. Margaret Battin has argued at great length that Christian Scientists have tried to convince their members that the unexamined anecdotal evidence of cures of church members based on prayer rather than medicine is more important than the enormous amount of statistically significant data that modern medical science has amassed showing the curative power of medicine.[46] The fact that the Christian Science leadership has consistently refused to subject its claims about the power of prayer to critical scrutiny, in anything like a double-blind test, leads Battin to say that Christian Scientists are not deserving of respect for their views; rather, they are to be morally criticized for deluding their members.[47]

I have a lot of sympathy for some of what Battin says. It strikes me that the evidence cited by Christian Scientists is at best mushy. This is one reason I urged that they should at least consider medical diagnosis as a kind of second opinion about how to cure their children. The evidence supporting medicine's curative powers seems as overwhelming to me as it does to Battin. Yet it is also undeniable that in many cases medical science cannot tell us what is the best strategy for curing a particular child. This is why cases such as the Newmark case should not be treated the same way as the Twitchell case. So, while I support the claim that Christian Scientists should be more open to testing the claims of efficacy of their curative methods, I do not think that their failure to do so means that they should be forced to accept medical authority in all cases. And I do not think that we should fail to respect this community even if it continues to resist critical scrutiny of its claims and methods of cure.

We now arrive at the third objection. It could be claimed that I have

46. See Margaret Battin, *Ethics in the Sanctuary* (New Haven, CT: Yale University Press, 1990). I am also grateful for the commentary Battin provided on an earlier version of this chapter at the 1994 AMINTAPHIL meetings in Charleston.

47. A similar point was made by Kenneth Kipnis in his commentary on an earlier version of this chapter presented at the 1994 AMINTAPHIL meetings in Charleston. Kipnis also raises serious questions about my construal of the legal issues, to which I will not here respond.

smuggled a major epistemological premise into this chapter. By construing the issue as one concerning conflicting perspectives or worldviews, where each struggles for domination over the other, I have abandoned the possibility that there is a truth of the matter, some criterion by which we could independently assess these viewpoints and find them wanting. Calling the positions of Christian Science and medicine "perspectives" seems to suggest that each has equal standing, and that to deny such equal standing is to fail to display equal respect for them. Conflicts between perspectives are seemingly claimed to be inevitable and unresolvable. Yet no argument is provided for why we should adopt this epistemological standpoint.[48]

It is true that I am at a loss in attempting to find an objective procedure that would tell us how to assess the Christian Scientist's claims about the power of prayer. But I am not espousing a cultural perspectivalism. There are certain statements that seem relatively uncontroversial, such as that it would have taken a very simple operation to remove the bowel obstruction from Robyn Twitchell, and hence to save his life. But there are other statements, such as that Robyn's life could also have been saved if people had prayed hard enough for him, that I would be hard pressed to deny even though I have a hard time believing them. I do not think that anyone really knows the truth about the power of prayer. If I am right, then it behooves us to adjust our laws so that we do not construct a presumption against those who rely on prayer rather than medicine. In a pluralistic democracy, especially where the truth of the matter is reasonably contested, laws should not be biased in favor of only one of two possible perspectives.[49]

48. This objection was raised, in private correspondence, by Kenneth Winston.

49. I am grateful to Peggy DesAutels for first stimulating my interest in this topic and for patiently explaining some of the intricacies of the Christian Science position. She, of course, is not responsible for any misconstruals of the Christian Science position that remain.

10

SCIENTIFIC WHISTLE-BLOWING AND

PROFESSIONAL SOLIDARITY

There is an increasing number of reported incidents of scientific fraud and deception within large research teams in universities, as well as in for-profit business corporations.[1] In addition, popular attention has increasingly been focused on cases of scientists who seemingly care more about research dollars than the truth of their research findings. This chapter was inspired by these recent cases, which call out for a reconsideration of our understanding of what professionals can and should do when faced with misconduct by their fellow professionals. In what follows, I will focus my discussion on whistle-blowing as the most difficult problem faced by socially responsive professional scientists.[2] The difficulty comes from the fact that scientific whistle-blowers must, on the one hand, risk personal loss and, on the other hand, break ranks with their communities and oppose their colleagues, seemingly undermining solidarity within those communities. Since the first of these problems was covered in a general way in chapter 6, in the present chapter I will focus mainly on the latter problem.

I will first describe some of the key considerations in scientific whistle-blowing. In the second section, I take up the difficult problem of the risk to solidarity and loyalty posed by whistle-blowing. In the third section, I nonetheless argue that it is professional communities rather than institu-

1. See Patricia K. Woolf, "Accountability and Responsibility in Research," *Journal of Business Ethics* 10 (August 1991).

2. One of the best collections of essays on this topic was published under the title *Beyond Whistleblowing*, edited by Vivian Weil for the Center for the Study of Ethics in the Professions at the Illinois Institute of Technology, 1983. This volume was based on a conference where many spoke eloquently about the problem of whistle-blowing in engineering and science, even though the volume's title may be seen, mistakenly, to imply that whistle-blowing is not an important ethical issue.

tional organizations that should protect and encourage whistle-blowing in science and other fields. In the final section, I draw some general conclusions about whistle-blowing based on my earlier reconceptualizations of integrity, solidarity, authority, socialization, and responsibility. These final remarks will help explain why professional ethics should focus on institutions, communities, and other social groups in understanding social and professional responsibility.

I. THE PROBLEM OF WHISTLE-BLOWING IN SCIENCE

Scientific whistle-blowing poses special problems in professional ethics. Generally whistle-blowing is defined as an act taken to prevent harmful behavior by a firm or organization.[3] For example, Gene James defines whistle-blowing as "an attempt by a member or former member of an organization to bring illegal or socially harmful activities of the organization to the attention of the public."[4] But whistle-blowing in science is rarely directed at firms or organizations. Rather, it is directed at the potentially harmful behavior of the whistle-blower's scientific colleagues. Scientific whistle-blowing involves the attempt by one scientist to bring information before the public about the illegal or socially harmful activities of a fellow scientist. Like most forms of whistle-blowing, scientific whistle-blowing is often an act of courage. But scientific whistle-blowing is unlike most other forms of whistle-blowing in that the whistle-blower breaks ranks with a member of his or her professional community as well as with those who hold positions of authority in the organization that employs the whistle-blower. For this reason it is often seen as an act of disloyalty both to one's colleagues and to one's employing organization.

Let us consider a very recent case of scientific fraud that occurred at a major medical college, and the attempts to expose it by a fellow member of this medical community, described in the following quotation from an investigative report.

> The lead researcher was Charles D. Bluestone, director of the University (of Pittsburgh's) Department of Pediatric Otolaryngology. Dr. Bluestone had strongly supported the routine use of antibiotics to treat acute infections of the middle ear. In 1987, however, Erdem I. Cantekin, who was then director of Dr. Bluestone's department, re-

---

3. See Marian V. Heacock and Gail W. McGee, "Whistleblowing: An Ethical Issue in Organizational and Human Behavior," *Business and Professional Ethics Journal* 6, no. 4 (winter 1987).

4. Gene G. James, "Whistle Blowing: Its Nature and Justification," *Philosophy in Context* 10 (1980): 99.

vealed that Dr. Bluestone had received about $500,000 a year in honoraria from drug companies, at the same time he was studying how effective the antibiotics were. He showed that Dr. Bluestone had not reported in his grant application to the NIH that he was receiving that money. He also charged that Dr. Bluestone had slanted his results to prove that the antibiotics were effective. Dr. Cantekin, in his own publication and using the same data, showed that the antibiotics did not help. The University of Pittsburgh, however, ignored the allegations against Dr. Bluestone and instead punished Dr. Cantekin. The Weiss report says the university "broke into Dr. Cantekin's office, packed his belongings, and moved them to the Giant Eagle Supermarket." The university also attempted to remove his tenure, froze his salary, and barred him from conducting research and teaching classes.[5]

This case is a classic example of what scientists fear may be the consequences if they blow the whistle on a fellow scientist.

The case described above occurred at the University of Pittsburgh, shortly after another University of Pittsburgh scientist became the first American scientist convicted in a criminal court for scientific fraud.[6] Yet university officials nonetheless sided so strongly against the whistle-blowing scientist that his professional career has been effectively ruined. The message sent to fledgling professionals is quite clear: retaliation for whistle-blowing will be swift and devastating; your supervisors will not only fail to come to your aid, more than likely they will seek to retaliate against you for doing what you thought was right. And worse yet, in many cases the profession will close ranks against whistle-blowers.

Scientists are often characterized as those who are supposed to pursue the truth as vigorously as possible. But some scientists are so focused on getting their theories into the public spotlight that they are tempted to falsify or plagiarize test results or to use morally questionable research protocols. The use of the data from the Nazi hypothermia experiments has raised the question of the limits to be placed on the scientific pursuit of truth—even though that truth may be quite beneficial—when political and moral harm may result from the pursuit of that truth.[7] There are

---

5. Stephen Burd, "Research Powerhouse under the Microscope," *Chronicle of Higher Education* 40, no. 41 (15 June 1994): A27.

6. The scientist in question was Steven Breuning, a psychologist at the University of Pittsburgh. See Alun Anderson, "First Scientific Fraud Conviction," *Nature* 335, no. 29 (September 1988): 389.

7. See Kristine Moe, "Should the Nazi Research Data Be Cited?" *Hastings Center Report,*

moral and political limits on the pursuit of scientific truth as well as on the pursuit of other professional goals. When the professional is a member of a large organization, the only way to stop certain forms of misconduct that cause harm may involve whistle-blowing.

Whistle-blowing becomes a relevant option for any scientist who finds out that her or his colleagues have engaged in scientific misconduct. The Royal College of Physicians defines scientific misconduct to include three categories:

Piracy is the deliberate exploitation of ideas from others without acknowledgement.
Plagiarism is the copying of ideas, data or text (or various combinations of the three) without permission or acknowledgement.
Fraud involves deliberate deception, usually the invention of data.[8]

While plagiarism is probably the most prevalent problem, fraud seems to be on the rise in science. Indeed, in one notorious case, a young medical scientist produced 137 articles in less than seven years, sixty of which have been determined to be fraudulent or ethically questionable.[9] Many of these cases of fraud occurred because the young scientist was not properly supervised or because other scientists were only too grateful to become coauthors of his research papers without having had to do any work on the research projects.

In scientific research, it is beginning to be recognized that moral standards need to take account of the fact that much of science is conducted by large groups rather than isolated scientists. As the *Responsible Science* study describes it:

Today, although many research groups consist of less than a dozen members, larger and more diverse research groups are becoming more common. The group members in large research teams differ in status; they include research investigators, undergraduate students, postdoctoral researchers, visiting faculty, and technicians. These individuals report, sometimes in an ill-defined manner, to a research

November/December 1984; and Mark Sheldon, "The Use of Nazi Data" (paper presented at a 1988 meeting of the Indiana Philosophical Association), as well as Sheldon's coauthored comment on Moe's essay in the *Hastings Center Report*, July/August 1989.

8. "Fraud and Misconduct in Medical Research: Causes, Investigation and Prevention," *Journal of the Royal College of Physicians of London* 25, no. 2 (April 1991).

9. Robert L. Engler et al., "Misrepresentation and Responsibility in Medical Research," *New England Journal of Medicine* 317, no. 22 (26 November 1987): 1383.

director who frequently has many more professional and institutional obligations than his or her counterpart of 20 years ago.[10]

The changing nature of research makes it especially important that the scientific community provide a haven for whistle-blowers, who are increasingly vulnerable to the vicissitudes of retaliation from various quarters within organizations that employ scientists.

The case of whistle-blowing at the University of Pittsburgh medical college illustrates the need for some kind of protection for scientific whistle-blowers. Until protection can be established for scientists against possible retaliation by organizations for doing what the scientists think is right, it is a mistake to continue to talk as if these professionals should blindly conform to professional standards. Professional associations, as well as the organizations that employ professionals, can have a profound impact on how professionals understand their moral responsibilities.[11] Fledgling scientists need to be socialized to regard whistle-blowing as an act of courage and virtue rather than an act of disloyalty.

II. CRITICAL SOLIDARITY AND SOCIALIZATION

Solidarity and socialization can often conspire to act to the detriment of the common good, as I argued in chapter 4. The case of scientific whistle-blowing provides us with an opportunity to examine in more detail how to transform those potentially detrimental factors into positive moral forces. Here is the problem: scientists are now quite reluctant to blow the whistle on fellow scientists because of a concern for them as fellow scientists, that is, as fellow members of a group with fairly strong bonds. The community of scientists, like many other professional communities, socializes its members to have great respect for each other's research programs. To blow the whistle on another scientist's research program is, then, to go against both strong feelings of solidarity and years of socialization. Such considerations should make us wonder about the moral value of these social factors.

Solidarity and socialization may result in negative as well as positive moral value. Throughout this book I have argued that they are factors that we need to take into account for any realistic view of morality. Sometimes what needs to happen is that solidarity is disrupted and socialization is

10. National Academy of Sciences, National Academy of Engineering, and Institute of Medicine, *Responsible Science: Ensuring the Integrity of the Research Process,* vol. 1, p. 70. This report was based on a two-year study by a very prestigious panel of experts who were charged to examine the incidence of misconduct in scientific research.

11. See May, "Professional Actions and the Liabilities of Professional Associations: ASME vs. Hydrolevel Corp."

changed, resulting in a refocused solidarity within a particular community. This seems to be the case in many professional communities today, not the least of which is the scientific community. Solidarity and socialization can go wrong when they are not critically pursued. By this I mean that solidarity, like loyalty, can often be blind; and socialization, like indoctrination, can stifle rather than foster critical appreciation of changing circumstances and risks of harm. I will say more about this momentarily.

One medical researcher who questioned various aspects of clinical trials run by a colleague said that she tried initially to voice her concerns in a constructive way within the organization she worked for. But instead of getting significant uptake from her superiors, she was told to remain loyal to the organization and to her fellow scientists. She articulates in the following account the incident that caused her to decide to blow the whistle.

> I was on the spot. I had to get with it or get out. I hated that. I was cornered. There was no compromise. Nobody from higher up came and said, "Why don't we do that or do this." They were just riding roughshod over me. I always like to feel I'm a person, not a cog in a machine.[12]

Solidarity and socialization are morally problematic when they make a member of a group feel willing to remain an anonymous cog in a large institution or community regardless of the misconduct that she or he believes is being perpetrated by colleagues. Seeing oneself as a responsive professional involves deciding for oneself whether one's colleagues are committing professional misconduct, and then, if they are, taking a stand that risks disrupting the calm, anonymous solidarity of one's professional group.

An ethic of responsibility is well suited to those who must decide what to do in the face of a professional colleague's misconduct. Anyone faced with such a predicament needs to be sensitive to the peculiarities of context, especially to such issues as

Who is likely to be harmed if the misconduct is left unpublicized?
Is one's judgment about the misconduct prejudiced by a dislike for the perpetrator?
How severe are the repercussions likely to be on the person who blows the whistle?
If there is significant likelihood that whistle-blowing will bring harm to the

---

12. The medical researcher's name is Dr. Grace Pierce and she worked for Ortho Pharmaceutical Corporation in the 1970s. This case is described in Myron Glazer, "Ten Whistleblowers and How They Fared," *Hastings Center Report* 13, no. 6 (December 1983): 35.

perpetrator's reputation or to the employing organization, is there some other way to stop the socially harmful practices?

Cases of whistle-blowing are hardly ever easy to adjudicate, and this is why most codes of professional conduct, which are based on an ethic of obligation or duty, are silent about whistle-blowing.

After a professional scientist has determined that harm will result from a particular practice, he or she must then decide whether the personal risks involved in publicly disclosing the morally questionable practice are worth it. If it is serious enough to warrant whistle-blowing, then the rest of the professional community becomes very important. Unfortunately, other professionals often see the whistle-blowing professional as a threat to the profession. As a result, it is rare for the whistle-blowing professional to receive support. But, as the *Responsible Science* study concludes, "Serious and considered whistle-blowing is an act of courage that should be supported by the entire research community."[13] In those cases where a professional scientist believes that the potential harm of a colleague's professional misconduct is quite serious, it is very important that the scientist be assured of the support of his or her scientific community so as to feel motivated to blow the whistle on the misconduct in question.

Professional solidarity and socialization can be a two-edged sword. It can create professional groups that feel above the laws and norms of the larger society, but it can also act as a motivational spur to altruism and against self-interest in that larger society. As professional communities gain in strength, they will probably manifest a bit of each of these tendencies of professional solidarity. Socialization practices in professional communities need to encourage their members to be more responsive to that dimension of the common good which their codes hold up as ideals of the profession. Solidarity enhances morality only when it is a critical solidarity, one based not on blind loyalty but on the consideration of context and circumstance that an ethic of responsibility would dictate. The critical dimension will provide a tool that I hope will aid in accentuating the more positive aspects of solidarity in professional communities. I next turn to a discussion of the use of solidarity as the most efficacious way for scientists and other professionals to protect themselves from retaliation before drawing some more general conclusions.

III. PROTECTING WHISTLE-BLOWERS

In this section I will argue that the best source of protection for whistle-blowers is the professional community of which they are members, not the

13. *Responsible Science*, vol. 1, p. 154, recommendation 11.

institutional organizations for which they work. In the case of the University of Pittsburgh medical college discussed above, the university was probably motivated by what was most profitable for itself. This meant attempting to keep a lid on the problem of scientific fraud so that it did not tarnish the university's image and cause its other scientific programs to come under scrutiny as well.[14] The research university is a highly bureaucratic institution that is ill-equipped to act in a way that is supportive of scientific whistle-blowers, who will undoubtedly disrupt the even functioning of the institution. Universities and other large organizations are not set up to put the interests of the larger community ahead of short-term gain for themselves. Organizational institutions will provide, at best, a weak protection for whistle-blowers.

Professional communities can provide strong support for whistle-blowing because the whistle-blower can be seen to epitomize all that is valuable about the profession, and what separates the profession from other institutions. The ideals expressed by most professions in their codes of professional conduct (such as serving interests of safety, justice, health) would be given real strength if the profession were willing to support those of its members who, in the name of these ideals, blow the whistle on professional misconduct by their colleagues. The often flagging public confidence in scientists, as well as in doctors, lawyers, and engineers, could be greatly bolstered if the public were to come to believe that strong professional associations would support their whistle-blowing members. This is especially apparent in those cases where the member blows the whistle because of a concern for public safety or welfare. Professional communities that offer moral support to their whistle-blowing members will send a clear message about the sincerity of their vaunted commitment to serve goals such as health, safety, justice, and truth—goals that will be recognized as quite different from the profit-oriented goals espoused by most of the employing organizations, which often cause them to retaliate against, rather than support, whistle-blowers.

In contrast to my view, Warren Schmaus has argued that it is a mistake to let professional associations police their own members.[15] He worries that professional societies would have a "conservative, inhibiting effect on conceptual innovation in science" if they were allowed to police their own members' misconduct, since they would tend to favor those members who

14. See Burd, "Research Powerhouse Under the Microscope," p. A24, where an unnamed government investigator is quoted as suggesting this analysis of the case.

15. Warren Schmaus, "An Analysis of Fraud and Misconduct in Science," in *Project on Scientific Fraud and Misconduct*, AAAS-ABA National Conference of Lawyers and Scientists (Washington, DC: AAAS, 1988), p. 103.

were well established and to disfavor those newer, less orthodox members. This is indeed quite a reasonable worry. It seems reasonable to think that most long-standing communities will favor those who have most contributed to the community. Schmaus seems to think that professional societies will lack the kind of objectivity needed in cases such as whistle-blowing, and instead proposes that whistle-blowing be enforced by the granting agencies upon which universities and businesses depend to support their research programs.

Schmaus is right to worry about the possible biases that exist within professional communities. However, the role that I have urged for them is not as controversial as allowing them to police their own members. I have merely called for them to offer moral support to their members who engage in whistle-blowing by protecting them from retaliation. It seems to me that there are no better avenues open to us for seeking this protection.[16] Granting agencies are controlled either by governments or by private corporations, both of which are bureaucracies that would have potentially strong biases favoring the existing status quo. Professional communities at least have a strong vested interest in the appearance of socially responsible activity on the part of their members that would seem to call for protecting their members against profit-oriented pressure.

Another serious objection to my proposal is that false accusations sometimes occur in cases of whistle-blowing, perhaps based on rivalries among competing scientists, and professional associations are not likely to be able to adjudicate these conflicts. Schmaus worries that in cases of this sort, the most senior or best-known rival will be favored by the professional association. It is also possible that a vigilant professional association would fail to detect false accusations of scientific wrongdoing in its zealous desire to appear to be supportive of whistle-blowers. Since both parties in scientific whistle-blowing cases are normally members of the same professional community, it will always be difficult for the professional association to side with one over the other of its own members.

These problems are serious, most especially because solidarity among professionals will often make it harder rather than easier to resolve disputes within the professional community. But as I argued earlier, professional as-

16. For a very good discussion of why legal protection of whistle-blowers is likely to be ineffective see Michael Davis, "Avoiding the Tragedy of Whistleblowing," *Business and Professional Ethics Journal* 8, no. 4 (winter 1989). Davis favors having a committee in every organization that "receives complaints about unethical behavior" and protects the anonymity of whistle-blowers. While I have no major conceptual complaint with this proposal, it seems less likely to be implemented, in the tens of thousands of organizations in question, than my proposal. Also see the discussion of this point in Michael Bayles, *Professional Ethics* (Belmont, CA: Wadsworth Publishing Co., 1981), pp. 140–1.

sociations need to instill a critical solidarity in their members. This means that these communities should not blindly side with one member over another because the one member is better known or has made more of a contribution to the community than the other. As I have tried to indicate, it is of the utmost importance for the maintenance of public trust in a professional community that its solidarity and socialization practices be seen as advancing the ideals of the profession, especially the ideals of service to the larger community.

It may seem that a scientific community could be hurt by continuing to support whistle-blowers who expose the misconduct of more and more of its members. Such increased public attention to the "rotten apples" of a profession may create a negative image in the public's mind of the profession at large. But as I have argued, scientific communities have quite a bit to gain by letting the public know that public service really is the highest aim of their profession. Such a public perception would offset any public perception that there are some members of the profession who misbehave, just as is true in any other stratum of society. Despite the problems with relying on them to protect whistle-blowers, professional communities remain the best and most likely source of moral support for whistle-blowers in science and many other professional fields. Let us turn finally to a reconsideration of some of the main themes developed in previous chapters to add more support to this conclusion.

IV. CONCLUDING REMARKS

As I argued in chapters 2 and 6, there are good reasons for professionals to try to restructure their groups so that they can achieve greater solidarity. Professionals are no longer predominantly their own bosses; they are increasingly supervised by managers of large organizations who are not members of their profession. This is nowhere better seen than in the scientific community, where teams of scientists work according to the division of labor for large organizations such as universities, hospitals, and business corporations. The dilemmas faced by professionals are often based on the opposition between professional values and organizational values. Such conflicts are increasingly discussed as one of the leading problems for professionals.[17]

Scientists and doctors identify themselves to a very great extent as sci-

---

17. See Robert W. Cooper and Garry L. Frank, "Professionals in Business: Where Do They Look for Help in Dealing with Ethical Issues," *Business and Professional Ethics Journal* 11, no. 2 (summer 1992). In this study the authors report that "simply not being pressured to compromise their own ethical values and standards by their immediate boss or the company environment/culture tends to be the way business can best help them in their efforts to behave ethically."

entists and doctors, even in their off-duty hours.[18] But they generally do not feel motivated to go to one another's aid. Their limited participant perspective has not allowed them to achieve solidarity. The lesson to be learned from professionals such as scientists and doctors is that even local solidarity is often very difficult to achieve.[19] But without that solidarity, there will be little protection for those professionals who try to act in the community interest to prevent or expose the harmful practices of fellow professionals. It is becoming increasingly clear that scientific communities need to protect their members who blow the whistle. This must start with a change in the socialization practices of scientists.[20]

As I argued in chapter 1, moral integrity is best understood as involving mature development over time, not necessarily unshakable commitment to the same principles over a lifetime. The moral integrity of scientists should correspondingly involve a commitment to a certain process of service, not necessarily to any particular rule or principle. The goal of serving the public that all professionals espouse should make professionals especially attuned to the idea of sharing responsibility for harms perpetrated by members of their communities. Of crucial importance to my communitarian, critical-theoretic approach to professional ethics is the idea that as members of various groups, people participate in forms of life that affect their responsibilities. The socially responsive scientist will recognize that his or her responsibilities sometimes involve whistle-blowing or support for whistle-blowers.

As I argued in chapter 2, individuals are able to form attitudes that are based on an understanding of the interests of a group as opposed to the interests of the individual members of a group. It is the formation of consensus that allows for the cohesiveness of a group, and such a consensus is reached through the mediation of various rituals and institutions that "socialize" individuals into the group.[21] The rituals create a sense of solidarity

18. In my daughter's preschool, a printed list of parents' names and phone numbers was circulated. One of the parents felt it important that his name be listed follwed by "M.D." It seems that he could not identify himself merely as a parent, but only as a doctor who was a parent.

19. Of course, another lesson may be that we are better off rather than worse off because already highly powerful groups such as doctors do not have solidarity since, if they did, they would be even more powerful. I have addressed this point in the previous chapter, "Challenging Medical Authority," sec. 1, "Two Christian Science Refusal Cases."

20. For a very good history of how the medical community has historically socialized its members concerning conflict-of-interest problems, see Marc C. Rodwin, "The Organized American Medical Profession's Response to Financial Conflicts of Interest," *The Millbank Quarterly* 70, no. 4 (1992).

21. See Habermas, *Theory of Communicative Action*, vol. 2, pp. 70–1. See also Habermas, "Individuation through Socialization: On George Herbert Mead's Theory of Subjectivity," in

among the members of a group, and other rituals stabilize and instill group identity in successive generations of group members. In the scientific community, a new tradition of protection for whistle-blowers would stabilize the group in important ways, both in terms of its own self-perceptions and in terms of how that community is perceived by the wider community.

As I noted in chapter 3, it is interesting that Durkheim, in examining many of the same issues I have examined, employs the term *conscience collectif*, which can be translated into English as either collective consciousness or collective conscience.[22] His use of this term shows that Durkheim meant for collective consciousness of professional groups and others to have a strong moral dimension. This is because a group needs to have a certain amount of moral authority to provide guidance for its members, and that authority is achieved through a consensus or shared consciousness about the group's goals. In the case of the scientific community, support for whistle-blowers would clearly indicate that the group's solidarity is not merely an egoistic feature of the group but a moral feature based on its larger goal of serving the public.

In chapter 4, I drew on the work of communitarians and critical social theorists in an attempt to provide a basis for a critique of certain methods and goals of bureaucratic socialization. Professional socialization should be sensitive to the pitfalls of other forms of institutional socialization and should remain committed to the kinds of personal, face-to-face educational processes that stress the importance of being socially responsive. Because of the community-oriented nature of professional life, professional socialization is the key consideration in any attempt to change the ethical practices of any professional group, such as scientists or doctors. But with changes in professional socialization should also come moral support for those who risk retaliation by acting on the ideals which the professional community values.

As I argued in the first half of this book, especially in chapter 5, moral integrity and responsibility should not be conceived as if they existed in a vacuum. Considerations of solidarity, socialization, and collective consciousness need to be considered as more than mere background factors against which ethical judgments are made. Rather, these social factors are integral to any adequate and realistic conception of the moral life. Social factors can both enhance and limit the moral domain. Without changes in

---

Postmetaphysical Thinking, trans. William Mark Hohengarten (Cambridge, MA: MIT Press, 1992).

22. In addition to the works cited in earlier chapters, also see the recently republished work by Emile Durkheim, *Professional Ethics and Civic Morals,* trans. Cornelia Brookfield (New York: Routledge, 1992).

patterns of professional solidarity and socialization, it is unreasonable to expect scientists to adopt inflated conceptions of integrity and responsibility.

Throughout the second half of this book, I have tried to provide a group-oriented picture of professional ethics that is informed by the insight that communities and institutions, as well as other social groups, affect both the responsiveness and the responsibility of professionals. The existence of professional communities means that the members share responsibility for what their fellow community members do,[23] and this sharing of responsibility increases responsibility for, rather than shields the members of professional communities from, the practices of the profession, especially those practices that risk harm to those outside the professional community. Science, medicine, engineering, law, and other professions should more adequately reflect the shared values of the population at large.[24] In this vein, I have presented a model of professional responsibility that does not see social interaction as a battlefield between isolated, irreconcilable interests. A progressive communitarian perspective on social theory and professional ethics, infused by considerations from liberalism and critical theory, will capture both aspects of a responsive self: as passive recipient and active participant in its social milieu.

23. See Mike W. Martin, "Whistleblowing: Professionalism, Personal Life, and Shared Responsibility for Safety in Engineering," *Business and Professional Ethics Journal* 11, no. 2 (summer 1992).

24. See Habermas, "Law and Morality"; and Habermas, *Moral Consciousness and Communicative Action.*

Aiken, William, and Hugh LaFollette. *Whose Child? Children's Rights, Parental Authority, and State Power.* Totowa, NJ: Littlefield, Adams, 1980.

Ake, Claude, "The African Context of Human Rights." In *Applied Ethics: A Multicultural Approach,* edited by Larry May and Shari Sharratt (Englewood Cliffs, NJ: Prentice-Hall, 1994). Originally published in *Africa Today* 34, no. 142 (1987): 5–13.

Anderson, Alun. "First Scientific Fraud Conviction." *Nature* 335, no. 29 (September 1988): 389.

An-Na'im, Abdullahi Ahmed. "Islam, Islamic Law and the Dilemma of Cultural Legitimacy for Universal Human Rights." In *Applied Ethics: A Multicultural Approach,* edited by Larry May and Shari Sharratt (Englewood Cliffs, NJ: Prentice-Hall, 1994). Originally published in *Asian Perspectives on Human Rights,* edited by Claude E. Welch and Virginia Leary, pp. 31–55. Boulder, CO: Westview Press, 1990.

Arendt, Hannah. *Eichmann in Jerusalem.* Rev. ed. New York: Viking Press, 1964.

———. *The Human Condition.* Chicago: The University of Chicago Press, 1958.

———. *The Life of the Mind.* New York: Harcourt Brace Jovanovich, 1977.

———. "Organized Guilt and Universal Responsibility." In *Collective Responsibility,* edited by Larry May and Stacey Hoffman. Savage, MD: Rowman and Littlefield, 1991. Originally published in *Jewish Frontier,* 1948.

———. *The Origins of Totalitarianism.* New York: Harcourt Brace, 1951.

———. "Thinking and Moral Considerations." *Social Research* 38, no. 3 (autumn 1971): 417–46.

Arrow, Kenneth. "Gifts and Exchanges." *Philosophy and Public Affairs* 1, no. 4 (summer 1972): 343–62.

Bar-on, A. Zvie. "Measuring Responsibility." In *Collective Responsibility,* edited by Larry May and Stacey Hoffman. Savage, MD: Rowman & Littlefield, 1991. Originally published in *Philosophical Forum* 16, nos. 1–2 (fall/winter 1984–85): 95–109.

Barnes, L. W. C. S. *The Changing Stance of the Professional Employee.* Kingston, Canada: Industrial Relations Centre, 1975.

Baron, Lawrence. "The Dutchness of Dutch Rescuers: The National Dimension of Altruism." In *Embracing the Other,* edited by Pearl Oliner, Samuel P. Oliner, Lawrence Baron, Lawrence Blum, Dennis Krebs, and M. Zuzanne Smolenska, pp. 306–27. New York: New York University Press, 1992.

Battin, Margaret. *Ethics in the Sanctuary.* New Haven, CT: Yale University Press, 1990.

Bayles, Michael. *Professional Ethics.* Belmont, CA: Wadsworth Publishing Co., 1981.

Baynes, Kenneth. *The Normative Grounds of Social Criticism.* Albany: State University of New York Press, 1992.

Blum, Lawrence. *Moral Perception and Particularity.* Cambridge: Cambridge University Press, 1994.

Benhabib, Seyla. *Situating the Self.* New York: Routledge, 1992.

Benjamin, Martin. *Splitting the Difference: Compromise and Integrity in Ethics and Politics.* Lawrence: University of Kansas Press, 1990.

Black's Law Dictionary. 5th ed. St. Paul, MN: West Publishing Co., 1979.

Bohman, James. *New Philosophy of Social Science.* Cambridge, MA: MIT Press, 1991.

Bouldin, Patrick. "Case Note on Newmark v. Williams." *Journal of Family Law* 30 (1991–2): 673–81.

Bourdieu, Pierre. *Distinction: A Social Critique of the Judgment of Taste.* Translated by Richard Nice. Cambridge, MA: Harvard University Press, 1984.

Bratman, Michael. "Shared Intention." *Ethics* 104, no. 1 (October 1993): 97–113.

Buchanan, Allen E. "Assessing the Communitarian Critique of Liberalism." *Ethics* 99 (July 1989): 852–82.

Burd, Stephen. "Research Powerhouse under the Microscope." *Chronicle of Higher Education* 40, no. 41 (15 June 1994): A24–A27.

Butler, Keith. "The Moral Status of Smoking." *Social Theory and Practice* 19, no. 1 (spring 1993): 1–26.

Camenisch, Paul. *Grounding Professional Ethics in a Pluralistic Society.* New York: Haven Publications, 1983.

Canovan, Margaret. *Hannah Arent: A Reinterpretation of Her Political Thought.* Cambridge: Cambridge University Press, 1992.

Card, Claudia. "Intimacy and Responsibility: What Lesbians Do." In *At the Boundaries of Law,* edited by Martha Albertson Fineman and Nancy Sweet Thomadsen, pp. 77–94. New York: Routledge, 1991.

Christian Science Board of Directors. "Christian Scientists and the Practice of Spiritual Healing." *Christian Science Sentinel* 93 (7 October 1991): 25.

Clark, Ralph W., and Alice Darnell Lattal. *Workplace Ethics: Winning the Integrity Revolution.* Lanham, MD: Rowman and Littlefield, 1993.

Clarke, Stanley G., and Even Simpson, eds. *Anti-Theory in Ethics and Moral Conservatism.* Albany: State University of New York Press, 1989.

Cooper, Robert W., and Garry L. Frank. "Professionals in Business: Where Do They Look for Help in Dealing with Ethical Issues." *Business and Professional Ethics Journal* 11, no. 2 (summer 1992): 41–56.

Davion, Victoria. "Integrity and Radical Change." In *Feminist Ethics,* edited by Claudia Card, pp. 180–92. Lawrence: University of Kansas Press, 1991.

Davis, Michael, "Avoiding the Tragedy of Whistleblowing," *Business and Professional Ethics Journal* 8, no. 4 (winter 1989): 3–19.

———. "Conflict of Interest." *Business and Professional Ethics Journal* 1, no. 4 (summer 1982): 17–27.

De George, Richard. "Ethical Responsibilities of Engineers in Large Organizations." *Business and Professional Ethics Journal* 1, no. 1 (fall 1981): 1–14.

———. *The Nature and Limits of Authority.* Lawrence: University of Kansas Press, 1985.

Deigh, John. "Shame and Self-Esteem: A Critique." In *Ethics and Personality,* edited by John Deigh. Chicago: University of Chicago Press, 1992. Originally published in *Ethics* 93, no. 2 (January 1983): 225–45.

Dennett, Daniel. *Consciousness Explained.* Boston: Little Brown, 1991.

Dewey, John. *Human Nature and Conduct.* New York: Henry Holt, 1922.

Douglas, Mary. *How Institutions Think.* Syracuse: Syracuse University Press, 1986.

Dreyfus, Hubert, and Stuart Dreyfus. "What Is Morality? A Phenomenological Account of the Development of Ethical Expertise." In *Universalism vs. Communitarianism,* edited by David Rasmussen, pp. 237–64. Cambridge, MA: MIT Press, 1990.

Durkheim, Emile. *Emile Durkheim on Morality and Society.* Edited by Robert Bellah. Chicago: University of Chicago Press, 1973.

———. *Professional Ethics and Civic Morals.* Translated by Cornelia Brookfield. New York: Routledge, 1992.

Eddy, Mary Baker. *Church Manual of the First Church of Christ Scientist, in Boston, Mass.* 1895. Reprint, Boston: First Church of Christ Scientist, 1936.

———. *Science and Health* 1875. Reprint, Boston: First Church of Christ Scientist, 1971.

Edwards, Carolyn Pope. "Culture and the Construction of Moral Values: A Comparative Ethnography of Moral Encounters in Two Cultural Settings." In *The Emergence of Morality in Young Children,* edited by Jerome Kagan and Sharon Lamb, pp. 123–50. Chicago: University of Chicago Press, 1987.

Emmet, Dorothy. *Rules, Roles and Relations.* Boston: Beacon Press, 1966.

Engler, Robert L., James W. Covell, Paul J. Friedman, Philip S. Kitcher, and Richard M. Peters. "Misrepresentation and Responsibility in Medical Research." *New England Journal of Medicine* 317, no. 22 (26 November 1987): 1383–9.

Fantasia, Rick. *Cultures of Solidarity: Consciousness, Action and Contemporary American Workers.* Berkeley: University of California Press, 1988.

Erikson, Erik. *Childhood and Society.* 2d ed. New York: Norton, 1963.

———. *Insight and Responsibility: Lectures on the Ethical Implications of Psychoanalytical Insight.* New York: Norton, 1964.

Feinberg, Joel. *Doing and Deserving.* Princeton: Princeton University Press, 1970.

———. *Rights, Justice, and the Bounds of Liberty.* Princeton: Princeton University Press, 1980.

Fisher, Lesley, and Sally Colter. "Should Nurses Strike?" *Nursing Times* 84, no. 5 (3 February 1988): 22–3.

Flanagan, Owen. *Varieties of Moral Personality.* Cambridge, MA: Harvard University Press, 1991.

Fiss, Owen. "Foreword: The Forms of Justice, the Supreme Court 1978 Term." *Harvard Law Review* 93, no. 1 (November 1979): 1–58.

Flores, Albert, and Deborah Johnson. "Collective Responsibility and Professional Roles." *Ethics* 93 (April 1983): 537–45.

Frankfurt, Harry. *The Importance of What We Care About.* Cambridge: Cambridge University Press, 1988.

Freidson, Eliot. *Profession of Medicine: A Study of the Sociology of Applied Knowledge.* New York: Dodd, Mead and Co., 1970.

Freud, Sigmund. *Group Psychology and the Analysis of the Ego.* Translated and edited by James Strachey. 1922. New York: W. W. Norton, 1959.

Friedman, Marilyn. "Autonomy and the Split-Level Self." *Southern Journal of Philosophy* 24 (summer 1986): 19–35.

———. *What Are Friends For?* Ithaca, NY: Cornell University Press, 1993.

Funk, Nanette. "Habermas and Solidarity." *Philosophical Inquiry* 12, nos. 3–4 (1990): 17–31.

Gevitz, Norman. "Christian Science Healing and the Health Care of Children." *Perspectives in Biology and Medicine* 34, no. 3 (spring 1991): 421–38.

Gilligan, Carol. *In a Different Voice.* Cambridge, MA: Harvard University Press, 1982.

Gilligan, Carol, and Jane Attanucci, "Two Moral Orientations." In *Mapping the Moral Domain,* edited by Carol Gilligan, Janie Victoria Ward, and Jill McLean Taylor, pp. 73–86. Cambridge, MA: Harvard University Press, 1988.

Glazer, Myron. "Ten Whistleblowers and How They Fared." *Hastings Center Report* 13, no. 6 (December 1983): 33–41.

Goldberger, Emanuel. *How Physicians Think.* Springfield, IL: Charles C. Thomas Publisher, 1965.

Goodin, Robert. *Protecting the Vulnerable: A Reanalysis of Our Social Responsibilities.* Chicago: University of Chicago Press, 1985.

Griffin, Donald. *Animal Minds.* Chicago: University of Chicago Press, 1992.

Guy, Mary E. *Professionals in Organizations.* New York: Praeger, 1985.

Habermas, Jürgen. *Between Facts and Norms: Contributions to a Discourse Theory of Law and Democracy.* Translated by William Rehg. Cambridge, MA: MIT Press, in press.

————. "Justice and Solidarity: On the Discussion Concerning 'Stage Six.'" *The Philosophical Forum* 21, nos. 1–2 (fall/winter 1989–90) : 32–53.

————. *Justification and Application.* Translated by Ciaran Cronin. Cambridge, MA: MIT Press, 1993.

————. "Law and Morality." In *The Tanner Lectures on Human Values.* Vol. 8, edited by Sterling M. McMurrin, pp. 217–80. Salt Lake City: University of Utah Press, 1988.

————. *Legitimation Crisis.* Translated by Thomas McCarthy. Boston: Beacon Press, 1975.

————. *Moral Consciousness and Communicative Action.* Translated by Christian Lenhardt and Sherry Weber Nicholsen. Cambridge, MA: MIT Press, 1990.

————. *Postmetaphysical Thinking.* Translated by William Mark Hohengarten. Cambridge, MA: MIT Press, 1992.

————. "Struggles for Recognition in Constitutional States." *European Journal of Philosophy* 1 (1993): 128–55.

————. *The Theory of Communicative Action.* Vol. 2, *Lifeworld and System: A Critique of Functionalist Reason,* translated by Thomas McCarthy. Boston: Beacon Press, 1987.

Hart, H. L. A. *The Concept of Law.* Oxford: The Clarendon Press, 1961.

————. *Law, Liberty, and Morality.* Stanford: Stanford University Press, 1963.

————. *Punishment and Responsibility.* Oxford: Oxford University Press, 1968.

Haugeland, John. "Mind Embodied and Embedded." Final draft, 1993, unpublished.

Haywood, Sarah, and Elizabeth Fee. "More in Sorrow Than in Anger: The British Nurses' Strike of 1988." *International Journal of Health Services* 22, no. 3 (1992): 397–415.

Heacock, Marian V., and Gail W. McGee. "Whistleblowing: An Ethical Issue in Organizational and Human Behavior." *Business and Professional Ethics Journal* 6, no. 4 (winter 1987): 35–46.

Herman, Barbara. *The Practice of Moral Judgment.* Cambridge, MA: Harvard University Press, 1993.

Hoagland, Sarah Lucia. "Some Thoughts about Caring." In *Feminist Ethics,* edited by Claudia Card, pp. 246–63. Lawrence: University of Kansas Press, 1991.

Hobbs, Jerry R. "Artificial Intelligence and Collective Intentionality: Comments on Searle and on Grosz and Sidner." In *Intentions in Communication,* edited by Philip Cohen, Jerry Morgan, and Martha Pollack, pp. 445–59. Cambridge: MIT Press, 1990.

Honore, Tony, *Making Law Bind.* Oxford: Clarendon Press, 1987.

Hume, David. *Treatise of Human Nature* (1739). Edited by L. A. Selby-Bigge. Oxford: Clarendon Press, 1968.

Ingram, David. "Dworkin, Habermas and the CLS Movement on Moral Criticism in Law." *Philosophy and Social Criticism* 16 (1992): 237–68.

James, Gene G. "Whistle Blowing: Its Nature and Justification." *Philosophy in Context* 10 (1980): 99–117.

Jaspers, Karl. *The Question of German Guilt.* New York: Capricorn Books, 1947.

Johnson, Mark. *Body in the Mind.* Chicago: University of Chicago Press, 1987.

———. *Moral Imagination.* Chicago: University of Chicago Press, 1993.

Jonas, Hans. *The Imperative of Responsibility.* Chicago: University of Chicago Press, 1984.

Jung, Carl. *Symbols of Transformation.* 2d ed. Translated by R. F. C. Hull. Princeton: Princeton University Press, 1956.

———. *Synchronicity.* Translated by R. F. C. Hull. Princeton: Princeton University Press, 1973.

Kant, Immanuel. *Grounding for the Metaphysics of Morals* (1785). Translated by James Ellington. Indianapolis: Hackett, 1981.

Kekes, John. *Facing Evil.* Princeton: Princeton University Press, 1990.

Kelsen, Hans. "Pashukanis's Theory of Law." In *The Communist Theory of Law,* pp. 89–111. New York: Praeger, 1955.

Kinports, Kit. "Evidence Engendered." *University of Illinois Law Review,* 1991, no. 2: 413–56.

Klein, Dories. "The Dark Side of Marriage: Battered Wives and the Domination of Women." In *Judge, Lawyer, Victim, Thief,* edited by Nicole Hahn Rafter and Elizabeth A. Stanko, pp. 83–107. Boston: Northeastern University Press, 1982.

Kohlberg, Lawrence. *Child Psychology and Childhood Development.* New York: Longman, 1987.

Kolenda, Konstantin. "Incremental Solidarity." *The Humanist* 49 (September/October 1989): 43.

Lakoff, George. *Women, Fire, and Dangerous Things.* Chicago: University of Chicago Press, 1987.

Larrabee, Mary Jeanne, ed. *An Ethic of Care.* New York: Routledge, 1993.

Laurendeau, Normand. "Engineering Professionalism: The Case for Corporate Ombudsmen." *Business and Professional Ethics Journal* 2, no. 1 (1982): 35–45.

Lévi-Strauss, Claude. *The Elementary Structures of Kinship.* Translated by James

Bell, John von Sturmer, and Rodney Needham. 1949. Boston: Beacon Press, 1969.

Levitan, Sar A., and Frank Gallo. "Collective Bargaining and Private Sector Professionals." *Monthly Labor Review,* September 1989, 24–33.

Lewis, David. *Convention.* Cambridge, MA: Harvard University Press, 1969.

Lockwood, David. *Solidarity and Schism.* Oxford: The Clarendon Press, 1992.

Luban, David. *Lawyers and Justice.* Princeton: Princeton University Press, 1988.

Lyotard, Jean-François. *The Differend.* Translated by Georges Van Den Abbeele. Minneapolis: University of Minnesota Press, 1988.

———. *Peregrinations: Law, Form, Event.* New York: Columbia University Press, 1988.

———. *The Postmodern Condition.* Translated by Geoff Bennington and Brian Massumi. Minneapolis: University of Minnesota Press, 1984.

MacIntyre, Alasdair. *After Virtue.* Notre Dame, IN: University of Notre Dame Press, 1981.

Manning, Rita C. "Toward a Thick Theory of Moral Agency." *Social Theory and Practice* 20, no. 2 (summer 1994): 203–20.

Martin, Mike W. "Whistleblowing: Professionalism, Personal Life, and Shared Responsibility for Safety in Engineering." *Business and Professional Ethics Journal* 11, no. 2 (summer 1992): 21–40.

Marx, Karl. *Contribution to the Critique of Hegel's Philosophy of Right* (1843). In *The Marx-Engels Reader,* 2d ed.Translated and edited by Robert C. Tucker. New York: W. W. Norton, 1978.

Mauss, Marcel. *The Gift: Forms and Functions of Exchange in Archaic Societies.* Translated by Ian Cunnison. London: Cohen and West, 1954.

May, Larry. *The Morality of Groups.* Notre Dame, IN: University of Notre Dame Press, 1987.

———. "On Conscience." *American Philosophical Quarterly* 20, no. 1 (January 1983): 57–67.

———. "Paternalism and Self-Interest." *Journal of Value Inquiry* 14, no. 4 (fall/winter 1980): 195–216.

———. "Professional Actions and the Liabilities of Professional Associations: ASME v. Hydrolevel Corp." *Business and Professional Ethics Journal* 2, no. 1 (fall 1982): 1–14.

———. *Sharing Responsibility.* Chicago: University of Chicago Press, 1992.

May, Larry, and Martin Curd. *Professional Responsibility for Harmful Actions.* Dubuque, IA: Kendall/Hunt Publishing, 1984.

May, Larry, and Marie Failinger. "Litigating against Poverty: Legal Services and Group Representation." *Ohio State Law Journal* 45/1 (1984): 1–56.

May, Larry, and John C. Hughes. "Is Sexual Harassment Coercive?" In *Moral Rights in the Workplace,* edited by Gertrude Ezorsky, pp. 115–22. Albany: State University of New York Press, 1987.

———. "Sexual Harassment." *Social Theory and Practice* 6, no. 3 (fall 1980): 249–80.

May, Larry, Marilyn Friedman, and Andy Clark, eds. *Mind and Morals.* Cambridge, MA: Bradford Books/MIT Press, 1995.

May, Larry, and Stacey Hoffman, eds. *Collective Responsibility.* Savage, MD: Rowman and Littlefield, 1991.

McCarthy, Thomas. "Complexity and Democracy: or the Seducements of Systems Theory." In *Communicative Action,* edited by Axel Honneth and Hans Joas, pp. 119–39. Cambridge: MIT Press, 1991.

———. *Ideals and Illusions: On Reconstruction and Deconstruction in Contemporary Critical Theory.* Cambridge, MA: MIT Press, 1991.

McElreath, Mark R. "Dealing with Ethical Dilemmas: Applying the IABC Code and the Potter Box to Solve Them." *IABC Communication World,* March 1993, 12–15.

McFall, Lynn. "Integrity." In *Ethics and Personality,* edited by John Deigh. Chicago: University of Chicago Press, 1992. Originally published in *Ethics* 98, no. 1 (October 1987): 5–20.

Meyers, Diana. *Self, Society and Personal Choice.* New York: Columbia University Press, 1989.

———. "The Socialized Individual and Individual Autonomy." In *Women and Moral Theory,* edited by Eva Feder Kittay and Diana T. Meyers, pp. 139–53. Totowa, NJ: Rowman & Littlefield, 1987.

———. *Subjection and Subjectivity.* New York: Routledge, 1994.

Miles, Stephen H., Peter A. Singer, and Mark Siegler. "Conflicts between Patients' Wishes to Forgo Treatment and the Policies of Health Care Facilities." *New England Journal of Medicine,* 6 July 1989, 48–50.

Mill, John Stuart, *On Liberty* (1859). Edited by Elizabeth Rappaport. Indianapolis, IN: Hackett, 1978.

———. *Utilitarianism* (1861). Edited by George Sher. Indianapolis: Hackett, 1979.

Millikan, Ruth Garrett. *White Queen Psychology and Other Essays for Alice.* Cambridge, MA: MIT Press, 1993.

Moe, Kristine. "Should the Nazi Research Data Be Cited?" *Hastings Center Report,* November/December 1984, 5–7.

Monopoli, Paula. "Allocating the Costs of Parental Free Exercise: Striking a New Balance between Sincere Religious Belief and a Child's Right to Medical Treatment." *Pepperdine Law Review* 18 (1991): 319–52.

Munson, Ronald. *Intervention and Reflection: Basic Issues in Medical Ethics.* 4th ed. Belmont, CA: Wadsworth Publishing Co., 1992.

Muyskens, James. "Collective Responsibility and the Nursing Profession." In *Collective Responsibility,* edited by Larry May and Stacey Hoffman. Savage, MD: Rowman and Littlefield, 1991. Originally published in *University of Dayton Review* 15 (1982): 53–61.

National Academy of Sciences, National Academy of Engineering, and Institute of Medicine. *Responsible Science: Ensuring the Integrity of the Research Process.* Vol. 1. Washington, DC: National Academy Press, 1992.

Nodding, Nel. *Caring.* Berkeley: University of California Press, 1984.

Nussbaum, Martha. *The Fragility of Goodness.* Cambridge: Cambridge University Press, 1986.

Oakeshott, Michael. *Rationalism in Politics and Other Essays.* Indianapolis, IN: Liberty Press, 1991.

Pashukanis, E. B. "The General Theory of Law and Marxism" (1924), translated by H. W. Babb. In *Soviet Legal Philosophy,* edited by H. W. Babb and John N. Hazard, pp. 111–226. Cambridge, MA: Harvard University Press, 1951.

Ramsey, Paul. *The Patient as Person.* New Haven, CT: Yale University Press, 1970.

Rehg, William. *Identity and Solidarity.* Berkeley: University of California Press, 1994.

Rhode, Deborah. *Gender and Justice.* Cambridge, MA: Harvard University Press, 1989.

Rodwin, Mark C. "The Organized American Medical Profession's Response to Financial Conflicts of Interest." *The Millbank Quarterly* 70, no. 4 (1992): 703–41.

Rorty, Richard. *Contingency, Irony, and Solidarity.* Cambridge: Cambridge University Press, 1989.

Rosanova, Michael Joseph. "Divorce-Related Mediation." *Perspectives on the Professions* 2, nos. 3–4 (September/December 1982): 2–6.

Ruddick, Sara. *Maternal Thinking: Toward a Politics of Peace.* New York: Ballantine, 1989.

Sabini, John, and Maury Silver. *Moralities of Everyday Life.* Oxford: Oxford University Press, 1982.

Sachdev, P. S. "Doctors' Strike—An Ethical Justification." *New Zealand Medical Journal* 99 (11 June 1986): 412–14.

Sandel, Michael. *Liberalism and the Limits of Justice.* Cambridge: Cambridge University Press, 1982.

Sartre, Jean-Paul. *The Critique of Dialectical Reason.* Translated by Alan Sheridan-Smith. 1960. London: NLB, 1976.

Schacht, Richard. *Alienation.* Garden City, NY: Anchor Books, 1971.

Scheler, Max. *The Nature of Sympathy* (1913). Translated by Peter Heath. Hamden, CT: Archon Books, 1970.

Schmaus, Warren. "An Analysis of Fraud and Misconduct in Science." In *Project on Scientific Fraud and Misconduct,* AAAS-ABA National Conference of Lawyers and Scientists, pp. 87–116. Washington, DC: AAAS, 1988.

Schutz, Alfred. *The Phenomenology of the Social World* (1932). Translated by George Walsh and Frederick Lehnert. Evanston, IL.: Northwestern University Press, 1967.

Schweder, Richard, Manawohan Mahapatra, and Joan G. Miller. "Culture and Moral Development." In *The Emergence of Morality in Young Children,* edited by Jerome Kagan and Sharon Lamb, pp. 1–82. Chicago: University of Chicago Press, 1987.

Searle, John, "Collective Intentions and Actions." In *Intentions in Communication,* edited by Philip Cohen, Jerry Morgan, and Martha Pollack, pp. 401–15. Cambridge, MA: MIT Press, 1990.

Sheldon, Mark. "The Use of Nazi Data." Paper presented at a meeting of the Indiana Philosophical Association, 1988.

Singer, Peter. "Altruism and Commerce." *Philosophy and Public Affairs* 2, no. 3 (spring 1973): 312–20.

Staub, Ervin. *The Roots of Evil: The Origins of Genocide and Other Group Violence.* New York: Cambridge University Press, 1989.

Sumner, L. Wayne. *The Moral Foundations of Rights.* Oxford: Clarendon Press. 1987.

Swan, Rita. "Faith Healing, Christian Science and the Medical Care of Children." *New England Journal of Medicine* 309, no. 26 (1983): 1639–41.

Tay, Alice Ehr-Soon. "The Law, the Citizen, and the State." In *Law and Society: The Crisis in Legal Ideas,* edited by Eugene Kamenka, Robert Brown, and Alice Ehr-Soon Tay, pp. 1–17. New York: St. Martin's Press, 1978.

Taylor, Charles. "Language and Society." In *Communicative Action,* edited by Axel Honneth and Hans Joas, pp. 23–35. Cambridge: MIT Press, 1991.

———. *Sources of the Self.* Cambridge, MA: Harvard University Press, 1989.

Taylor, Charles, Amy Gutmann, Stephen Rockefeller, Michael Walzer, and Susan Wolf. *Multiculturalism and the Politics of Recognition.* Princeton: Princeton University Press, 1992.

Taylor, Gabriele. *Pride, Shame, and Guilt.* Oxford: The Clarendon Press, 1985.

Thalberg, Irving. "Socialization and Autonomous Behavior." *Tulane Studies* 28 (1979): 21–36.

Titmuss, Richard M. *The Gift Relationship: From Human Blood to Social Policy.* New York: Pantheon Books, 1971.

Tuomela, Raimo, and Kaarlo Miller. "We-Intentions." *Philosophical Studies* 53 (1988): 367–89.

Turiel, Elliot, Melanie Killen, and Charles C. Helwig. "Morality: Its Structure, Functions, and Vagaries." In *The Emergence of Morality in Young Children,* edited by Jerome Kagan and Sharon Lamb, pp. 155–244. Chicago: University of Chicago Press, 1987.

Unger, Roberto Mangabeira. *The Critical Legal Studies Movement.* Cambridge, MA: Harvard University Press, 1983.

Vandivier, Kermit. "Case Study: The Aircraft Brake Scandal." In *Ethical Issues in Business,* 3d ed. Edited by Thomas Donaldson and Patricia Werhane, pp. 290–303. Englewood Cliffs, NJ: Prentice-Hall, 1988.

Walker, Margaret Urban. "Feminism, Ethics and the Question of Theory." *Hypatia* 7, no. 3 (summer 1992): 23–38.

Walzer, Michael. *Thick and Thin*. Notre Dame, IN: University of Notre Dame Press, 1994.

Weber, Max. "Politics as a Vocation." In *From Max Weber,* translated and edited by H. H. Gerth and C. Wright Mills. New York: Oxford University Press, 1946.

Weil, Vivian, ed. *Beyond Whistleblowing*. Chicago: Center for the Study of Ethics in the Professions at the Illinois Institute of Technology, 1983.

Wells, Paula, Hardy Jones, and Michael Davis. *Conflicts of Interest in Engineering.* Dubuque, IA: Kendall/Hunt Publishing Company, 1986.

Whitbeck, Caroline. "A Different Reality: Feminist Ontology." In *Beyond Domination,* edited by Carol Gould, pp. 64–88. Totowa, NJ: Rowman & Allanheld, 1983.

White, Stephen K. *Political Theory and Postmodernism*. Cambridge: Cambridge University Press, 1991.

Williams, Bernard. *Moral Luck*. Cambridge: Cambridge University Press, 1981.

———. *Shame and Necessity*. Berkeley: University of California Press, 1993.

Wilson, James Q. *The Moral Sense*. New York: Free Press, 1993.

Winslow, Betty J., and Gerald R. Winslow. "Integrity and Compromise in Nursing Ethics." *Journal of Medicine and Philosophy* 16 (1991): 307–23.

Wolf, Susan. "Moral Saints." *Journal of Philosophy* 79, no. 8 (August 1982): 419–39.

Wolfram, Charles. *Modern Legal Ethics*. St. Paul, MN: West Publishing Co., 1986.

Woolf, Patricia K. "Accountability and Responsibility in Research." *Journal of Business Ethics* 10 (August 1991): 595–600.

Wyschogrod, Edith. *Saints and Postmodernism*. Chicago: University of Chicago Press, 1990.

Young, Iris. *Justice and the Politics of Difference*. Princeton: Princeton University Press, 1990.